The Pagan Leadership Anthology

An Exploration of Leadership and Community in Paganism and Polytheism

The Pagan Leadership Anthology

An Exploration of Leadership and Community in Paganism and Polytheism

Edited by
Shauna Aura Knight & Taylor Ellwood

Megalithica Books
Stafford England

The Pagan Leadership Anthology: An Exploration of Leadership and Community in Paganism and Polytheism
Edited by Shauna Aura Knight and Taylor Ellwood
© 2016 First edition

Editor: Shauna Aura Knight and Taylor Ellwood
Layout: Taylor Ellwood
Cover Design: Shauna Aura Knight

ISBN: 978-0-9932371-6-4
MB0180

Set in Estrangelo Edessa and Book Antiqua

A Megalithica Books Publication
An imprint of Immanion Press
info@immanion-press.com
http://www.immanion-press.com

Dedication

To the Ancestors, to all who have gone before, to those whose shoulders we stand on.

To the Descendants, to all those who will come after us, to those who will stand on the foundations we build today.

To the Leaders, to all of you who have stepped into Service, into creating and supporting communities, to those of you who have done this work and who continue to do this work, and to those of you who will step into this work.

Table of Contents

Section 5: Delegation and Volunteers

Section 6: Building the Long Term Infrastructure of the Pagan Community

Section 7: Conflict Resolution and Dealing with Crisis in Groups

Section 8: Recognizing and Dealing with Burnout

Introduction
Shauna Aura Knight

When Taylor and I sat down together for a lunch meeting at a Pagan conference, I wasn't expecting him to ask me to edit an anthology of Pagan leadership. I didn't even think he knew who I was. I did know one thing for sure: this kind of anthology would be an incredibly useful resource for the Pagan community. And so I agreed, even though I knew I was making one of my own typical mistakes as a leader—taking on too much work and risking burnout.

But sometimes it's worth the risk, and this is one of those times.

Working on this anthology brought me face to face with some of my own leadership shadow. I knew that my workload "plate" was already full, and I knew I was at risk of dropping the ball. *And at times I did.* I hadn't quite planned on this leadership anthology taking me on a journey through the Underworld of my own shadows, of looking into the mirror of my challenges as a leader.

What I've found, over and over, is that we (leaders) are often the cause of many of our problems. Because we're human, and we make mistakes. There are things we're good at, and things we aren't good at. I'm good at sitting alone in my Writing Cave and writing. I'm not so good at the more social and communication side of things. I'm an introvert, and when I get overloaded, I tend to go into avoidance mode. It should be obvious, but that's not a great pattern of behavior when I'm the one responsible for keeping in contact with people about a project, and answering in-depth questions people have about the anthology, or following up with people on edits or biographies or other information.

Put simply: Writing books is far different from editing them, and I found my skills were far more suited to the former than the latter.

I see this sort of thing happen all the time in the Pagan community, too. Pagan leaders are often asked to fulfill roles that they aren't actually suited for, but they do it out of a desire to serve, and because there may be nobody else to fill that job.

There's an axiom I teach in my leadership workshops: Play to your strengths. We, as leaders, don't have to be good at everything. Not every writer is a good leader. Not every leader is a good writer. In the Pagan community, the visionary is often asked to manage volunteers and delegate, the administrator is asked to do public speaking, the artist is asked to be the accountant, the introvert is asked to be the social greeter.

I came face to face with this as I worked on this anthology: Not every leader is good at everything. And not every leader needs to be good at everything. Many leaders have talked to me about dealing with burnout—and a number of essays in this anthology deal with burnout so it's clearly a consistent problem for our communities—and one of the consistent patterns I see is that leaders who step into roles that they aren't suited for burn out far faster.

There are so many different facets to leadership, and a core piece of leadership goes deeper than learning communication techniques or learning about conflict resolution or group dynamics. It goes into knowing ourselves. It's crucial to be aware of our own strengths and weaknesses, and to work hard to not agree to take responsibility for an area where we are weaker. I know for myself, taking on the tasks and responsibilities in areas where I'm not as good at the work definitely leads me to blowing deadlines, dropping the ball completely, or the dreaded Pagan leader burnout.

And yeah—there are times when you do what you have to because the project is important enough, as I did with this anthology. Having done this project, I know a lot more about myself and what I'm good at and what I'm not good at. This means I can get myself off the leadership hamster wheel…that is to say, so that I don't continue setting myself up for failure. Remember—a lot of times, we as leaders cause our own problems.

This anthology offers a lot of tools and techniques, and a lot of stories. It offers stories of things that went well, and it offers stories of problems in groups. While some of the essays fall into the category of doing our personal work as leaders, I'd offer that most of the essays at least touch on some aspect of knowing ourselves.

Being a leader, and working to be a better leader, means

being self reflective. If you can't acknowledge what you don't do well...if you can't acknowledge the things you consistently screw up...then you can't change the pattern.

Some of the essays on volunteer management were a huge look in the mirror for me. In short, I realized some of why I'm not great at managing volunteers. It was freeing, in a way, to realize why I've failed at this aspect of leadership, because now I know that to run a larger event, I need to engage a leader who is good at those things instead of trying to shoehorn myself into a role that I'm going to do poorly.

Something else that came up for me while editing this anthology is that I don't necessarily agree with what each author wrote. I walked a bit of a tightrope while reviewing and editing the essays. I had to be able to discern the difference between, "I disagree with this and find it unethical," and "I disagree with this but recognize there are a diversity of leadership styles and ethical systems and this might work well for some."

In fact, if you read this book cover to cover, you'll find several essays that outright contradict one another in approach. That's part of the power of an anthology like this—that it's a cornucopia of ideas and thoughts and processes and experiences, and it's up to each of you, the readers, to determine which suggestions are going to work for you and your group, and which aren't a good fit at all. It's up to you, the reader, to sometimes hold the paradox that two people are writing conflicting advice, and yet, both suggestions may be correct, accurate, and useful. Some of the approaches and advice might even make you downright uncomfortable.

And maybe that's the gist of leadership; it isn't always comfortable.

Going deeper, it's important to notice when you aren't comfortable, and to know why. Sometimes, being uncomfortable is a sign that this isn't working for you, that it's not the right fit. And sometimes, being uncomfortable is a sign that you have deeper personal work to do, shadows to confront, mirrors to look into and behaviors to address.

Working on this anthology forced me to look into the leadership mirror a number of times, both as I read the essays themselves, and as I dealt with my own issues in the process of managing the anthology along with Taylor Ellwood.

I'm forever grateful to Taylor for the opportunity to work on this anthology. He's so much better at managing anthologies than I am and I'd have been lost without his support! I feel incredibly privileged to have had the opportunity to make this book a reality with him, because truly, this book is a fantastic resource. There are essays in this book that are absolutely priceless pieces of advice whether you're an aspiring leader or long-time Pagan elder.

I'm also grateful to all the authors who wrote something for the anthology. They wrote about their experiences, their expertise, about tools and techniques that you're sure to find useful. They also wrote about their mistakes, the pain they went through as they learned this the hard way, and they are sharing those experiences so that you can benefit...so that you don't have to make those mistakes...or even just so that you know that *you aren't alone*, that others have been through this, that it's not just you.

I hope you will find this book a treasure trove of resources for anyone in a position of leadership and service.

Shauna Aura Knight
November 2015
Milwaukee Wisconsin

Section 1
Personal Work

The Necessity of Social Skills
Rev. Bill Duvendack

If you're reading this, you're most likely living in a Western world society. If you're reading this and you're not, then I am not sure how much of this will be applicable, so please understand that I am writing this from that perspective. The Pagan community as a whole is not known for its leadership skills but guess what? A lot of subcultures in society aren't! However, what separates the Pagan community from the rest of the varied subcultures in our society is that a lot of the core current beliefs and perspectives within the community are counterculture in nature. Some even take this to the extreme, exhibiting prepubescent behavior to the tune of being confrontational and/or rebellious just to "prove a point" or to show individuality.

One of the reasons for this tie into counterculture is that the Pagan community on average and as a whole gained its main momentum from the counterculture movement of the late 1960s and 1970s. True, being counterculture has always been there, but what occurred during that time is a rapid expansion to a wider group of people than previously reached. A large part of this was fueled by the rapidly expanding information age. This rapid expansion is why we are at where we are today, yet it has also left us with a large growth opportunity in the community. Now is the time for leaders to step up as we shift further into the new century and aeon.

The area of greatest growth that I will address in this essay is the area of social skills for the aforementioned reason. The Pagan community is a community of people that have been counterculture for approximately the last 50 years or so, and as those that are knowledgeable with metaphysics know, when a person or group of people identify with a particular energetic signature, they take on the traits of said signature. This isn't necessarily a conscious choice, but rather it happens on the finer planes level, usually subconsciously. This has been discussed and written about in many pages over the years, so I see no reason to cover trodden ground. For those that are interested, any common search of sociological studies will reveal much information about traits of different social and occupational groups. Beyond sociology, other academic areas of study have covered this from different perspectives as well, so ample research can be found for the curious seeker. In magick this is known as tapping into the egregore and receiving the traits and characteristics of said egregore.

An easy starting place for those that are interested is to start with the self. We can control our actions and our behavior, thus making it fertile ground to sow the seeds of change. When we change the inner world, the outer world reflects this change following the path of least resistance within the realm of universal and natural laws, moving through karmic pathways as it manifests in day to day life. When one becomes serious about their spiritual growth and their desire to assist others, one recognizes their strengths and growth opportunities. When these are realized, the question then becomes whether to develop the growth opportunities present, or to delegate those weaknesses to others that show they have the requisite skills, and they have proven their moral fiber; however, that is determined by the group and peers in question.

Part of this personal assessment lies in recognizing where certain areas cannot be delegated. Take, for example, social skills. Social skills are not necessarily something that we can ask another to do for us. They are part of the skill set that it takes to get through life. With them, we can move through society a lot better and faster than if we didn't have them. By navigating interpersonal relationships and different societal structures, we can not only incur a lot of personal growth, but we can achieve success regarding the manifestation of our Will. While social skills are not a must, they definitely make life easier.

Not all people are raised with them, though, and usually what we encounter through life are people that have that skill set somewhere between black and white, somewhere on the sliding scale of grey that is reality. The ability to get along with people through the use of manners and other subtleties is something that becomes very valuable in order to advance what we are here to do. Lacking them can make life quite hard, though, and thus the starting point is to discover our strengths and growth opportunities. Each person has social skills, but not everyone had a supportive environment in which to foster their development. While the average person may not care about such things, to the leader, it is of the upmost importance to cultivate these skills, tailoring their use to the individual's preference.

Through the use of social skills at a leadership level, we cultivate two major things: 1) leading by example, and 2) respect. Of course, there are other things that come along with this, but they are unique to individual people. These are the two that I would like to focus on for the sake of this essay. We'll look at them closely, and I will share perspectives to consider as food for thought. By beginning with broad strokes, we can get a macrocosmic view of the role of social skills in the Pagan community at least as it pertains to the United States and the Western world.

Let's begin with respect. There is a Japanese Zen koan that sums it all up very well: "The student chops wood, carries water, the master chops wood, carries water." There is no task beneath a true leader in the Pagan community. Does this mean that the leader should do every task that is available? No, not at all. A good leader will delegate tasks in accord to those that are most skilled and can be trusted to do the job right. This koan is all about humility, and staying connected as you move through the ranks into a leadership position. This koan also addresses the fact that when it comes to all things in life, the key to success lies in the fundamentals.

In the context of this essay, the fundamentals are the basics of interaction with people. By knowing the right time to say the right thing, we put ourselves in a position to deal with people in a more productive and conducive way. We not only get to know our community more intimately, we also make valuable contacts and impressions on people.

The challenge lies in that one of the fundamental principles of current Paganism is the counterculture mindset mentioned above. It's more challenging to navigate the social graces of counterculturism, but not because it's any more of a difficult situation to navigate. Rather because most people operate social skills from a cultural perspective, not a countercultural perspective. Each culture and subculture has its societal norms to follow, and because of this, each one is different in nature. In the case of Paganism, those differences are to be celebrated. This counterculture basis is one that can be difficult to work with, though, for this makes it closed off from the whole, which ultimately works to its detriment. A challenge that exists is that it goes against the norm, and while sometimes this is a good thing, there are times that it is not.

For example, a business person that is a Pagan may have a hard time conforming to what the overall Pagan community considers normal. I have seen this multiple times. Generally, they adapt fairly quickly, but sometimes the communities that they find themselves in judge them harshly, and rather than seeing them as one of themselves, they shun the individual. In other industries this wouldn't necessarily be something to note, but in Paganism it is a huge point to consider. Paganism is a spiritual belief system, and thus that kind of behavior can seriously damage someone spiritually for years to come. As an extension of that, the karma of that shunning falls on the shoulders of the people that should know better, if they practice what they preach.

Conversely, it is hard for someone that is deep in counterculture to navigate the ways of big business and the professional world in general. Just like Paganism, big business and the professional world have their own culture, too, and if it is not learned, the individual may feel left out and shunned. The scientific perception that if something is true, so, too, is its converse, has almost never ceased to amaze me. We live in a polarity reality, and because of that, opposites exist, sometimes complementary, and sometimes conflicting. I believe the duality here is clear.

This concept of duality is an important one when it comes to social skills, particularly when it comes to the Pagan community. Understanding that every point has a counterpoint is something that can serve the individual very well. This is especially true when considering points of view and perspectives in a workshop or group discussion format. By respecting someone that has a different view and pausing to consider that it is as valid as your view, we increase our openness to learn from one another. This awareness often times breeds solutions to problems that would not otherwise be obvious. This also breeds thinking outside the box for solutions to growth opportunities.

Too many times people believe that finding a solution is

an "either or" scenario, when in reality it is that type of thinking that created the problem in the first place. Diplomacy is what is really being addressed here, and it is one of the biggest social skills to cultivate. There is no reason to *not* practice it, especially since the Pagan community is, at its core, a spiritually-oriented community; or at least it should be. Sidestepping polarity solutions to the best of our ability is something that should strongly be considered at the leadership level. Yes, I realize that sometimes this cannot be avoided, but by and large it can be. All it takes to accomplish this is a skill I like to call the art of the spin. To ceremonial magicians, this can also be called "being initiated into Hod." Being a wordsmith can help to accomplish this.

Vocabulary is a double edged sword when it comes to the Pagan community, and to people in positions of leadership no matter the subculture. On one hand I highly appreciate someone that is direct and uses monosyllabic words to convey a point. There's something refreshing about honesty and directness. However, I have found that often time rudeness comes along with this. Sometimes the people that are the most direct, honest, and blunt, are also the rudest, and when it comes to getting things done, particularly in leadership capacities, rudeness is detrimental at best, and immature at worst. It is possible to be direct and honest without being rude. The way to accomplish this is through choosing words carefully and respecting the opinions of others, especially since their opinions are just as valid as yours. We will all die at the end of our lives, and we all share certain biological functions, so it is wise to remember this even footing to remove the psychological pitfalls that would otherwise be present.

It is often time wise to increase your vocabulary to find the most appropriate word for the current situation. When I was in college, I took a page out of Aleister Crowley's book and carried a thesaurus and AP stylebook with me to browse through when I had the opportunity simply to better myself through language. I found this quite effective because I learned a lot and extended my vocabulary quite a bit. Being aware of our language can help us navigate life overall, for often time people judge us, incorrectly or not, based on the words that we say. Hence it is wise to be aware of this fact so that we can adjust when it would be to our benefit. I'm sure that the answer for each person lies in the middle of these two very opposite views. After all, most times reality is a sliding scale of grey rather than two black and white polar opposite perspectives. By addressing our individual vocabularies we create a dialogue of respect because we see every point as valid and as something to consider. However, it is wise to be aware of the fact that just because every view is valid doesn't put every view on the same footing.

Just because we can do something doesn't mean we should do something, and this is an important principle to keep in mind as we develop ourselves personally and professionally. Discernment is the principle that comes to mind here, and at a leadership level discernment is a very valuable skill to have. The key to successfully using discernment lies in the aforementioned concept of respect. If we respect someone and/or an idea, then we can better process it because we're approaching it from the mental plane rather than an emotionally charged perspective. Sometimes this is hard to do because generally in the Pagan community we're discussing emotionally charged themes, but I assure you based on my own experiences, discernment is worth the cultivation for many reasons.

There's an old saying that "discretion is the better part of valor," and that has always struck me as a very powerful concept due to the fact that every belief system has a concept of valor attached to it. I have found that this is also very true because by being discerning we eliminate what is unhealthy and unnecessary, and truly focus on the things that matter. Socially this applies in a very important yet subtle way.

Often times people don't stop to think about what they're doing and why. For example, if you're against war, there is absolutely positively no reason to go to an anti-war rally. It is much more intelligent and energetically wise to go to a pro-peace rally. Often times the thoughtfulness that comes from discernment can be applied in many ways, and can be a powerful tool for growth when it comes to leading a community. The foundation of discernment is respect, though, so first we must learn to respect. A challenge that comes with this is the fact that respect is earned, and should never be given freely. For example, if someone is constantly confrontational and generally for no reason, then whatever they say really can't be respected.

However, if someone is confrontational because they're pointing out an objective issue that needs to be addressed, then they can be respected for their view, and while their methods may not be stomachable, their ultimate goal may be valid, and thus worth considering.

In short, all of this can be summed up in one skill set: critical thinking.

Now that we've covered respect in great depth, particularly regarding how to respect and where it can lead to, let's move on to the second point I would like to address: leading by example. When one gets to a position of leadership in the Pagan community, they now have more responsibilities that they chose than they had before. One of those responsibilities is that they can now be held accountable to those that they lead, in whatever capacity that leadership may be.

As an extension of this, I've seen leadership roles vary from community to community, at least nationally here in the USA. Sometimes the leadership role lies in simply being the only elder in a given area, while in other communities the leadership role is brought about because it was forged in fire and steel through various immature witch wars. Whatever the criteria, the fact of the matter remains that leaders are held to a higher standard; and really, this should be something that is carefully considered before stepping into a leadership role. It is both an honor and a privilege, but it is also a sword of Damocles.

The easiest way that I have found to address this is to become the best possible leader you can be, and part of this entails honesty. Not every leader has all the answers, but every wise leader knows this, shares this, and seeks the answers. Leading by example simply means to do the best you can each and every day, and to evolve as is necessary for a healthy, productive, and prosperous life. If people in any given community see a leader that has serious flaws (sexual abuse of station, as an example), then that community will be scarred and not able to evolve until the wound is healed. Or, perhaps, they will see that behavior as an acceptable form of behavior, and will copy it, thinking that they are consequence-free with their actions.

Often times a community cannot be blamed for their behavior if they have not been shown a different or better way.

True, each individual is responsible for their own actions, but often time people gravitate to the Pagan community from another spiritual or religious community, and thus they honestly don't know any better because it is all new to them. I have seen countless times older high priests take advantage of this in order to have sex with young, naïve people.

If we want a healthy Pagan community, regardless of the level (local, national, international), then all of us must become healthy on all of the planes to the best of our abilities. For each one of us this is a subjective experience and takes hard work. Patience is our best friend when it comes to creating this due to the fact that a lot of times what we're making healthy are things that didn't occur overnight, and thus they won't necessarily be healed overnight as well. Everything regarding this point can be brought back to the Hermetic Axiom: "As above, so below, as within, so without." By addressing our inner life, we actively change our vibration that ripples out to the outer world, and when this occurs, dynamic changes occur. When these changes occur, they affect others, albeit usually subconsciously. This not only impacts how people see us and responds to us, but it also affects the overall vibe of the environment that we find ourselves in. This can change a toxic environment into a healthy environment, but often times it takes time for the change to occur. Part of the reason for this is that people usually have to see that a new way is better; they generally don't take it on blind faith. Can you tell I live in Missouri in the USA? We're the "show me" state, so show me, don't tell me!

Part of the responsibilities of leadership has to do with leading an authentic life, and the enemy of the authentic life is hypocrisy.

Integrity is something that is wise to develop in a position of leadership. Doing what you say, and saying what you do, cannot be stressed enough, for this is how spiritual maturity is attained. Hypocrisy is never good, and can be quite damaging at the leadership level. If a leader says one thing but does another, then how can they be a good example for people to look up to? Hypocrisy in a spiritual setting is a characteristic of a different spiritual paradigm, and thus can be quite damaging in the Pagan community. A true, competent leader does what they say they believe. In this way they cultivate trust in the community they find themselves in towards them and their leadership skills.

Everyone has a closet, and most closets are full of skeletons, but the difference between handling this in a healthy fashion or not lies in personal integrity and honesty. I'm not advocating pouring it all out there for everyone to see, but rather when something comes up having to do with that, being honest about it and discussing it where applicable. Denial is just a river in Egypt, as the common phrase goes. By owning those experiences and lessons that have occurred to us, we not only disarm our critics, we step into a greater awareness of our personal power. This should carefully be considered ahead of time before stepping into a leadership role. If we say one thing and do another, then the fabric of the community is intentionally weakened overall.

I say intentional because by the time one gets to a leader level they usually know what hypocrisy is, so thus subconscious hypocrisy isn't even a thought. I do realize that often time people don't realize they're being hypocritical, but by the time one gets to a level of leadership, this is worked through; at least from a proactive growth perspective. This view on hypocrisy also bleeds over to the personal honor code as well.

Another way to lead by example is by learning to be of service, and not live in an ivory tower, isolated away from the general community. Too many times I have seen "leaders" isolate themselves from the whole of their community rather than becoming engaged in their community. Yes, there is something to be said for taking care of the self first and prioritizing wisely and appropriately, but there is also something to be said for being engaged in the affairs of the community, and interacting with them on a regular basis. This is part of being of service which is something that goes along with being a leader. If one claims to be a leader and never engages in their community, then how in touch are they with said community?

Of course I'm not saying that 100% involvement in the community 100% of the time is what is desired, but rather the work should be done to interact with the community as much as possible in a healthy way. Isolation, especially from the view of self-importance, is one of the most effective ways to become out of touch and obsolete with your community.

At this point it would be wise to share with you where I'm coming from when I say this so that you can see my perspective, and so that you can see how it can be done. I work a full time job, own my own business, and am the current president of 2 non-profit organizations, one of them being a church. I am also a member of multiple magical organizations. My time is valuable and precious, yet I do my best to keep in touch with people in my community in a few different ways.

The first way is through social media, and the second is by engaging in local events. Whenever possible, I present material for free to the local Pagan community. I prefer to be in the trenches of the community rather than aloof. Because of my busy schedule I'm not as engaged as I might like to be, but the community as a whole understands this.

Those that live in ivory towers are usually the ones that aren't those great of leaders anyway, for they slowly lose their connection with the people, focusing on the ego rather than the greater good. I don't share this information here with the focus of self-aggrandizement, but rather to illustrate the fact that time can always be made for the community that you find yourself in if you apply yourself and walk your talk. If time can't be found, then perhaps looking in the mirror and figuring out better time management skills should be on the near future agenda.

In these brief words I hope that I have conveyed basic ideas and reasons to have excellent social skills when it comes to being a leader in the Pagan community. Quite honestly an entire book could be dedicated to the necessity of social skills, but others have already written them. I'm reminded here of Dale Carnegie's classic: "How to Win Friends and Influence People," but there are plenty of other books out there that can be referenced for guidance. All it takes is a commitment to be better than you were before, and a willingness to work. Even if this self-work is not focused on becoming a leader in the Pagan community, these concepts can be applied to many areas of life and can be quite useful when it comes to spiritual growth in general.

Power, Pitfalls and Projection: Leadership in the Pagan Community
Kenn Day

Any role of leadership within the Pagan community carries with it the responsibility of power. This power is the capacity to influence the thoughts and actions of those who look up to you. Being unaware of this power can cause harm both to individuals and to the community as a whole. This is especially true of those whose charisma and vision have lent an aura of power beyond the boundaries of their own traditions. This projection of power carries with it a lot that feeds the leader's ego. You are granted importance, people listen to you, your opinion is sought. This can seem very attractive, but without substance and integrity, the power can corrupt.

In terms of leadership, power has one important aspect: The power that is unconsciously projected onto the leader by the follower. This is that quality which sets the leader apart, raises them above the ordinary, and makes their words more important than those of others. As with all forms of power, this form carries with it the weight of responsibility.

In this case, it is the responsibility not to act or speak in any way that seems to be lacking integrity. To do so gives the impression that you are condoning such actions and speech.

I learned this lesson many years ago in the registration line for Starwood, one of its first years up at Brushwood. I was standing in line with Elisheva Nesher. We were among the first twenty or so to get in line for the Sunday afternoon "cattle call". This was when all those who had attended the previous festival registered for Starwood. The registration desk was a little late in opening, and we were still standing in line when I needed to take a break. I hurried to the port-o-let, expecting to have my place waiting for me when I returned. When I got back, Elisheva pointed at 100 or so folks who had showed up since I left and said something along the lines of: "It's not enough to not do evil. You must also not *appear* to do evil." I'm a bit slow, so it took me a minute to realize that she meant that, just because I knew that I was not cutting to the front of the line, didn't mean that all those other people knew that. "One of the curses of leadership," she said with a smile as I went to the back of the line.

I am still working on some of the more subtle aspects of this lesson. Perhaps the most difficult is that, sitting in my own skin, I am just an ordinary person, with a balance of strengths and weaknesses, much as anyone else. As such, I have no expectation that others would look at my words and actions as a guide for their behavior.

This internal perspective is entirely at odds with that of someone watching me from outside, someone who sees me as a guide through the difficult, confusing and sometimes terrifying territory of their own spiritual crisis. It is their perspective that I need to be conscious of not only when I am teaching a workshop or leading a ritual, but in my everyday life as well. I have sat with a student who came back years after we had completed out work together, to confront to me about suggestions that I made for her practice, which turned out to be overwhelming and painful. I asked her why she accepted my guidance at the time, and she said, "You were my teacher. I assumed that you knew better than I did."

That is really the root of it all.

It would be easy to say, "I didn't ask anyone to project their perceptions of power onto me," but if you have presented a workshop, written a book, led a study group or become the high Priestess of a Coven, you have done exactly that. You have offered yourself as a canvass, however unintentionally, for others to project onto. Part of the responsibility of leadership is to recognize and accept these projections while not allowing them to define you. What I mean by this is that the projection of power onto you is an important part of the growth process for those who look to you for leadership, but the power remains inherently theirs—not yours. There will come a point in their process where they are ready to take that projection back, and it is your job to hand it back to them with grace.

At the root of the issue of leadership is the question of how to wear the mantle of responsible power without letting it become an ego trip. My initial answer, many years ago, was to create a persona based on my own idea of the perfect teacher. I developed this gradually, and it served me well—to a point. However, it was rather like being on stage the whole time, which was exhausting and which kept me at a distance from my students. Over the past decade, I have begun to deconstruct this persona, trusting myself instead to be a person of integrity, who has vision, knowledge and substance that is of value to those who are seeking.

This has led me to an experience of leadership as radical vulnerability, with no armor and no distance between myself and those whom I am in service to. I remind my students at most workshops that the most valuable things they will take away will not be the words I speak, but the experience they have of those teachings transmitted through me from my own teachers.

This is not always a comfortable position. It is a place of constant change, challenge and self-confrontation, but it is also supremely rewarding. My work gives me the opportunity to be of great service in the lives of others, in a way that is authentic to my deepest self. This is not something to be ignored. For someone with a vision that can provide guidance and clarity to others, I think it is wrong to not take up the work of a teacher and leader.

For all the work I have done, I am well aware that I can and do still make mistakes. I can only hold this position by learning from these mistakes, by doing my own work and embracing the transformations that arise from this work. I must live in integrity, not only when I am at an event where others might look up to me, but in every moment of my life. I must struggle to speak and act with kindness and compassion, rather than my habitual judgmental and critical mind. Otherwise, I have nothing to offer those who chose to project the role of leader onto me.

Ultimately it is this challenge and deepening that makes this process so rewarding: Taking on this work has made me a better person, bringing me more and more into alignment with my soul.

Leadership in the Pagan community is not something to be entered into just to feed the ego. Too often, this approach leads to the pitfalls of irresponsible leadership, which are damaging both to the leader and to the community. Learning to be a good leader takes attention, integrity, and compassion. With these qualities, one can grow into the role of leadership, shouldering the responsibilities along with the power.

Being Seen:
Carefully Navigating Leadership
Phoenix

Those who step into leadership in the Pagan community are unlikely to do this in hopes of becoming rich, famous, or powerful. In the Pagan world there are way more leaders schlepping ritual tools, dealing with group process, and planning for the month-to-month needs of their groups, than there are "big name Pagans" getting books published and earning an annual salary for their teaching commitments.

Most of those in Pagan leadership have done a lot of hard personal work to get to a place where they actually have something to offer those on the path behind them. And they step into this role (often reluctantly) to give a hand to their community members, to share what they have learned through their own explorations. By doing the personal work, Pagan leaders have learned some tools, tips, and tricks that may hold value to others and by stepping into leadership they share these things with their communities.

And yes, no matter if you are the High Priestess of a small coven, a planning member for a community ritual group, or a published "big name Pagan," stepping into leadership means that you are stepping into *being seen*.

Being seen means exactly that, having your name out there, having people know who you are, being someone responsible for the goings on of a group, and bearing the weight of responsibility. Being seen means that people will make assumptions about you; you could end up being the target of unhappy feelings, blame, triggers, and so on.

Carrying not only the responsibilities that you are aware of, but all of the unspoken extras that come with group process, can be exhausting. This weight has lead to the downfall and burnout of many skilled and talented leaders. Leaders aren't super heroes, they are human, and all of the pressure of being seen can come on suddenly and be rather unexpected.

But it isn't all struggle and challenge, otherwise we would have no leaders. There are some upsides. It isn't all pressure and stress. There is a certain level of respect that comes with being in the limelight along with opportunities.

Having the desire to be seen is a normal, healthy part of human nature. We all have a desire to be seen. This might be the longing for a parent, lover, friend, to see you or it might be on a bigger scale; for your home, community, or the whole damn world to know your name. On whatever scale you want to be seen is your own special unique need, but all of us humans have this desire on some level.

When it comes to being seen in leadership there are some pros and some cons. It's good to hold awareness around these things before diving into the realm of leadership.

PRO: *Validation* - Being seen can help you feel validated for all of the hard work you've done. As a Pagan leader you've worked hard to put together your coven, plan that big ritual, put together that festival, or write that book. When other people see the work that you've done and acknowledge that work, it makes you feel good. After all you deserve it.

CON: *Projection* - Stepping into leadership, being seen, putting yourself out there, also means that you get the projection of those looking at you. People will make assumptions about who you are and what you believe, these assumptions may or may not be true, but you get to be a big movie screen that holds all of the ideas other people are creating about you. In Pagan leadership you also get to hold all the triggers. You might say or do something that creates a breakthrough for another person (good or bad) and this can be equated to you, not to their own process. There really isn't anything that you can do about it except remain humble.

PRO: *Purpose* - Many who step into Pagan leadership do so because they feel it is their calling. There isn't a set "priesthood" in the Pagan community; like you will find in most Christian churches. Finding your purpose in Pagan spiritual leadership can feel more challenging; the path isn't as clear. But many who walk that path feel like they are following their purpose, work, and place in the world. Leadership can confirm that yes, you have a purpose and it is clear that you've done the hard work to put you in a place of honoring that. Well done!

CON: *Imbalance of Power* - In teacher/student relationships it is not uncommon for the student to hand over their power to the teacher. This is partly due to projection, people will see the leader as having some special skills, talents, or access to information that is more than what the 'layperson' might have access to. If this imbalance of power is left unchecked it can quickly turn into serious problems in group dynamics, eventually creating inflated egos for those holding leadership. If you don't have a firm grasp of your own identity this may lead you to think that you really *do* have all the answers and can do whatever you want. Not good, not healthy, and not good ethics.

PRO: *Opportunity* - When you are noticed, and seen, for your leadership skills, ritual talents, and so on, it can open up more doors to use or share those skills more often. This can help you to be seen on a larger scale or by a bigger community. Opportunities will follow you when your skills are seen and noticed by others.

CON: *Loss of Privacy* - As you are seen you also lose some of your privacy. When you step into the limelight people are likely to overstep their bounds, ask more of you, expect more of your time and attention, and push your boundaries without knowing that they are doing so. People will want to know more about you, they will want to get to know you on a personal level, be your friend because you hold 'status', and depending on your online presence, you might run into people who feel like they already know you.

Boundaries and Expectations

When it comes to leadership there are a lot of expectations. People may expect you to know it all, to always keep your composure, to have an excellent daily practice, and to do no wrong. You may find yourself up on a pedestal, being held to higher standards than others. This can feel amazing and it can be also feel exhausting or unfair. If you don't have firm personal boundaries and a strong sense of self you might start believing your own press.

Putting yourself into the front of the pack, letting your skills shine, and stepping out into leadership comes with challenges, but ultimately if you have gifts to share you just gotta do it! The goal is to stay grounded, calm, humble, and let your light shine. So how can you navigate the potential choppy waters of being in leadership while avoiding burnout and keeping to your principles?

This is really the biggest challenge in being a Pagan leader. No matter how much you love to plan ritual, love to lead classes, and love to help others, at some point you are likely to feel the stress and weight of these responsibilities; maybe even to the point that you just want them to go away. How can you stay in a position of leadership and keep your own sanity?

Maintain Your Daily Practice - Yes, this is the most obvious and simple answer, but it is also the most powerful. Keeping your personal practice strong and firm is one way to help you stay connected to your own path and spiritual development. When we step into leadership we don't stop our own development.

Stay In Touch with Your Own Leaders - If there is a leader, teacher, or mentor that helped you along the path, keep working with this person, even if this is only on a spiritual plane. Your teachers are a way to help you remember those that came before you. These mentors can also help to bring you back down to the ground when you might start getting a little inflated or lift you up when you are feeling overwhelmed.

Don't Do It All - You might want to lead all the Sabbats, all the Esbats, teach all the classes, be available for mentorship, and speak at all the gathering you can, but pace yourself. If you take on too much too often you are likely to hit a wall and end up getting burnt out. One of my mentors told me, "You won't know your boundary for burnout until you've crossed over it, so be careful." When you are asked to do something don't just say yes. Take a moment to think about it, pull a tarot card, ask your allies, and check in to see if the commitment is really something you can, and should, take on.

Take Breaks - It's important that you have people who can take on some of the work to help you out. If there aren't any of those people currently around then you need to start looking at who you can bring up. Training others to do the heavy lifting is important. Part of being a good leader is helping others step into leadership too. This is how our traditions carry on.

As in most things in life, it is important that you find the balance in this work. When you step into leadership you bring some of your life in to the world, there is no greater work that you can do. Learning to navigate the waters, being centered and humbled in leadership will help you to remain in a place where you can serve your community for long into the future.

On Courage
Manny Tejeda

It is certainly clear from reading advertisements of Pagan events that the Pagan community has and supports individuals who have been ascribed the role of leader. Some leaders rise to position because of their authorship of popular Pagan texts or blogs. Others are recognized by becoming Elders of their community; while others still—and perhaps more rarely—earn the title of leader as an outcome of their devotion or commitment to their community work. At the core of these "promotions" to the role of leader is a social measurement of their contribution to the community through their varied forms of service, which regrettably is sometimes all too often confounded with profit. Many Pagans leaders often have other roles that include business within the community.

While there is surely nothing problematic with earning a living through community service or involvement, one might rightly argue that there is a paucity of Pagan leaders at national or international levels with credible followings who became prominent solely on their selfless service. There are certainly a few Wiccans, Druids and non-Aligned Pagans who offer visions about the role of Paganism for the future as an important spiritual pole that can address many difficult, modern problems. However, there are still very few individuals who would risk personal alienation from the community to address grim and difficult issues within it. As such, many Pagan leaders fail to challenge the community on sobering issues such as abuse and violence possibly because the perceived threat from non-Pagans cautions unity over division. But, no doubt, many Pagan leaders sidestep difficult challenges because of real or perceived risks of being ostracized by other Pagans (the latter being more serious if the leader's livelihood is dependent on the Pagan community).

Yet, while many Pagan leaders abjure the controversy around such issues as those mentioned earlier, these kinds of issues remain grave problems and are precisely the types of problems that forward-looking visionary leadership—through thoughtful and courageous plunges into controversy—can respond to, and thus begin addressing serious community challenges while also uniting the community further.

For such difficult problems, two elements of leadership intersect in a space that is at once uncannily Pagan and yet uncomfortable to embrace: courage and integrity. Aristotle described the virtue of courage as perseverance against adversity, balancing both boldness and fear. The Hávamál—a a poem within the Poetic Edda—offers courage as a critical virtue that fosters our voice to be bold while also recognizing that we must be accepting of challenges in all aspects of our lives. The research on courage bears out these associations of it as virtue, as well as strength of character or disposition (Lopez, O'Byrne & Peterson, 2003; Peterson & Seligman, 2004). In contrast to the view of courage as a state or characteristic, courage is also seen and admired as a *process* involving the effort to accept reality, discern solutions and engage a struggle to better circumstances (Finfgeld, 1999; Sereka & Bagozzi, 2007). As Koerner (2014) points out, the courage literature appears to have consensus on the essential components of courageous behavior: (1) a noble and worthy goal; (2) intentional behavior; and (3) the presence of personal risks and obstacles. When we explore those difficult issues that challenge the Pagan community, such as abuse, the relevant connection is both powerful and clear. It is inherently a worthy task to challenge abusers. Leaders must build a plan to affront and manage the problem; and they do so exposing themselves to personal risk and obstacles. Doing so is clearly a manifest virtue.

Integrity, on the other hand, is somewhat more elusive, at least when reviewing the research literature. One might question whether there is enough development of Pagan Ethics in manner independent of Abrahamic codifications of moral behavior to answer the question of integrity to what or whom. After all, many Pagans adhere to less indicatory commandments than those found in Abrahamic texts. The Wiccan Rede is certainly one such example. But this argument is narrow. Pagans have long followed unwritten codes that are supportive of social justice and inclusivity. Pagans have—near universally—focused their service on a reverence for community and environment. And individuals who foster these actively are typically seen as spiritual leaders who are examples of Pagan virtues. Even cursory attendance at Pagan festivals should make obvious—to even the most self-focused person—how the community strives of unconditional acceptance of all members, the practice of respect, and a reverence for Nature.

The research on integrity, as mentioned earlier, is much less developed. Trevinyo-Rodriguez (2007) proposed a systemic model of integrity that encompasses the personal space, social situation and moral circumstance as the focal essentials that dictate leader integrity. The concept of integrity presumes the presence of a personal moral core that becomes a tool for discerning the cultural and ethical relativism of interpersonal and community problems (deBakker, 2007; Hartman & DesJardins, 2011; Carter, 1996). The over-arching direction of the limited research, however, is that integrity is a manifestation of a behavioral *authenticity* among leaders that ultimately shows a consistency between the personal action and the personal ethical core.

Looking at the lives of powerful change-makers in society, such as Rev. Martin Luther King, Emmeline Parkhurst, Virginia Prince and Harvey Milk, we recognize their deep commitment to social justice was consistent with elements of behavioral courage (regrettably including the tremendous personal risk), their beliefs about society and the equality of its members as well as how their actions were dependably in concert with their personal beliefs and ethical core. Their vision about social justice inspired others to continue their work and produced armies of individuals promoting equality. Likewise, the empirical literature supports such observations of leaders as well. Sosik, Gentry & Chun (2012) reported that behavioral displays of both integrity and courage were the two most important factors of chief executive level performance. They further suggested that performance gains were the result of exemplar behaviors that were consistent with an organization's mission, even during tremendous adversity. In other words, leaders who walk the talk, inspire others to do the same and work hard at fulfilling a mission.

The question then becomes, of course, how does this research inform the Pagan community about leadership? And how might Pagan leaders use this research to better serve the community; given, in particular, the prominence the many Pagans place on courage and integrity? Foremost in application and deeply important to recognize, the Pagan community is not a monolithic block for which a single brand of leadership applies. However, it is undeniably true that courage and integrity are important Pagan values. And, it is important to note that the lessons about courage and integrity do come from research that attempts to supersede the vagaries of a single group by highlighting the systematic effects of these variables as they apply in many circumstances.

The preface of the argument and research presented here is that courage and integrity are values that are highly consistent with the expectation that Pagans place upon themselves, especially when in community. As leaders rise out of their communities, so too should our leaders live these values. Living openly and in one's ethics are mainstays of participation in Pagan festivals. They represent essential elements about how Pagans relate within the shared space of community. The processes of respect, collaboration, consensus and supportive criticism are bulwarks of Pagan gatherings and reflect the values that leaders must not only share but live out. We can witness these in all activities. For example, Pagan decision-making through discernment and consensus are inherently both acts of trust and courage. Indeed, the very act of offering trust requires courage, especially when interacting with non-Pagans in daily life. Integrity—as the research suggests as living to an ethical standard—is precisely how to "*be*" within the Pagan community.

As these characteristics are not alien to the Pagan community, so too, can they not be alien to the expectation one must have of Pagan leaders. Courage is abundant in Paganism. Being Pagan is by its very nature an indisputably dangerous undertaking. The Pagan community has countless stories of how discrimination by outsiders has undermined the opportunity to congregate, freely exercise religion, and even promote an eco-centric lifestyle. Pagan sensibilities demand a constant vigilance toward outsiders because we have been targeted untold times by ignorance and bigotry. Indeed, Tejeda (2014) found evidence of systematic discrimination of Pagans in the workplace noting that such biases appear to limit economic and financial opportunity for many in the Pagan community.

However, courage need not always be an act of risk as it relates to an external constituency. There is risk from within the

Pagan community when confronting difficult issues. Unsurprisingly, many Pagans are concerned that rocking the boat or exposing our own community weaknesses will display fractures and perceived frailty (or perhaps even a lack of legitimacy) to the outside community. Yet there is no religious community that functions effectively without serious self-reflection. And there is no effective religious community with leaders who challenge it to strengthen it. It is the fear of challenge that produces weakness.

But there are examples of powerful Pagans raising questions and promoting reflection. The late Elder Margot Adler, for example, once raised the issue of Wiccan privilege within Paganism. This was not only an insightful remark about the power of the majority group within the Pagan community but also an act of courage and integrity. Her observation was a self-reflection that power must be challenged even if it is one's own. Moreover, the act of addressing privilege was consistent with reflections on promoting inclusivity, reducing harm, and promoting justice: all inarguably, core Pagan values.

Weick (1995) suggested the people act — and thus create — their identities as part of the social fabric in which they exists. So, the role of leader begins with the courageous internal recognition that each of us can — and must — be called to lead. There is perhaps nothing more important that I hope to convey than the essential truth that each person is called to this service and that every person is capable to being empowered and empowering others. The empirical research has unfailingly shown us that leadership resides in the behavioral. As Pagans we are trained to recognize the spiritual nature of our actions — an act, in and of itself, far too courageous for many others to undertake. Moreover, the essence of Paganism calls our integrity into constant relief as the way we approach community. One could rightly argue that Paganism calls the community to authenticity.

Indeed that last term, authenticity, describes a leader who is "perceived by others as being aware of their own and others values, moral perspectives, knowledge and strengths; aware of the context in which they operate and are confident, hopeful, optimistic, resilient, and of high moral character" (Avolio & Gardner, 2005, p. 321). Authenticity demands self-reflection and an interactional sincerity between the leader and the community. They promote positivity through social identification and emotional contagion while striving to create constructive social exchanges. Bluntly, I think to many of us, that sounds like a Pagan gathering.

The question of courage nonetheless remains open though. Courage still requires a confrontation of the self, and the identity that is portrayed to others. It is, unfortunately, a lacking quality when it is subordinated by worries of rejection or, perhaps more insidiously, clothed in niceties to avoid sounding confrontational, upsetting people, or changing a situation. In my own opinion, the latter is more dangerous. Our own needs to be recognized and accepted are powerful deterrents to promoting change and raising our voices for the less powerful. It is the major transformational challenge that each person-leader must resolve.

I opened this essay by raising issues that continue to surface as ongoing challenges within the Pagan community. Such issues as violence and abuse, whether emotional, sexual or physical, occur within any community where one person is perceived as powerful or even holds initiatory power over another. Predatory behavior is everywhere and the community challenge is vigilance and response. I raised these issues to highlight the importance of courage and integrity—core Pagan values—that the research literature is now recognizing as so critical to leadership by promoting authenticity. Confrontations of abusers require that courage and integrity, bears the risk that others might support the abusers, and demands that community and personal integrity be upheld. And while the Pagan community is replete with leaders, we still struggle with imbuing that leadership with courage in order to confront many difficult issues.

Courage demands that we not fear fractures and leadership prepares to unite in community. Integrity exposes how we live our values and authenticity prepares us to confront challenges. These are combinations that Pagans have promoted as virtues beyond even our written histories. They are embracingly familiar.

There is no shortage of Pagan challenges in the broader context of the general society. But there is also no dearth of challenges within the Pagan community. Transgender pagans are avoided by some groups because of a self-imposed (and misguided) need to recognize a sexual binary in deities. Pagans with physical, intellectual, or emotional challenges continue to encounter barriers to participation in the Pagan community. The number of Pagans of Color within the community still remains shockingly low for unclear reasons. However, these challenges also represent how courage can be invoked to promote change within the Pagan community. By the virtues of our own value system, every Pagan is leader potential, shaped by our community to be authentic. And in that sense, we simply await our courage to be given voice.

Works Cited

Avolio, B.J. & Gardner,W. (2005). Authentic leadership development: Getting to the root of positive forms of leadership. *The Leadership Quarterly, 16(3)*: 3-21.

Carter, S. (1996). *Integrity*. New York: NY: Basic books.

De Bakker, E. (2007). Integrity and cynicism: Possibilities and constraints of moral communication. *Journal of Agricultural and Environmental Ethics, 20(1)*: 119-136.

Finfgeld, D. L. (1999). Courage as a process of pushing beyond the struggle. *Qualitative Health Research,* 9: 803-814.

Hartman, L.P. & DesJardins, J. (2011). *Business ethics: Decision making for personal integrity and social responsibility*. New York, NY: McGraw hill Publishing.

Havamal. http://www.pitt.edu/~dash/havamal.html Retrieved August, 30, 2014.

Koerner, M. M. (2014). Courage as identity work: Accounts of workplace courage. *Academy of Management Journal, 57 (1)*: 63-93.

Lopez, S.J., O'Byrne, K. K., & Peterson, S. (2003). Profiling courage. In S.J. Lopez & C.R. Snyder (Eds.) , *Positive psychological assessment: A handbook of models and measures*: 185-197. Washington, D.C. : American Psychological Association.

Peterson, C. & Seligman, M. E. P. (2004). *Character strengths and virtues*. Washington, D.C.: American Psychological Association.

Sereka, L. & Bagozzi,R. (2007). Moral courage in the workplace: Moving to and from the desire and decision to act. *Journal of Business Ethics, 89*: 565-570.

Sosik, J.J., Gentry, W.A. & Chun, J.U. (2012). The value of virtue in the ipper echelons: A multisource examination of he executive character strengths and performanc. *The Leadership Quarterly, 23*: 367-382.

Tejeda, M. J. (2014). Skeletons in the broom closet: Exploring the discrimination of Pagans in the workplace. Journal of Management, Spirituality & Religion. DOI:10.1080/14766086.2014.933710

Trevinyo-Rodriguez, R.N. (2007). Integrity: A systems theory classification. *Journal of Management history, 13(1),*: 74-93.

Weick, K. E. (1995). *Sensemaking in organizations.* Thousand Oaks, CA: Sage Publications.

A Balm for a Pagan Plague:
High Priestess' Disease
Sable Aradia

If you've been at all active in the Pagan community, you have probably heard of this particular ailment. It describes the spiritual malaise that causes some of us to develop an inflated sense of our importance and "power trip" on being a Wiccan Priest(ess). In this essay I'm going to discuss this problem frankly, explore its possible causes, and suggest solutions for it. While I am sure that many of my observations can be adapted to other Pagan traditions, I am writing from a Wiccan perspective because that is all I can address with authority as that is what I know.

Symptoms

Symptoms of High Priestess' Disease include: arrogance, inability to accept criticism, emotional explosions, a compulsive need for control, feelings of abandonment, impatience, a sense of not being taken seriously or of your accomplishments being disregarded, and becoming frustrated when people disobey or disregard your requests or instructions. Recognizing these indicators in yourself, or in your students, is the first step to recovery.

Causes

Contrary to popular belief, I don't think that this epidemic is due to defects of character. I believe it is a natural part of the process in the study of the Craft and that some of us handle it better than others. It is caused by the nature of the Work that we do as Witches.

Learning to Manage Power

I like to joke that in Wicca, women learn how to take their power, and men learn how to give it up. What I mean by this is that Wicca is a space where the traditional roles of power are broken down or deliberately remodeled. The gender divide is only one of the most obvious examples of this. When I do public rituals with my husband and Priest, the newspaper reporters always go to talk to him first, because they assume that he is the one in charge. When someone has been involved with Pagans for a while, they come to talk to me first, because they know that the odds are that the person in charge is me.

While I certainly will agree that this perception is changing in Western culture, the unconscious bias still exists. And so many women come to the Craft from a disadvantaged place, attracted by the feminist viewpoint and the lack of a glass ceiling. I was no exception. I am probably a Witch today because I was always mystically-inclined and I felt that most churches did not want female religious leaders. And since women are often not taken as seriously as men are, when they find a role that gives them leadership, they often become a little drunk on it. This is probably why we call it "High Priestess' Disease."

But this is hardly the only example of power intoxication in those who come from disadvantaged groups. Wicca is, by definition, a counter-cultural movement. According to Berger, Leach and Shaffer, we attract all kinds of outsiders, minority groups, and just plain "weirdos" (and I mean that with all the due affection of being one of those "weirdos" myself.) We attract GLBT men and women, geeks, nerds, rebels, and people with disabilities. We attract more than our fair share of scholars and people with anxiety disorders. Whenever people who have lacked power are suddenly given it, there is always a chance that they can run away with the headiness of it.

Breaking the Ego

Wicca is a mystic's path. Ultimately, its greatest mystery is union with the Divine; what we call "Drawing Down the Moon" and "Drawing Down the Sun." In order to achieve that, we must break down the dross of our personalities. Not all of our personality, just the stuff that interferes with our ability to channel our Divine Selves. Think of it as a refining process. We are trying to become better conductors. Pure gold is the best conductor for electricity, and pure copper follows that, but elements are rarely pure in nature and so they must be melted, tempered, and beaten in order to reach that state of purity. We are no different, and frankly, the process hurts and we resist. However, the more we resist, the greater the pain. Someone who is suffering from High Priestess' Disease is having their ego challenged and they are resisting alchemical transformation of the spirit. That is why Wicca demands that we choose this path of our own free will.

We don't handle this process very well as Witches. I believe that's because this form of our religion is so young. It may help to look to the teachings and practices of other spiritual paths for ways to deal with this complex and confusing process.

Growing Up

Growing up is the process of coming into our own, of defining our personalities and our innermost selves as being different from that of our parents, of testing our limits, and ultimately accepting responsibility for our own lives. Becoming a High Priestess or Priest is no different. We must define our spiritual selves as being different from that of our "Craft parents"; we must define ourselves as spiritual people; we must test our limits, and the Rede demands that we accept responsibility for all of our actions, intentional or not. In other words, those new to being Wiccan clergy often have the exact same arrogant swagger that teenagers do who are convinced that their parents are the world's biggest idiots and they have invented new and better ways to do everything. As any parent could tell you, if they are in that space, there is simply no talking to them.

Prevention

If you can head the behaviors off at the pass, you can prevent the development of the disease. If not, you must confront them on a case-by-case basis.

Successful Power Management

Sharing power fairly is an important part of the Craft. Many groups deal with this by consensus decision-making, while others deal with it by establishing a firm hierarchy and delineating a process by which other groups, created under someone else's leadership, may form.

In the first case, often a covert leadership forms in the place of an overt leadership. As long as power is being distributed fairly and all are being given a chance to facilitate (and respected when they are), this is probably just fine. Making sure this process is respected is a cure to power-hunger. Make good use of Talking Sticks, mentorship and shared facilitation, as well as other time-honored methods of power sharing.

In the second case, usually a Priestess who has obtained a Second Degree in an initiatory tradition has the right to "hive off" and form her own coven if she doesn't want to remain under the existing High Priestess' leadership. As coven leaders, encourage budding Priestesses and Priests who are getting too big for their britches to do so, and take note of your own behavior when you have a rash of defections.

In either case, arrogant leaders who refuse to share power or to help others to build their own groups will soon find themselves without groups to lead, whether they led the old group, or the new. That's a good wake-up call.

Ego-Death

I like to tell my students that one of the keys to successful Wiccan life is developing a "right-sized ego." Many of us do not appreciate our own significance. We are taught to be humble, and this leads to false humility and an undervaluing of ourselves and our capabilities. Arrogance will cause us to be so busy looking at our own noses that we trip over our feet and look ridiculous, but not appreciating our own capabilities undervalues the hard work of others. When we are comfortable with ourselves we can engage in honest assessment. For instance, I am a reasonably talented singer/songwriter. I know many who are better, and many more who are worse. I am probably good enough to make a living at it if I want to, but not good enough to leave a legacy of lasting value. I am comfortable with this.

Initiation is also an excellent coping mechanism. Especially in the Second Degree, we are forced into an ordeal that causes us to confront our fears and our personal issues head-on, because ego is usually a defense against fear–be it fear of hurt, humiliation, pain or fear of death and loss. Initiation helps us to face the transition from one state to another and recognize the pain. If you do not have a formal initiation, in my experience, your path as a Witch will cause life to provide an on-the-spot "initiatory experience" for you!

The firm transition from one state to another is intended to shock the ego into taking a nap and allowing the transformation. It is a valuable tool, like a Rite of Passage marking the transition to adulthood, but it's not always successful, and some traditions don't have initiations. However, those traditions usually speak of the Hero's Journey and the Mysteries of the Dark Goddess, and the same lessons are learned there.

Growing Up

I find that if Witches are stuck in the acute stage of High Priestess' Disease, refusing to grow up is usually the cause. I described "growing up" as "accepting responsibility." Victims of High Priestess-itis don't do this well. They always have an excuse, or someone else to blame. You can't confront your issues unless you admit to them. Be willing to be vulnerable, and to apologize for your mistakes and make restitution for whatever your part was in it, whether the harm you did was intended or not.

Treatment

Treatment is much more difficult than prevention. Long-term care or "shock therapy" is needed. I advise teachers not to take it upon themselves to deliver the shocks, however, other than with initiation. The gods do well enough at that without our help. We can, however, help with long-term care. Teach (and study) the Rede; teach (and practice) honest self-assessment, and encourage (and practice) regular confrontation of the Shadow-Self. I have a meditation for this on my YouTube channel; you are welcome to use it.

In some cases, professional therapy may be called for. There's no shame in this. The Craft is not an easy path. There's a reason that the weird old Witch at the edge of the woods and the mad, wandering Wizard are stereotypes. Take advantage of modern psychology or ancient shamanic wisdom, and if you delve too deep and find something in there you can't handle, get someone to help you.

Prognosis

High Priestess-itis is 100% preventable and in most cases responds well to therapy, but defense systems of the ego often prevent the afflicted from seeking treatment. Untreated, it leads to alienation, loneliness, and constant confrontation of the ego. In other words, the personal issues of the victim continue to rear their ugly heads again and again and again until lessons are learned, locking her or him into destructive patterns, characterized by the victim's exasperated cry, "Why does this $%&* keep happening to me?!" This pattern might continue for years. I find, however, that those who genuinely wish for help will actually recover, so don't be afraid to reach out and ask.

Works Cited:

Berger, Helen A., Evan A. Leach and Leigh S. Shaffer. *Voices from the Pagan Census: A National Survey of Witches and Neo-pagans in the United States.* Columbia, SC: University of South Carolina Press, 2003. Print.

The Myth of the Higher Standard
Mya Om

I have doubts. I have pressure points. I have a temper. I am a perfectionist. I am demanding. I cannot stand to see a perceived injustice. I do not always stand up for myself. I have low self-esteem. In the darkest corners of my soul, I constantly feel as if I am an imposter, that no one likes me, and that I am unworthy of success because I have done things that I regret. This is my private persona, and it bleeds through to my public self, especially when I feel called to put myself on display.

I can speak to a conference room full of professionals, including other attorneys, CEOs of Fortune 100 companies etc... it does not faze me in the slightest. I can stand there as Mya, the Attorney, the Risk Manager, the Litigator, the highly educated woman that I know am, and speak with all confidence about any number of topics. But put me in a room with a bunch of Pagans and suddenly, I have nothing to say. I am insecure and I self-censor myself—being a published author has not changed that, in fact it has made my condition worse. I worry about being held to a higher standard, about saying something stupid or something that can be taken out of context. I worry about being seen as arrogant, a snob, elitist or Gods forbid, a Big Nose Pagan. I lie to myself and say it is because I am humble, in reality I am terrified.

You see, in my identity as a Pagan, as a Witch, I allow you to see me—my authentic self—and not the professional persona I have built up for the rest of the world. It is akin to that dream of standing in front of a classroom of students in my underwear. The idea of being judged and found lacking terrifies me, to the point where I once vowed that I would not teach, accept students, or even use my author pseudonym at Pagan events. I am more often assistant #1 at the Lotions Potions Notions booth at various events, than I am Mya Om.

When I wrote my first book, *Energy Essentials for Witches and Spellcasters*, I did it because I felt I had something to say and to add to the Pagan discourse. Energy work was something I understood very well and it was something I perceived was not being discussed, at least not in any sort of formal sense within the larger Pagan community. I expected the manuscript to be rejected. It wasn't. I expected my "friends" to be happy for me when it was accepted for publication—they weren't. Instead, I went from being the oft silent girl, who volunteers for different Pagan events, to that girl who wrote a book that was published by Llewellyn. Critics and detractors I didn't even know I had come out of the woodwork. The funny thing is—my identity did not change. I was still me, but the reactions to me had changed. In the years since that first book came out, I wondered if I got the reaction I did because I was only in my twenties when I wrote it; if it was jealousy, or if it was because I never really put myself out there as an expert, teacher, or leader until after the book came out.

Don't worry; I did not spend much time worrying about these so-called friends or their reactions. I was too busy growing up, going to law school, falling in and out of love, traveling and learning how to love myself (flaws, insecurities, pressure points and all). The question you might have now, is if I'm over what happened, why I am writing about all of this?

Two reasons:

I want you to understand that on a fundamental level—regardless of personal accomplishments, where I am in my career, etc.—that how you might see me is not the same as I see myself. I am just me. I try to make ethical choices, to do the right thing, and to be a good example. Unfortunately, I am far from perfect. I have regrets, a history, and scars.

I want you to understand that merely being in leadership position, regardless of if it is in a spiritual sense, political sense, or in a career sense, does not make the person infallible, and ultimately the fallibility of the person should not diminish the religion, the community or the office itself. My faults belong to me; they do not belong to an office I may hold, or my job title, or a community position I hold etc....

When a child pornography scandal erupted in the broader US Pagan community in March 2014, there was a huge push within said community to assert that Pagan leaders needed to be held to a "higher standard." My problem with the idea of a "higher standard" is that it is a nebulous undefined concept. What is a "higher standard?" Do I know? Do you know? And if neither of us knows, how can we expect anyone to comply with it? Is it like the Supreme Court's definition of obscenity/pornography, where Justice Stewart is famously credited with saying "I don't know what it is, but I know it when I see it[1]"?

Don't misunderstand me, *child pornography is not acceptable* for anyone. I'm pretty sure asking someone to not have child pornography is a pretty low bar to set when it comes to standards of behavior, ethics and leadership. The larger issue that this scandal exposed is the lack of uniformity when it comes to ethics, expectations, and roles within the larger community.

In my opinion, at least, the events surrounding the child pornography scandal, and the subsequent revelations that inappropriate conduct had been going on for a number of years with this person was not only a failure of *leadership*, it was a failure of the *community*.

My primary training is in Wicca, and I try to hold to the ideals of the Rede—and its "harm none" ethics. However, the Pagan community is comprised of individuals who have very diverse beliefs, ideologies, ethics, and practices. Given the diversity in practices, experience, and ethics, how can we even begin to define what the standard of behavior ought to be? And without even that base standard, how can we really examine the idea of the "higher standard."

Instead, what I believe our community needs is something else—we need a Social Contract.

The Social Contract

In 1762 a Frenchman by the name of Jean-Jacques Rousseau wrote a small treatise titled *Of the Social Contract, or Principles of Political Right, Du Contract Social ou Principes du Droit Politique[2]*, if you prefer the original French. Without turning this manuscript into a thousand page discourse on the history of political rights, the American & French Revolutions and the rise of secular political authority—because I would only be reiterating what historians and political theorists have already written about at great length, and because I don't want to bore you silly—

---

[1] See Jacobellis v. Ohio 378 US 184 (1964)
[2] J. Rousseau, Of the Social Contract, or Principles of Political Right, 1762 available at http://www.constitution.org/jjr/socon.htm

Rousseau's social contract examined the question of whether there can be any legitimate political authority. In the end, Rousseau concluded that in a desired Social Contract, each member of the community gave up the same rights and took on the same obligations as every other member.

Rousseau's work was considered very controversial during his time because he challenged the idea that rulers had a divine or god given right to rule; he opined that rulers and nobles, instead of being given a free pass merely because of their position as kings/queens etc., should be held to the same standards as everyone else. In Rousseau's world this meant that in any society there should be two parts (1) the sovereign— which is made up of all of the members of the society and (2) the government—which is made up of people who enforce or apply the rules established by the "sovereign." If the government failed to uphold with will of the sovereign, then it was the responsibility of the sovereign to replace the government.

Rousseau's theory works well when there is a political body in place—so for an actual government like the United States, where there are representatives or other people with clearly defined authority. I am not suggesting that Pagans adopt a governing body, for one I doubt you'd get anyone to agree on the structure or on who should be represented and to what extent. Second, I do not see the Pagan community becoming a dogmatic institution like the Catholic Church. Finally, the Pagan community is not a political institution so it is unlikely that a replication of Rousseau's ideal government would work for us.

Why bring Jean-Jacques if I am not recommending setting up a Pagan government or legislative body? First, because I don't like not attributing ideas to the people who came up with them, and second, because I agree with his analysis, if not the application.

To summarize:

There is no god or goddess given right for an individual to be held up as a leader in the Pagan community—this applies regardless of the individual's ego, how many books he/she has written, or how many Facebook friends and followers on Twitter they have. It also applies regardless of how many successful events he/she has hosted, or whether or not the person is considered a "draw" or "attraction."

People who put themselves into leadership roles *are not* any better or worse than the rest of the members of the community. They have the same human limitations, foibles, flaws, and faults as the rest of the members of the community.

It is the responsibility of *every* member of the Sovereign, as Jean-Jacques put it, or the community, to hold each other, perceived authority figures, so called leaders etc... accountable for their conduct. If you wouldn't let Joe Shmoe get away with certain behavior, then Big Nose Author or Community Leader doesn't get to get away with it either.

There is **No** "**Higher Standard**" — the standards of acceptable behavior apply to every member of the community.

There is **No** "**Lower Standard**" — the standards of acceptable behavior apply to every member of the community.

Everyone gives up the same rights, and takes on the same burdens — this means you too. If you see something, say something. If people in "authority" don't listen to you, then as Jean-Jacques suggested, replace them.

As a community our Social Contract is not with our "leaders", as these people may come and go, they may be virtuous people or closet villains. Rather our Social Contract is with each other. There are no Pagan police that are going to enforce the rules of ethical conduct. We don't have a president who can kick offenders off of Pagan Island. What we have, and all we really have, is each other.

I do not propose establishing a set of rules or protocols that the larger Pagan community must follow. Rather what I suggest is accountability for each member of the community. As outlined above, everyone — even those who are in leadership positions whether by choice or default — are held to the same standards of conduct as everyone else. The question of whether something constitutes acceptable conduct I leave up to the Sovereign/Community to define.

Individual Groups & the Social Contract

In the last section, I discussed the idea that the broader Pagan community needed a Social Contract as a way of realizing the each member of the community is held to the same standard of behavior and has the same obligations to each other as the "leaders" do. In this section I am going to zoom in a bit and examine the idea of a Social Contract, from the perspective of a smaller community (Coven[3]).

Just as I initially suggested that the broader Pagan community needed a Social Contract with each other, I feel as well that smaller groups—where the level of intimacy can be significantly greater than in the broader community—would benefit from developing a Social Contract with each other. This Social Contract should be based on the same ideas discussed in the last section, but should be tailored towards the individual beliefs, morals, and ideology of the group itself.

At the initial phase of forming a Coven no one really expects things to go wrong, and so the group members often do not discuss the question of what to do when something does go wrong—I see this as a kind of honeymoon phase, where all the members are eager, they are on the same page, and things are going great.

The Social Contract is not for the honeymoon phase—the Social Contract is for six months, or a year, or two years down the road when interests start to diverge, when new members have joined the group, or when interpersonal issues start to come to the forefront and communication breaks down. In the life-cycle of a Coven this is known as the implosion stage, when internal forces start to pull the group apart. The implosion stage can also lead to the infamous Witch-Wars which may cause strife and spillover into the larger community. It would be ideal if all of those disputes could be nipped in the bud; unfortunately, Covens are made up of human beings. Coven members, Coven Leaders, just like community members and leaders are not perfect. Disagreements happen, relationships end, feelings get hurt.

The questions the Coven must answer are:

---

[3] I am going to use the term Coven going forward, but this can be applied to any type of organizational structure where individuals interact. From a traditional Wiccan sense the term Coven evokes certain ideas with respect to structure, membership etc… Here I am using the term in a broader sense as any gathering of Pagans, Witches, Magick Practitioners etc… and not in the traditional Wiccan sense.

- How are we going to deal with the inevitable disagreement?
- What standards of behavior are we going to expect from the people involved?

All too often Covens fail to address these questions initially, and when something does go wrong the situation turns into a spectacle worthy of a teenage drama—mean girls anyone?

Establishing accountability and behavior thresholds at the outset helps to keep the emotion out of the Coven's decision making. This doesn't mean that the Coven will always be successful in heading off conflict; rather, it will help to establish a framework through which conflict can be resolved amicably and hopefully with class. To borrow some lines from a famous movie, the goal should be more of "now is the end, let her go in peace;" instead of "now is the end, let her go in pieces" ending to the conflict.

Below are some questions that individuals may want to think about when developing a Social Contract between the coven members:

- How would I treat someone if he/she hurt my feelings?
- How would I expect someone else to treat me if I hurt his/her feelings?
- How would I react if I found out that someone said something negative about me to another group member, on social media, or to a member/leader of another group?
- What should I/we do if someone does something illegal, immoral, or which violates my/our ethics?
- What is my/our stances on drug/alcohol use? Sex? Nudity? Allowing Minors with/without parental consent into the Coven or to participate in rituals?
- What would happen if I dated/was married to/or was otherwise in a relationship with someone in the Coven and we broke up? Or what would happen if two Coven members

were dating/married/in a relationship and the relationship ended?—what happens if it ended badly?

- What is my/our stance on manipulation/coercive behavior? On baneful magick? On using witchcraft against or on another person without his/her permission?
- What is my opinion on gossip? What constitutes gossip? How would I/we deal with gossip and/or hearsay?
- If two or more group members disagree about something, how will the group handle the disagreement? -would you expect people to pick sides? To get a neutral arbitrator?
- How would I/we terminate the relationship with someone in the Coven? Would we tell other people why/how the relationship ended?
- Under what circumstances would someone be kicked out of the Coven? What steps would be taken to accomplish that goal?

Discussing these and other questions that may come up is a good first step in determining not only how the group may react in a certain situation but also how individuals may react as well. It may be tempting to treat this as an informal discussion, but I recommend writing down the outcome of this discussion and either incorporating it into the group's bylaws (more on that later) or at least keeping a record of them for use when the inevitable situation comes up—and be prepared to stick by them.

No one person, group, or situation is going to be exactly the same. My advice: approach the situation from a perspective of allowing all of the people involved to maintain their dignity and respect. Keep it off the social media sites, off your personal blog, and don't repeat unconfirmed rumors to other Coven members or to members of the larger community.

From a personal perspective, I understand that asking these questions may seem like a lot of unnecessary work. Phrases like: "Why fix something that isn't broken?" and "We're all adults here; we can handle a bit of conflict when it comes up," immediately to come to mind.

After several decades of experience and living through more than one witch war, I can emphatically say:

- Conflict/conflict resolution is something that needs to be discussed.
- You cannot count on people to behave like adults in situations where feelings are hurt, tempers are involved, and egos are bruised.
- Individuals are called "individual" for a reason; views on just about everything may differ even within people raised in the same family. In the long run it is better to ask than it is to assume.
- Do not expect that the High Priest/High Priestess/Coven Leader will be able to solve all conflict—(1) They may actually be the source of the conflict (2) The High Priest/High Priestess/Coven Leader is human and may not be equipped to deal with a particular situation. (3) Each member of the Coven is responsible not to the High Priest/High Priestess/Coven Leader but to the other Coven members and to their own self.

The idea here isn't that any person gets a free pass on bad behavior—rather the simple premise behind this article is that each person needs to take responsibility for his/her own conduct and hold other members of the community to the same level of accountability. Community leaders, High Priests, High Priestesses etc. are not here to act as the morality police or as referees or judges. It is up to the Community in general, and to individual groups in particular to define what the acceptable standards of behavior may be.

Section 2
General Advice

Leadership 101: Respect
Raine Shakti

Throughout the course of modern history, Pagans have rarely organized on a large scale. Small groups have met in groves and fields or people's homes with potluck meals and shared duties. We take pride in our heathen beginnings and on our lack of rigidity. However, there are many lessons that can be learned from organized religion and from the corporate world that can help us to truly build Pagan leaders who are taken seriously. While these lessons are broken down below, they all boil down to one thing: Respect.

Many Pagans would protest loudly and voraciously if they were accused of being disrespectful and would point to their abiding respect for nature, the right of other people to worship as they see fit, their respect for diversity, and a myriad of other respects as evidence that they are, in fact, respectful. While all of those facts are certainly true in most instances, many Pagan leaders show disrespect on a regular basis for their Gods, for their followers, for themselves, and for the act of ritual itself.

Respecting Our Gods

Asking our deities to do things that are not in our best interests and not in the best interests of others shows certain disrespect for their power and the help they offer us so freely. This disrespect is multiplied when we involve others in these requests. Unfortunately, this is a disrespect that I've been guilty of on more than one occasion. I went through a brutal separation and divorce four years ago and, immediately after my ex walked out the door, my moods were swinging rapidly between wanting vengeance and wanting him back, and my magick and my requests to the Gods mirrored those swings.

When I was seeking vengeance, I would channel all my negative energy into whoever he was seeing at that particular time. I would ask the Gods to give him what he deserved, which in my mind was not loving/healing but was every hellacious thing that the universe had to offer. My magick and requests were somewhat successful as his girlfriend broke up with him on the very day our divorce was final and subsequently lost his job. He went off his rocker and threatened suicide and a host of other misfortunes befell him. However, all this magick did was to strengthen the unhealthy ties between us and leave me thinking less of myself.

On the days when I was lonely and afraid and wanted him back, I'd do magick to bring him back to me no matter what. We had an Anubis statue that we had gotten at the Parliament of World Religions in 2003 and when we split up I offered to give it to him. However, before this, I did a ritual and asked Anubis to bring him back to me no matter what. Again, all this magick did was to keep the unhealthy tie that bound us together and create more misery for me. Anubis also knew that our getting back together was not in anyone's best interest, and every time we started getting closer, something would happen to drive a wedge between us again.

I've never involved others in my questionable magick, but I've seen other Pagan Leaders succumb to the temptation of raising power in ritual and channeling it into questionable endeavors. The worst of these instances was when a fellow priestess led a ritual to goddess of questionable morals. The energy raised was then directed toward her ex. I bowed out of participating in this ritual, but I heard about the power that was raised and directed toward her ex and I was glad I chose not to participate.

Lesson Learned: Follow the Wiccan Rede

The Wiccan Rede, *"That it harm none, do as thou wilt,"* states clearly and unequivocally that we should not harm others. However, this is a very hard rule to live by in the magical realm as just a quick flick of the finger or an angry thought can send our rage raining down on someone. It is all the more powerful when we deliberately ask our Gods to assist us. Being a Pagan leader means that I need to respect myself and my Gods enough to take the high road. This doesn't mean I roll over and accept abuse, but it does mean that instead of using magick to harm I choose to use my magick to protect. What I've found is that when I deliberately choose to not seek revenge, the universe has a way of taking care of things. However, when I interfere, I often end up hurting myself in the process.

Respecting Yourself

Leadership speakers and corporate gurus make a lot of money standing in front of people and peddling their wisdom. In contrast, many Pagan leaders barely eke out a living and give their wisdom away for free because they believe it is part of their ministry, or they don't want to be viewed as taking advantage of their brethren.

There is a fine line between respecting ourselves enough to charge for our wisdom and taking advantage of other people. There many factors that go into determining what, if anything, to charge including how long the workshop is, how much the upfront investment in supplies and or travel costs is, and how much other leaders charge for similar workshops. Charging a fair price for your services shows (yourself and others) that you value yourself and what you have to say enough to charge for it.

Self-sufficiency is another way to demonstrate that you respect yourself and others. It is a hard, cold fact of life that the world does not owe anyone a living. However, I have seen Pagans who have chosen to live on welfare and food stamps because they believe that there message is so important and they are so special that they shouldn't have to work a "square" job. It may sound cold and harsh, but I do not believe that anyone's message is so important that other people (i.e. taxpayers) should be unwillingly conscripted to pay for it. I have to be honest and say that after reading that Vicki Noble had chosen to be on food stamps so she could write, I lost a lot of respect for her as I choose to write, build a Pagan ministry, and support myself, and although the road may be longer, it brings me a deep sense of self-respect.

An ex-friend who considers himself an elder in the Pagan community is another person who believes that his message and ministry are so important that he shouldn't have to work a square job. He accepts food stamps, he grumbles when budget cuts reduce his dole, and he regularly skirts tax laws to support his ministry. When I first met him, I was so shell shocked from my divorce that I didn't step back and ask myself what kind of message he was truly sending. However, when I took a step back, I realized that his message was one of arrogance as he believed he was too important to follow the tax laws and support himself.

My views on self-sufficiency may be radical, and I truly applaud anyone who chooses to downsize their lifestyle to support their dreams. I also applaud people who offer assistance to our Pagan leaders; however, I believe we are all responsible for our own lives and if we choose to downsize then we shouldn't complain about it and we should not expect others to unwillingly support our dreams.

Lesson Learned: Value our Skills

Valuing our skills means that we set reasonable prices when we offer our services. It also means truly thinking about what we can afford to give away and what we need to charge for. For instance, a Pagan Priestess may choose to charge for weddings and separation rituals, but may choose to offer funeral services as part of her ministry. She may choose to charge for readings, but facilitate seasonal rituals with a request for a love offering. I'm personally choosing to participate in Pagan Pride events and offer a free shortened version of a workshop I normally charge for. My decision is based in part on a spirit of giving back to my community, but it is also about building my reputation.

Lesson Learned: Be Self-Supporting

Being self-supporting means paying your own bills and not relying on others to do things you can and should do for yourself. This is not to say that being self-supporting means never asking for help as there are times when we all need a helping hand. It does mean doing what you can to ensure there is a fair exchange of energy or that you help someone else when they're in need. For instance, if you need cash, you might barter your services so there is an equal exchange.

Lesson Learned--Follow the Rules

People decry greedy corporations that play shell games to avoid paying income tax, but many Pagans skirt the same rules by taking cash for services and underreport their earnings. Not being honest about their earnings shows a lack of integrity and a lack of respect for the Gods, because if someone truly believes the Gods will take care of them, then the Gods will take care of the taxes as well.

Respecting Others

There is a rule in many companies that meetings start on time and if someone doesn't show up on time, it is their responsibility to get caught up. And if the leader does not show up within five minutes of the scheduled start time, everyone leaves and it is the leader's responsibility to reschedule the meeting. In contrast, I've participated in many Pagan rituals that don't start on time because the leader is chronically tardy or chooses to wait for someone who is running late because they don't what to hurt that person's feelings by starting without them. What they fail to realize is that starting late is disrespectful to all of the people who planned ahead and made it to the ritual on time.

Respect for others doesn't just apply in group settings; it also applies if you are a Pagan Elder who meets with students or others for spiritual counseling or teaching. I used to meet with a Pagan Elder who worked in an occult store and even though my appointment was for 7:30, there were often evenings where I would wait for him until 9 pm because he had other customers. At the time, I thought I was learning patience, but time and distance from this person has made me realize that all I was doing was allowing myself to be disrespected.

Pagan leaders also have the responsibility of respecting other people's boundaries and carefully choosing how they relay messages seen in readings or other situations. The aforementioned reader also took it upon himself to tell me my son was unemployable, even though my reading had nothing to do with my son. That comment was the beginning of the end for my friendship and spiritual relationship with this person as I started to pay careful attention to how he treated me and others, and I realized that his attitudes were very misogynistic as one of his favorite past times was talking about how he loved all the skin that was on display during the summer. The fact that he spoke about this openly gave me the impression, rightly or wrongly, that he was incapable of truly accepting women as equals.

Lesson Learned: Timeliness

Starting rituals or gatherings on times shows others that you respect them and that you respect their other commitments.

Lesson Learned: Be Kind and Respectful

There is too much ugliness and abuse in the world. As Pagan leaders we have a responsibility to set an example to others by living our lives with kindness toward others and respect. There may be instances where we see things in readings that are uncomfortable, but we have a choice as to the words we use to convey them and we can choose to be kind or unkind. It is also important to remember that our attitudes speak volumes about who we are, and if we are disrespectful to one group of people, that exhibits disrespect for people in general.

Respecting the Ritual

Olympic opening and closing ceremonies are very public ritual events that seem to unfold like magick on our television screens with pageantry, ritual, and very few glitches. These events appear so flawless because of the months of planning that went into them. In contrast, many Pagan rituals appear disorganized with people forgetting their lines, supplies left at home, or other glitches occurring. Although the planning involved in a community ritual does not reach the level of planning required for the Olympics, the elements are the same:

- **Ritual Design**—Good rituals are well thought out and designed around a central theme. They incorporate the correct components and they flow.
- **Venue**—Ritual venues should be chosen with care to ensure that they are quiet, appropriate for the ritual, and will comfortably hold the number of expected participants.
- **Participants**—One of the most beautiful parts of Pagan rituals are their participatory nature, and while there is always some room for choosing

participants at the last minute, it's important that some thought goes into choosing who will play the main roles in each ritual.

- **Script** — Depending upon the complexity of the ritual, the number of participants, and the purpose of the ritual, a complete script can be written for the ritual or a rough outline can be created that leaves room for creativity and ad libbing.
- **Logistics** — Very few rituals will require the kind of logistics that the Olympics require, but even the simplest rituals need a little bit of logistical planning to ensure that the alter is set up correctly, cakes and ales are arranged for, and copies of the script are available.
- **Rehearsal** — Ritual rehearsals don't have to mean completely setting up the ritual space and going through the script line by line, the rehearsal can just be a "table walk through" after the ritual is planned and scripted. A walk through involves giving an overview of what's going to be said and done to make sure that everyone understands their role and what will be said at a high level.

Lesson Learned: Be Organized and Prepared

Taking a little bit of time ahead of time to plan and organize your ritual will make it a better event for everyone involved. Participants will enjoy a ritual that seems to flow easily and leaders will be better able to enjoy the ritual as they've taken care of all foreseeable problems. Chances are that something may still go wrong with your ritual, but because you've taken care of everything you could in advance, you'll be better able to deal with those unforeseen circumstances.

Lesson Learned — Rehearse

Taking a little bit of time ahead of time to walk through the ritual and make sure everyone knows what they need to say and where they need to be will help things go so much more smoothly. From a personal perspective, I've learned that even when my dress rehearsals in front of the mirror are disastrous, I always seem to get the words out correctly when it is show time and I know that's because I took the time to practice saying thing things different ways and I worked out all the giggles ahead of time.

As we continue to reclaim our Pagan heritage and achieve more respect in the world, it will do us all well as Pagan leaders to remember to show respect to our Gods, ourselves, our followers, and our rituals.

A Dynamic Adventure
Rev. Judith Laxer

I didn't know I was founding a ministry when I offered that first Goddess worship service in September of 2000. I'd been a Priestess for about a decade and I simply wanted people who didn't belong to a coven, circle or grove to have a place to gather with others of a like mind to engage in the sacred. I knew that Pagan practice wasn't even referred to as 'worship' and I knew it should occur out in nature whenever possible. Still, twelve people came to that first service in my office, and they encouraged me to do it again the next month. Over fifteen years later, Gaia's Temple is a thriving spiritual entity whose community is strong and loving.

As I walked my Priestess path, I came to understand how crucial it was for those who honor and respect Mother Earth as a sentient being to stand strong as Her advocate. My work as a Priestess became the priority in my life, and when I felt sure that I had a specific role in what Joanna Macy calls 'The Great Turning', I made a decision. I garnered all my courage and decided not to let fear and the cellular memory of persecution that haunted me constrain my calling.

Sounds a bit affected to call it that. A "calling" seems so trite, a cliché. And yet that is exactly what it is. I heard the call of the Goddess. In the late 1980's and early 90's, watching the news about impending environmental disaster and yet another warmongering deed, I heard Her call through the noise and chaos and inequity of our patriarchal world. Discovering the Great Mother Goddess and Her nurturing and balanced ways awakened my ability to hear Her call for feminine wisdom in leadership to bring equilibrium. In responding, I stepped forward with nothing but my faith and a history of experience in the performing arts, my two greatest loves that dovetailed perfectly.

Providing leadership has brought strong challenges along the way, most of which have tested and spurred powerful growth in me on a personal level as well as a public one. I didn't have a mentor, a guide, a teacher, no colleagues who were also doing what I was. I didn't know anyone else who had founded a ministry. I still don't. All the other clergy I knew in my interfaith community were supported by houses of worship that had already been established. I had no one to run things by, no one else's experience to learn from. I was charting uncharted territory with intuition as my sole compass. It was risky, but exciting because there was no one to answer to and my own creativity and ideas had free reign.

I wrote alternative versions of ancient myths and told them in my best storytelling voice. I picked songs and chants that supported my 'teachings' (my word for 'sermons') and wove them into the offerings. Each month I produced another service honoring nature and the qualities of compassion and relatedness in an attempt to bring balance in the world. All my theatrical skills came perfectly to bear in these creations and I reveled in my new found profession.

Conversely, all mistakes were mine and their impact landed squarely in my lap. The consequence of every blunder was my fault and mine to attempt to amend. It's a misunderstanding that control is glamourous. Leadership humbles.

Four years after that first offering, the Temple had grown such that it was time to formalize it. I wanted those who were generously giving financial support to the ministry to receive benefit from doing so. We needed to become a non-profit organization with church status so that financial contributions would be tax deductible. I invited five of my most trusted friends at the time, one of whom was obtaining her Masters degree in organizational development (a bit of luck there!) to join me in forming a Board of Directors that would work together in a circle model and on consensus. This was in alignment with the feminine values I so strongly held dear.

Circle model meant all voices would be heard on all issues. No one voice or opinion would hold more weight than anyone else's. We agreed that consensus meant no decision would be made unless everyone either agreed to it or would approve it, even though it might not be what they would prefer. A conflict resolution protocol was drafted and agreed upon. This kind of foundational work takes time. It was incredibly detailed, sometimes excruciating in its particularities, but worth every minute spent. Once these foundational pieces were in place, the focus of the board shifted to maintaining the financial health of the Temple, as it is meant to do. No matter how spiritual your organization is, the pragmatic aspects of it must be developed and strongly rooted in practicality in order for it to endure. I liken this to the essential labor that goes on backstage so that everything in front of the curtain looks effortless.

Circle model and consensus are magnificent in theory, a beautifully feminine praxis that promises to bring great transformation to hierarchical organizations. And it is often difficult in practice. Hearing all voices is easy enough and so is decision making when everyone agrees. But when they don't, that talking stick can be passed around and around to no end. There is value in taking the time to process, but not everyone has the patience for it. Many times, especially at the beginning, I wanted to override the method and jump to a conclusion, any conclusion, just to move on. Patriarchy runs deep. Power-over is seductive.

No matter how much you want all voices to be heard equally, the truth is that the founder's voice carries the strongest influence because it's their baby, their vision, and usually they are carrying most of the burden, doing most of the work. As the founder of Gaia's Temple, my greatest challenge, as well as the place of my greatest growth, has been in maturing to the point where I can hear and withstand opposition and consider other plans and ideas that are not my own without succumbing to egoic measures that tear at the integrity of the group. My mistakes in this arena are the ones for which I hold the most regret.

In a confusing conflict over intellectual property rights, for example, I lost a potential Priestess who only wanted to be able to use her written words as she might need them in her future. In my eagerness and assumption that I knew what was best, in wanting to control ideas that should have been freely given to the world, in my own fear of plagiarism, I unwittingly stepped on toes and hurt feelings and consequently lost someone who possessed the potential to stand with me in leadership. Something, to this day, I dearly need. Lesson learned.

These kinds of losses propelled me to develop a healthy working relationship with my inner patriarch so that I can remain strong in my vision, yet flexible in how to implement its stewardship. This required a willingness to confront and heal in the places Carl Jung calls 'shadow', the unconscious aspect of the personality which the conscious ego does not identify in itself. Here's a resource if you'd like to learn more about how this works: http://changingminds.org/explanations/identity/jung_archetypes.htm

Tricky stuff, the shadow. Messy. Hard to maintain looking good when involved in that healing. It taught me how important kindness is. And having an objective friend and/or therapist who is not associated with your organization to help with clarity and perspective.

To keep my ego in check and dysfunction at bay, I have to regularly check to make sure I do not become too identified with my own ministry. I have to watch the righteousness, which is an occupational hazard when you spend time in the pulpit, even if you don't call it a pulpit. Before I learned to manage my ego--an ongoing endeavor for sure, we don't just weed the garden once--I felt I needed to be in control of everything, from the big picture of the Temple's purpose in the world right down to where the candle should be placed on the networking table. Of course, this brought me to the brink of burn out, and an underlying resentment began to seethe.

In one of my shamanic journeys for guidance, Hecate informed me that I had better start asking for help. She reminded me that no one, no matter how energetic and inspired, works alone. That I must deeply question and then shed the identity that had me believing this work was a burden. She told me that no one would think less of me if I asked for help, and in fact doing so would model the good practice of how that is done. Of course She was right. Asking for help was easier than I thought once I found the bravery to show my vulnerability. I accepted the help that came, even if it seemed easier to do it myself. Not only was this a great relief to me, but it strengthened the community. Everyone wants to feel needed and most derive satisfaction from giving.

In group process, when someone had an idea or wanted to implement a policy and all my psychic senses told me it was not going to work, I learned how necessary it is to explore the possibility anyway. Several times along the way I have been the one who agreed to a plan although it was not what I would have preferred simply because someone else's passion for their idea was so strong. I didn't want to dim their light or thwart their commitment to the Temple.

Some of these plans were costly in their failing, but it would have cost the organization more dearly in support and buy-in to have prevented them from happening. The failed experience itself speaks louder that any one individual can about whether a plan worked or not and therefore letting it, not you, bring the message home, preserves relationships. That is, of course, if you don't go on to lay blame afterwards but instead, chalk it up to a necessary learning experience.

On the subject of blame: don't do it. Just don't. Don't blame others and don't blame yourself. Determining how something went wrong is necessary and important to avoid future mistakes, but blaming is not. All blaming does is cause rifts, turning good blood bad. Pagans who want to emerge as powerful spiritual leaders in these opportune times can't afford to lose one drop of good blood. There is a huge distinction between beating someone or yourself up for a mistake and simply acknowledging that a mistake has been made.

Early on, I was in collaboration with another organization. When their leader stepped down, causing the quality of our teamwork to decline, I informed the new leadership that I could no longer maintain the original agreement. I believed I followed standard business protocol in how I relayed this information, but it was like throwing vitriol on an already raging, yet hidden, fire. I was the messenger who delivered an unwelcome, unwanted truth and, completely in the dark about the goings on behind their scenes, I unknowingly walked right into their roiling, sputtering inferno. I was perfectly scapegoated for being the reason their organization fell apart. I recovered as best I could, bandaged my scorched heart, and—regretting the loss of some who to this day have never returned to the Temple--moved forward sadder but wiser.

Leaders are visible. Often we are the face of the organization. Because of our front line position, we are the ones who take the hit. As the leader, I must take responsibility for everything that occurs in my organization. It is not glamourous. It is not sexy. It is not fun. But it is right action. I must be big enough to take responsibility for everything without taking one little bit of it personally. Quite the challenge. Yes, I am a leader, but I am also a sensitive and emotional human being. When I keep in mind Mahatma Gandhi's brilliant words "be the change you want to see in the world" it becomes easier to model the very best behavior, even under duress and in crisis.

Dignity, integrity and maturity have never steered me wrong. Kindness matters. The crucial effects of these simple truths might very well be the direct reason an organization will ultimately survive. As time goes on it becomes clear to me that the content of my teachings is just one aspect of this Pagan ministry. How I conduct myself is equally, if not more, important.

As a leader, people in your community, even those working closely with you, will project their shadows onto you. We all do it. I know I have. I wish this weren't true, but I have experienced being the target of others' scarcity, abandonment, and martyrdom issues, to name just a few. I have been put on their pedestal and then torn down from it. I have been envied, and copied. Some have taken credit for and even tried to sabotage my good work. I have been admired for my leadership and then resented for it. I've been loved for living my truth and being in service, and hated for the very same reasons. I have felt others' jealousy seep silently through even the tightest crevices. I have been the mirror into which people either love or hate what they see reflected. Human frailty often trumps our loftiest and most spiritual understanding and attempts.

I have found that the best thing to do is to refrain from trying to do anything at all about it. Let The Fates take care of it. Don your psychic shield as the most important part of your regalia and stay focused on being in service. If you are in leadership for the glory and the fame, you are not there for the right reason, which you will discover soon enough. If, however, you are living your authenticity and your path brings you to leadership, trust that whatever it takes is worth it.

Leadership is a dynamic adventure, not a static position. It requires flexibility along with steadfastness. Leaders must enact dedication and perseverance, especially when failure threatens on the horizon or even as close as your own pocket. I believe dedication and perseverance are born of deep faith. Therefore, the esoteric aspects of spiritual leadership require care and tending in a disciplined way for longevity. They are equally vital to your healthy success. The invention and offering of the rituals and worship services is creative and spiritual, and requires continued inspiration.

The ancient aphorism applies here: Know Thyself. What inspires you? What takes your breath away? What makes you want to drop everything to engage with it? If an afternoon viewing art in the museum or a walk in the woods helps you feel connected to life in an exhilarated way, make sure to do it. If going into trance among the Deva of the plant world in your garden conjures ideas that can't be stirred up any other way, get out there and shift your consciousness. Make dates with what brings you enthusiasm. And then keep them.

Stay in deep and intimate relationship with the Gods, and in this way strengthen your faith. In what ways do you commune with the Divine? In what ways do the Gods communicate to you? Through an oracle? In a dream? Do They whisper in your ear, send you a vision, proffer signs in the natural world? I work hard to keep that channel open, honing my oracular skills, making offerings to Them at my altar. I journey between the worlds and cast frequent spells to stay connected to the energy of the Divine Beings who help me from that numinous realm. Because just as Hecate, the Crone of Wisdom at the crossroads said to me: *No one works alone.*

On another note completely—because the work, tasks, details, energy and presence required for good leadership is taxing--preserve your home as sanctuary. Perhaps it is just my Cancer Moon talking, but this will ensure your well-being. Leaders need a peaceful place to restore, and all efforts to create and maintain beauty and harmony in the place you call home are worthy ones.

Despite the mistakes and the painful lessons, my years of spiritual leadership have taught me to be resilient, to remain available, to trust. They have brought more joy, growth and grace than anything else. A beautiful ministry for the Goddess exists because of it. Knowing we are in Her service is our greatest blessing, bringing with it deep and soulful satisfaction.

Walking the Walk:
The Nature of Leadership at Four Quarters Interfaith Sanctuary

Sophia Kelly Shultz[4]

It is around 2 PM on a hot, sunny late August day. There hasn't been any appreciable rain at Four Quarters Interfaith Sanctuary in the past month: my van throws up a cloud of red dust as I drive up the hill and past the Labyrinth.

Thank the gods, I'm finally here. My drive from southern Maryland has left me completely frazzled. On all but one leg of the drive, I had encountered traffic stoppages; I had hoped to get to the Land before noon so that I could open up my tent and set up my vendor's booth before it got too hot. The next stop would be Hemlock Hole.

At least I was here. I was off the highway, and I was Home –

--until I drive around the corner and what to my wondering eyes should appear but a not-so-miniature Stone and eight full-size Stone workers – a hundred yards ahead of me.

Well, crap. Another traffic jam. I've come in on a part of the Stones Intensive: as a prelude to the actual Stone pulls to take place later in the week the Stone Crew is moving the Stone – in this case all 6 tons of it-- from its former location at the top of the hill across from the Labyrinth to a place where the Tribe will be able to pull it into the Stone Circle.

I throw the van into "park," turn off the engine, and get out.

The members of the Stone Crew are so focused on the Stone that they don't see me until I've walked up to them and asked if I can help.

*I have never used rollers before, but I know how they work. These particular rollers are newly-cut, and have been fitted with heavy rope so that the Crew can keep better control of them. As the Stone moves over the rollers, Crew members remove the rear roller and **run** back to the front of the Stone, where they can position it in time for the Stone to bite into its surface. I take up a rope and begin to learn a new skill.*

---

4 The anecdotes, which are based on my own personal experience, are not intended to lionize me, but to provide a thread of continuity within this article.

Using rollers requires intense focus and teamwork. Naturally, there are those who give orders, but in this scenario the ones giving orders are doing at least the same amount of work, and not just in their heads. The crew is The Crew.

Today the orders are given by 19 year old Coriander Woodruff, who is already experienced with this phase of the Stone-raising process. She alternately walks beside or stands on the Stone to help it remain level and better move over the rollers, periodically consulting with Mike McConnell. His years of experience put him in the position of leader of the Stone Crew, but he treats Coriander with respect. This slip of a young woman takes directions from him, sometimes under protest, and sometimes he has to admit that she is right.

Coriander has grown up at Four Quarters. Though she and her family live some hours away, they have spent large chunks of time on the Land. As a little girl she participated in the Seed Stone Pull at Beltaine; as a teenager, she now leads it. She joined the Stone Crew as soon as she could, and now she is standing on the Stone shouting directions.

We move on: one of the Crew counts down so that we know when to allow the Stone to bite into our roller.

"Three...Two...One...go!"

It's not as easy as it sounds. The Stone does not move at a consistent pace: neither the road nor the bottom of the Stone has a uniform surface. Those on the rollers must all maintain focus and control the directions of their rollers to keep the Stone going straight down the road. An error could send it over the side of the hill and into the ravine.

"Sophia, watch your HANDS!" Coriander shouts.

"I'm okay!" I reply, grateful for her attention.

We reach the top of the High Meadow, and stop for the day. We drink water, dust ourselves off, and finish saying our hellos. I walk back to my van, neither frustrated nor angry. One person could not have moved this Stone alone, but together we have gotten it from main parking to the High Meadow. As I start the van, I feel kind of cool. Once again, I've walked the walk.

Four Quarters Interfaith Sanctuary, one of the most well-established modern organizations whose members fall under the classification "Pagan," is located in the southern part of Bedford County, Pennsylvania. The original tract, often referred to as "the Land" is 150 acres surrounded on three sides by a horseshoe bend in Sideling Hill Creek. Its cliff, meadow, wetland, and mature forest habitats distinguish it as the most ecologically diverse tract in the county. Rated as exceptionally clean by the State of Pennsylvania, spring-fed Sideling Hill Creek plays an integral role in the formation and perpetuation of all of these biomes. A new, 110-acre tract features, among other things, steep cliffs to provide privacy for members' religious practices and rolling fields perfect for rituals and events.

To Four Quarters members, the entire Land is sacred. This sentiment is expressed in the altars that can be found from Hemlock Swimming Hole to the Fox Altar to the Vendors' Green; in the hilltop Labyrinth, Upper and Lower Drum Circles, Sweat Lodge, and, most especially, in the work of years: the Stone Circle.

Visible on Google Earth (if you squint—there are trees in the way), the Stone Circle has been growing steadily for the past 20 years. Occupying a hilltop oak grove, it currently consists of 48 megaliths, the largest of which weighs 8 tons—all of which were pulled and raised "the old fashioned way": with ropes and rollers and sweat and sinew. The Circle is Four Quarters' centerpiece, hosting not only weddings, hand fastings, memorials, baby blessings and other rituals, but also less formal activities such as workshops, yoga classes and meditations. Children play in the Stone Circle. During Stones Rising, which is held over the Labor Day weekend, drummers play the Native American spirit drum there. The Circle provides a common thread to all who come to Four Quarters, especially for anyone— members and non-members alike—who can say "I helped raise that Stone."

A visitor today will also find many other structures thoughtfully built into this beautiful landscape. The kitchen, dining pavilion, bunk house, and shower houses provide amenities such as hot showers and sheltered dining to members and guests alike, and hand-crafted bunk beds for those among them who are unused to camping. During events, the Coffee Dragon provides round the clock hot beverages and a place for visitors and members to meet and socialize. Gravel-paved roads allow members and visitors alike to bring their equipment into even the most remote parts of the camp.

Four Quarters was not always so well appointed: when the Land was purchased by Orren Whiddon in 1994, there was one barely adequate road and a dilapidated farmhouse. Finding a tract of land that met Whiddon's criteria had made his search a long one. First, its features had to provide a natural boundary for members of all paths to practice their spirituality in private, and, no less important, the land had to have the perfect site upon which his dream--the creation of a Stone Circle--could come to fruition.

Orren—and the other pioneers who first lived on the Land—faced extraordinarily challenging circumstances in those first years. It was these fiercely dedicated people who founded Four Quarters Interfaith Sanctuary, created the first policies, wrote and conducted the first rituals, and assured the continued care of our sacred ground, the Land and the Stone Circle.

Leadership and the Board of Directors

"These Bible study groups for married couples are getting bigger and bigger," the man across the table from me said to the guy sitting next to him. "There's a waiting list; we really need some more people to volunteer to host them."

"I know," the other man sighed, shaking his head. "People just don't seem to get that they need to volunteer for things when they want them to happen."

"At my church," I interjected, because although their conversation was clearly intended to be between the two of them, it was being conducted at a dinner meeting in front of six other people, "we are very good at getting people to walk the walk."

Both men seemed startled, and possibly a little irritated. How dare I eavesdrop--let alone comment upon--their private conversation! "And how do you accomplish this?" the one on the left inquired skeptically.

"Like this." I put my hand on my husband's shoulder and smiled. "David, you've done such a great job today, we'd like you to take over this project."

Both of them looked utterly flummoxed. Apparently, although this sort of interaction might be perfectly normal to a Four Quarters regular, to them it was a novel idea. "Where do you go to church?" the other one asked, his polite tone only barely concealing a challenge.

"Four Quarters Interfaith Sanctuary," I replied matter-of-factly. "It's about three hours southwest of here: I go out once a month."

Another pause. "So," the left-hand man ventured, "it's non-denominational?"

"I prefer the term **interfaith,**" *I replied. "It implies that we have faith."*

Although many find the title "church" off-putting in this context, the mission of Four Quarters Interfaith Sanctuary is to provide a place for like-minded people to gather, and, more importantly, to protect the Land and the Stones[5]. Twice-monthly Moon Services have been conducted continuously since 1995, and, since there is no stated liturgy or ordained ministry, these services are led by people of all different spiritual paths.

There are no benefits to being a member of the Church of Four Quarters; if anything, a Church member might find themselves getting more involved — sometimes so involved that they will end up on the Board of Directors.

Four Quarters Interfaith Sanctuary is governed following the episcopal model, in which decisions concerning, among other things, legal matters, ultimate oversight of Church operations, and financial concerns are voted on and consesus-based. In the event of a disagreement, final authority rests on one person, in this example, the President. Seated Board members also include the Vice President, Prothonotary, and Member at Large. Serving below them are Members' Advocates.

The leadership ethic does not end with Board meetings. By "walking the walk," Board members and Members' Advocates pass on standards of behavior, care for the Land, involvement, and responsibility.

---

[5]The recognition, honor and preservation of the many different cultures and traditions that have developed, through time, similar expressions of Earth Four Quarters is a religious association of people, drawn to the Earth and its cycles, the natural world and its polarities; and seeing in them the manifest expression of spirit.

Protecting and furthering the growth of EarthSpiritedness; by maintaining the responsible and public identity of a Church, and providing the support of the Church to all people on allied paths; is a central mission of Four Quarters.

To hold, honor and care for the Land, in a ritually responsible and focused way; and to provide access to that Land for the spiritual needs of anyone; is a central mission of Four Quarters.

Fostering communication and cooperation among the people; by organizing open religious gatherings and festivals upon the land; is a central mission of Four Quarters. Spiritedness; is a central mission of Four Quarters.

By an Act of The Board of Directors
The Church of Four Quarters, 25th October 1995

In the event of a dispute, members are encouraged to speak to one of the Members' Advocates. It is not the Members' Advocate's responsibility to insert themselves into any given situation so that they can force a solution. If anything, it is their responsibility to step back and encourage the members to solve the problem themselves. Only after the members' attempts at finding a satisfactory outcome have proven unsuccessful does the Members' Advocate become actively involved. This process encourages members to be accountable for their own part in a negative interaction — and usually the dispute will end amicably without further Board involvement.

Board members are required to ensure that the content of Four Quarters sponsored events[6] reflects the Church's mission statement. Often, but not necessarily, they are among the lead planners; there are occasions when they remain onlookers, offering advice and a helping hand wherever needed. Experienced Board members guide and delegate whenever possible, providing Four Quarters members an opportunity to work on their own, becoming ritualists, costumers, and prop managers, and learning — most importantly--the niceties of convincing other members to participate.[7]

Seeing the Need: Leadership Amongst Members

Getting to the Hemlock Hole, the swimming hole whose depth is best suited for children, has always been a little challenging. Each spring, members would build stone steps down to the shoreline, and each winter, floods would wash them away. Members viewed this cycle with the pragmatism with which Hawai'ians view the march of Pele's lava over their houses. The creek was the creek.

I still don't know how, but one year I ended up in charge of this project. I was not a Members' Advocate yet: I was still just a humble vendor, finding my feet as an active Four Quarters member.

We labored through a cold, drizzly April day and together my team built what people would later call "the best steps to Hemlock Hole ever."

The next year, however, the spring floods left us not only without steps, but with an eight-foot vertical drop--in other words,

---

6 These events are Beltane, Fires Rising, Drum 'n' Splash, Body Tribal, Stones Rising, Samhain and Yule

7 The most crucial of these niceties is a sense of humor.

there was no slope into which we could build the steps.

It was the first morning of the work weekend[8], and I had already seen the condition of the bank. Therefore it was not surprising when Orren sat down with his cup of robust Farmhouse coffee and said, "You can't build steps to Hemlock Hole this year."

"I know," I replied.

"You're going to have to raise money to buy steps for Hemlock Hole," he continued. "Something that's lightweight and can be pulled up during winter or if we have a flood."

I was astonished. Previously, Orren had been dead set against putting anything other than the stone steps down to the swimming hole--and he didn't even like those. All of a sudden--**now**--he wanted **me** to raise money for real steps?

"And you're going to have to raise about $2500."

Have I mentioned that I had no experience with fundraising?

Well, if there was anything other than the Stone Circle that was close to the hearts of most Four Quarters members, it was Hemlock Hole. I guessed I could give it a shot.

Best get started right away. That meant a Facebook page and inviting all my friends.

Next, I made an announcement at the Beltane members' meeting[9]. I suppose that I handled it like a revival: "Do you like swimming at Hemlock Hole?" I asked, and there was a chorus of "Yes!" "Have you **been** down to see Hemlock Hole this weekend?" I asked. There was a somewhat less enthusiastic response. Yes, many people had seen it, and had had the same reaction as I.

Now that they were primed, I announced the fundraiser.

Over the course of that summer, various people stepped up to help the cause. Two members bought a case of glow sticks and sold them to attendees at Mountain Madness, an outside electronic music event, for a considerable markup. Some of our most talented artisans donated items to be offered for raffle, giving one of our Members' Advocates an opportunity to demonstrate her prowess at convincing people that they desperately needed to buy raffle tickets.

---

8 Work weekends are scheduled throughout the year, but people wishing to volunteer are encouraged to show up whenever possible to build/fix/do Useful Things.

9 *Members' meetings are held at Beltane and Stones Rising, and serve as a forum for the Board to keep members up to date on subjects such as finance, construction projects, and outreach, and for members and non-members alike to voice concerns, ideas and to raise questions.*

By the end of the season, we had raised enough money to purchase the steps, and by the following spring they had been installed.

I think that I realized what I had accomplished when a long-time member came up to me and said, "You got money out of Pagans? Amazing!"

Generally speaking, unless they are involved in politics or business, people do not go gently into leadership roles. Today's world gives us too many other things to worry about; why aspire to being a Pillar of the Community when you're trying make sure there's a roof over your family's head and food on the table? Leadership requires energy, of which we have only a finite amount. Would we draw from the energy we necessarily expend on work, family, or the hobbies that serve to relieve the pressures of everyday life? You already have a demanding boss; why would you want to put yourself in the unenviable position of having to meet somebody else's expectations — or, worse, requiring that someone meet yours?

We have all heard stories of wealthy and politically influential families "grooming" younger family members to take up the reins of power when their elders retire. This centuries-old practice has yielded mixed results: witness the British royal family's ups and downs.

At Four Quarters, potential leaders are not groomed. Members of the Board of Directors allow opportunities for leadership to present themselves and then pay attention to which individuals rise to the occasion: who steps up in what capacity and how they comport themselves. For some this is a natural and quick progression; for others it takes a little longer.[10]

Likewise, the method of getting people involved varies depending upon the target and the task at hand. As I mentioned above, in the case of *building* the stone steps to Hemlock Hole I found myself leading the work crew (as I recall, because I

---

10 I am a very good example of the latter: when I came to Four Quarters for Samhain of 2005, I was looking to be a vendor and nothing but a vendor. Being a stubborn person, I actively avoided participation of any kind. However, in 2009, things changed: that year, I was asked to participate in ritual (that was with 15 minutes' lead time); I found myself making costumes and charms for a role I was to play in a Body Tribal; and writing letters to the Board of Directors expressing my concerns about various matters instead of splashing them all over the Forum. Now, in 2014, I am a Members' Advocate, and am active in many aspects of Four Quarters operations.

dreaded the very idea of mothers and fathers carrying their children down that hazardous drop); in the case of *raising money* for the aluminum steps, I found that I had been hornswaggled-- in other words, I was told that I would be the one heading up this effort because I had been the one who'd been in charge of the "get people safely down to the creek" project to begin with.[11]

Outside of Four Quarters, it may be possible for a person to be enticed into getting involved with promises of rewards and recognition. The best analog for this is the person who gives money to their local PBS station so that they can get a cool gift: to give something, be it money or time, many people feel that they should get something.

It is not standard operating procedure regarding helping out at Church sponsored events for volunteers to get preferential treatment such as breaks on the cost of grounds fees or festival admission. Today's volunteers did not set out for a reward, or to become tomorrow's leaders, they set out to fill what they perceived as a need — and in many cases, *found their calling* in the process.

Perhaps members — and even non-members — find it easy to volunteer once they ascertain that they would be part of a *team* led by a *member of the team* rather than a grunt working with a group of other grunts directed by an individual who is Almighty and likely to smite them if they ask the wrong question or fail to carry out orders correctly.[12] It is a testimony to the standard of Four Quarters leadership that if someone who heads up an event or other project is complimented for the work he or she has done, they are quick to point out that they had a great team working *with them*.

A case in point is the kitchen, which is staffed by volunteers who love working alongside our serve-safe head chefs — and *love* is the proper word when the work involves laboring long hours in a very hot kitchen. Members and visitors alike acknowledge their Herculean efforts in many ways — usually with cheers from a dining pavilion full of happy patrons- -but with the exception of some outside events, expression of

---

11 Some refer to this as being "voluntold"; I dislike this term because I feel that the terms "volunteer" and "told" are mutually exclusive.

12 Of course, there have been isolated instances of verbal smiting, usually when the volunteer's enthusiasm had put his or her own safety at risk.

this appreciation does not often involve money.

Likewise, our fire-tenders, called The Order of the Bracers, chop cord after cord of firewood, usually in the hot summer sun, endlessly rake the Upper Drum Circle in order to keep it free of rocks that could injure dancers' feet, ensure the safety of all who enter the Circle, and work late into the night to maintain the fires for drumming and dancing. In addition, they maintain and set up kerosene lanterns for ritual and provide all things fire-related wherever required. These volunteers are often thanked by event planners and those drumming or dancing, but on a more individual level.

The Sweat Lodge staff also chops vast quantities of firewood and maintains structures for this important spiritual work. Like the Bracers, they labor long hours—often missing rituals or even the opportunity to visit with people outside of the Sweat Lodge—they are engrossed in tending the lodge's fires, cooking for each other or pouring the sweats themselves in the brutally hot lodge. They are like the Bracers, providing for the safety of those who partake of their services, and here too they receive abundant thanks from individuals who have partaken in their rituals.

Although for the most part these groups feature a conspicuous absence of titles, is important to point out that each still has a hierarchy which is based upon the level of experience each member has achieved. Responsibilities are fluid; volunteers with the most longevity train newcomers, and have been sufficiently equipped to take over in the event that a recognized leader is delayed, or, for whatever reason, unable to meet a commitment.

In the case of the fire tending, there are two classes: Initiates and Bracers. Initiates the learn basics of fire tending from the Bracers, and, when they appear ready, take their "Trial by Fire"--a day during a major festival during which they are given the responsibility of arranging and caring for all things fire related from lanterns to the fire in the Drum Circle. If they successfully fulfill these responsibilities, they become a full-fledged Bracer, and are presented with a pair of the leather wrist bracers—the symbol that gives their fire tenders their name.

Inspired by the work of these leaders, and often as a way to express gratitude for their work, new people volunteer to help. They don't know it, but they are already leaders: their willingness to step up and wash dishes or chop firewood will inspire others to do the same.

Leadership and the Next Generation

I became Vendor Coordinator because I saw a need – and as an act of self-interest: without someone filling this position, the behavior of the vendors generally occupying the Merchants'' Green might deteriorate; people would set up wherever they pleased; rules like "no vehicles on the Green after the festival has started" would be less easily enforced.

Okay, I admit it: I'm a control freak and no one was in control.

*I've been vending for over thirty years. I have seen difficult vendors; I have **been** one of the difficult vendors. I've learned what vendors want and don't want, and how to deal with the clueless, the forgetful, the entitled, and the passive-aggressive. I would say I've seen it all, but I just know that there's someone out there thinking of me as they perfect their new Stupid Vendor Trick. But mostly I have learned that I enjoy this work, even as my blood pressure rises to touch the crowns of the pines under which we vend. I like being able to help, to find people to assist in raising booths, carry merchandise, fetch and carry tools. I like being able to say, "yes, I've got a mallet, here you go," and "is your booth adequately secured?" I like passing on the knowledge I've gained from others regarding the weather. "If you see a storm coming over that ridge, button it up and run."*

I want them to do well.

This year we had a new vendor whose specialty was henna. She arrived at Drum'n'Splash with two children, a shy thirteen year old girl and an uncertain-looking ten year old boy. They had a wonderful weekend, and I was very pleased when they returned for Stones Rising.

However, there was a problem: while her daughter was more than willing to find the friends she'd made at the previous event, her son spent her entire set up looking like he was going to hold his breath until he turned blue. She informed me that he was determined to be miserable; he had apparently decided that he hated camping in general and Four Quarters in particular.

Since it is notoriously difficult to get people to sit down and have henna applied when there is a grouchy ten-year-old in the booth, I decided to take a walk up to the Coffee Dragon, and was pleased to find young Odin Victorious sitting in the otherwise empty gathering space.

Odin is eleven years old. He is gregarious, intelligent, and thoughtful, and more than once I have observed him taking charge of some of his contemporaries. Of course, he is still an eleven-year-old boy, subject to the hormonal whims of boys his age. I knew I must be cautious.

"Odin!" I said cheerfully.

"Yes?" he asked, studying me with caution.

"I need your help."

He looked at me skeptically. "What do you need?" he asked in a voice that indicated he had a sneaking suspicion that I was going to ask him to do something like rake the Drum Circle.

"There is a callow youth in the Merchant's Green," I said, probably more dramatically than I needed. "He has decided that he hates Four Quarters and camping. Odin, I need you," I paused for maximum effect, "to help him to see the light."

Odin grabbed his box of Magic: the Gathering cards and stood up. "Take me to him."

Three minutes later the vendor's son was a changed boy, laughing and joking with Odin. Smiling, his mother waved to me and then got back to setting up.

I had not saved the day for her, Odin had. Four Quarters' next generation of leadership does its work with the gentle art of persuasion – and a box of game cards.

It is an understatement to say that children are valued at Four Quarters: they *are* valued, but they are also respected and nurtured. They wrestle in the meadow, sit in the Coffee Dragon drinking cocoa (though after an occasion when a group of kids used up the cocoa in record time—two days into a five-day festival--cocoa distribution is now handled through whoever is running the operation), and play at being pirates in the Stone Circle. We watch over them as they grow from babies to children to teens to young adults. In ritual, they call to the Ancestors or the Children Yet to Come—be it formally, speaking before all who are gathered, or with the fresh voices of babes in arms.

Parents accept that they are responsible for the well being of their children, but they also know that in the Kids' Tribe, the older children look after the younger ones. They grow together-- not without bumps, bruises, and conflicts amongst themselves — until the older ones become pre-teens and drift off in an adolescent amoeba and those they cared for take their place leading the younger children.

Traditions—many, but not all, service-related—connect children to the spirit of Four Quarters. Racing rubber duckies or dancing and playing in the sand around the fire in the Drum Circle in the early evening are pure fun. Pulling the Seed Stone at Beltane, helping with the Loaves of the Corn Mothers at Stones Rising[13] [14] or serving water and snacks to the Stone Crew and all involved in the work allows children the opportunity to work together towards common goals. Each of these activities allows room for growth: today's children participating under their parents' watchful eye will become the teenagers passing their knowledge on to the younger children.

So is Four Quarters' next generation of leaders formed. As with adults, not every child becomes a leader. Some, like Odin, will be natural leaders; others will be more like me, brought into leadership kicking and screaming. All of this is done in the hope that Four Quarters' next generation will have leadership strong enough to organize and carry out the continued raising of Stones.

It is dusk. Stones Rising attendees have gathered around a Stone lying on a sled near the Labyrinth. Unlike the one I encountered in the road, this one does not count its weight in tens of thousands of pounds: it is "petite"--less than a thousand pounds.

This is the Night Pull. We will pull this Stone in silence, our way lit by torches and fire spinners. The excitement in the air is palpable. We have already appointed torch-bearers and people to lead each rope. Now it's time to get moving!

Mike McConnell steps up onto the Stone. "You know," he says in his characteristic drawl, "I'm tired. Today I've dealt with clogged toilets, firewood and all kinds of other crap. I don't feel like moving this Stone. So Coriander, it's on you to do this pull."

Coriander's eyes grow wide. Everyone shouts, whoops, and cheers as she steps up onto the Stone with Mike, who is looking very smug. He's managed to keep this a surprise.

Coriander may be surprised that she has been given the responsibility for an actual pull, but those of us who know her and have

---

[13]The Seed Stone Pull, mentioned earlier, involves the children pulling a 500 pound Stone and raising it in the spot where the new Stone will be raised that Labor Day. This serves to teach them not only teamwork but the skills they will need to raise 16,000 pound Stones when they are grown.

[14]The night before the Stones are raised, children and their parents participate in baking bread for the Tribe. Whether they stay all night, for a couple of hours, or for an hour, the children see the fruits of their collected work the next morning as they help to distribute bread to all present.

seen her in action, are not. This is an exciting announcement for everyone: it is the passing of a crucial leadership tradition to the next generation of Stone People. We all know that Mike will head up the pulling of the other Stone, and the raising of both, but for the moment we are experiencing an extraordinary moment, a moment that makes us proud.

She composes herself with considerable aplomb. "Everyone line up next to your ropes!" she shouts. "Alternating on either side. DON'T PICK UP THE ROPES YET!"

I smile. This could be Mike giving these directions – with the same tones and inflections.

Time for me to run to the front. It's my job to make certain that none of the line leaders walk into a tree or embankment, and that we have adequate light for the journey. I maintain order on the lines, try to keep them straight, and I am the only one besides Coriander and Mike who is allowed to yell "STOP!"

Bringing the Stone down from the Labyrinth is arguably the most complex part of this pull: we will have to execute a number of maneuvers in order to get it onto the road and past the gate. Each time we stop, Coriander directs the people on the ropes to take, for example, several steps to the right or left, or to peel off and re-form on the other side of an obstacle – for example, a tree. We progress slowly – not easy with so many enthusiastic hands ready to pull this Stone straight to the Circle. Coriander wants to get this right.

We've made the final turn and are starting on the straight part of the road. Any changes in course will be fine-tuning now: moving the lines a couple of steps to one side or the other. Still, it's necessary to watch to be certain that the leaders don't end up in the trees (unless it's intentional).

One of the lines is most definitely about to enter a copse of trees. "STOP!" I yell.

And from the Stone I hear those words I have heard so many times from Mike McConnell, now shouted by Coriander: "WHO YELLED STOP?"

"I DID!"

And, as with Mike McConnell, the response to that, somewhat moderated: "Okay!" Then, "This line, take two steps to your left and line up with your leader!"

Back to work. In this moment, I have seen the future of Four Quarters leadership.

It looks pretty damned good.

What I Wish I had Been Told
Peggy Thompson

As I sit here, staring at a blank page, I realize that I don't know where to start. Educating and training Leaders is one of my passions, I've taught Event Planning, Leadership Theory, Recruitment and Retention, and even Parliamentary Procedure- but for this essay, I don't know where to start. There are so many different aspects of being an effective leader that it's easy to become mired in details and eventually the idea of "Leader" simply becomes a list of chores that one must accomplish in order to succeed. Being an effective Leader is one of the most exhausting things I have ever done, but it's also one that carries an immense amount of personal satisfaction.

Over the years, I've had many (many) people give me advice, suggestions and commands about what leadership is, and how to be a leader. In the beginning, I tried to do everything the "right" way, and I jumped in with both feet. I threw away tradition and suggestions and ultimately spent much of my time "reinventing the wheel". Next, I tried to listen to each person, I held tradition as an immutable object that no force on this planet could change. This tactic led to frustration because I ended up doing everything myself—I was told that people never follow through and it's up to the "leader" to make sure nothing went wrong.

Finally I started educating myself, I went to conferences and took a leadership theory class. I learned what my leadership style was, and how to use this knowledge to be more effective. This brings me back to this essay and the horrible blank page before me. I asked myself, "When I was starting out, what advice do I wish I had received? What would have made me a better leader, before I made all the mistakes?" What follows are the tips and suggestions that I've kept and used, and passed on when I've taught.

- **Make Lists,** the more lists you make, the better organized you are. Creating a list helps you to organize your thoughts along specific lines (i.e. a list of supplies, chores, or volunteers). One difficulty leaders encounter is doing too much. By making a list of things you're doing, or need to do, it's easier to see that maybe you're doing too much and need to delegate or reduce involvement. When I plan events, I've even had a list of my various lists so that I don't forget anything.

- **Ask for help.** We (leaders) have a habit of feeling as though we have to do as much as possible, even when we feel overwhelmed. Take time to ask for help, even when we don't actually "need" help. Sometimes taking the time to ask someone to give us a hand makes others feel more involved, which leads to everyone feeling more ownership of a group or an event.

- **Spouses make great sounding boards, but bad co-leaders,** co-chairs and co-coordinators. When spouses are working on something together, many times it leads to people feeling less connected and heard in an organization. It also becomes very easy to make plans and decisions over dinner, instead of during a meeting where everyone has a chance to speak. Whenever possible, choose someone who isn't related to you to be your second-in-command or co-chair.

- **Take time to take classes** that teach skills like group facilitation. Group facilitation is a great way to take a group of people that have difficulty agreeing on items, or reaching decisions, and walk them through a process where everyone feels heard and a decision that benefits the group as a whole can be reached.

- **Take time to go to leadership conferences,** or leadership theory classes. Conferences and classes are great ways to meet other leaders who are struggling with the same things you are. It's also a way to explore how you view leadership and helps you to develop your own skill set.

- **Elders are important.** Listen to them, acknowledge what they have accomplished and have been through.

Because of the struggles of our Elders, we can hold public ritual, practice openly, and face much less discrimination than when our Elders were young. Take the time to hear their stories and ask questions. Remember that our Elders deserve respect for what they've done.

- **We don't have to do what our Elders tell us to do.** Our Elders deserve respect, but times have changed and what worked twenty years ago is not necessarily what works today. For example: Craigslist, Facebook and Twitter have changed how we recruit and retain members. No longer do we simply run around town hanging flyers and hope people contact us.

- **Don't get mired in tradition.** Just because something has been done one way, doesn't mean that you can't change something. You might find that you have drawn people to an event or organization who never thought about coming before.

- **Praise in public, criticize in private.** This is very important. No matter how frustrated and angry you become, always tell that volunteer in private. Furthermore, don't give generalizations, give specifics. For example, if a volunteer is supposed to be at the Welcome Table and they're taking a smoke break every 20 minutes, don't just tell them they need to stop taking smoke breaks and they need to sit at the table; tell the volunteer you noticed that about every 20 minutes they're wandering away to take a smoke break and you're concerned that this leaves the table empty. Maybe the person is actually uncomfortable talking to strangers, and doesn't know how to tell you—so instead, they take frequent smoke breaks. On the other hand, if someone is doing a good job, make sure you pause and tell them.

- **Remember that each of the people you work with are volunteers**. Few people you work with will have the dedication and drive that you have. A good leader will remember that part of leadership is cheerleading — making sure your volunteers feel valued and showing them how much good they're doing. Make sure you talk to your volunteers about how attendance has increased at an event, or this year you have more members- find a way to quantify what your group has accomplished.

- **Make sure you thank your volunteers.** Buy a large box of Thank You notes and some Post-it notes, when you notice someone doing something, write who it was and what it was on a sticky note and stick it to a Thank You note, then every week or so, sit down and write the notes and mail them off. If you're planning an event, make sure after the event is over that every volunteer receives a Thank You note, and try and give each note something specific that that person has done. Sending the notes via "snail mail" is a great way to give the recipient a quick thrill at getting actual mail.

- **Take time to create a position description for each position in your organization,** and if your organization already has these, once a year look at each description and update them if necessary. There are two reasons for this: First, it refreshes in your mind what each person in your organization is supposed to be doing, and you can assess if people are (or aren't) doing their jobs. Next, if things have changed, you can update the jobs descriptions. One example is that a group that is just starting out might have one person in charge of Recruitment and Retention and that person's position would include Social Media and a Website. As the group grows, eventually a new position needs to be created to handle the website and social media. If you never look at the position descriptions, one person can be given more and more responsibility until they simply burn out (and because they're doing so much, they can't be replaced).

- **Sometimes groups end.** There's no shame in taking a group that isn't working and deciding that it's time to disband. When a group is no longer able to function, or fulfill its mission statement, it might be up to you to speak up and say that it's time to close the group. Sometimes a group ends because its mission has been accomplished and the group naturally disbands because their work is done, other times the group becomes mired in in-fighting and cannot move forward.

- **Plan for your own obsolescence.** Many times leaders become entrenched in a position, and even though they're burned out and tired, they can't step down because no one is there to take over. From the first day that you step into the position, have an eye on who will take over once you're done. After you become acclimated to the position, start training whoever will step up when you step down. Ideally, you should never be in a position more than three years, more than that and a number of things begin to happen. First, the longer you're in a position, the more likely it is that you can't easily step down. New leadership brings new ideas, the longer a person is in a position, the easier it becomes to institute "tradition" and then it becomes harder to create change. Finally, when someone is in a position for too long, it's harder for the membership to accept a change in leadership when it happens. I remember the first event I coordinated, I spent two months hearing, "that's not how (so-and-so) used to do it." I hated hearing that.

- **Institutional documents are important!** These are your by-laws, constitutions, policies and procedures, etc. Well written documents help the organization by outlining exactly how it's to be run, and the documents help you as well because the documents will tell you exactly what's permissible and how to accomplish the goals of the organization. Take time to learn these documents, and use them to guide your actions.

- **There's no shame in walking away from a group that is abusive** or refuses to put policies and procedures in place that will protect you and the group. There are a lot of groups out there that still believe in the Shoebox Bank, or that it's ok for the group's money to go into the personal bank account of one of the members. There will always be people and groups that don't operate ethically, and sometimes you don't realize this until you're brought into the "inner circle". Your spiritual, mental and physical well-being is more important than any group or event, if something isn't "right", walk away.

- **Beware people who constantly insist that consensus is the only way** to run an organization. I have seen people browbeat, denigrate, and abuse others to make consensus happen. If you're part of a group that insists on consensus, take time to find a workshop or class on how to use it ethically. Consensus isn't everyone sitting around going "yup, I agree", it's a systematic way of making sure everyone's voice is heard, and if someone disagrees finding out what the stumbling block is and correcting it. I prefer using basic Parliamentary Procedure, but using that effectively also takes some training (there is a *Dummies Guide to Parliamentary Procedure*, however, that is very effective).

My last two pieces of advice are actually the most important. Both of them came from a leadership conference I attended ten years ago, and they are the two things that I tell every person who asks me questions about leadership.

- **You are going to screw up.** It's inevitable. Listen to the advice of others so you don't make their mistakes, but never forget you are going to make your own mistakes. This is part of the journey, learn from your mistakes and pass the wisdom you've learned on to others. There's nothing wrong with making mistakes, but own up to those mistakes and find ways to avoid the situation in the future.

- **Have fun! Laugh!** Leadership is stressful and hard, but don't forget to see the humor in what you are doing.

Learn to laugh at yourself; don't take anything too seriously. Laughter will help you to release stress. I believe that if you can laugh you can find a solution. It seems like whenever a group I was working with was having a "crisis", if we could find some humor we could find a solution. If we simply sat around talking about how horrible the situation was, we just went "round and round" and never moved forward.

These tips and suggestions are just that, take what works for you and discard the rest. There are plenty of conferences, workshops and classes available—take some time to explore options for learning more about Leadership, it will help you in your journey. Being a leader is a very powerful thing, Good Luck.

Making It Up As I Go Along
H. Byron Ballard

I avoid the notion that I'm a leader, thinking of myself as an advocate and an ally instead. I'm an old leftist and have Moon in Scorpio so the word "leader" is triggering in some deep ways. The work I do is just that—the work I do. I fell into it when my daughter was small and the Pagan community was sparse here. So, twenty years, give or take.

When well-meaning people tell me how lucky I am to even have a Pagan community in my town, I want to snarl at them and growl—it wasn't luck. It was perseverance and trial-and-error and long hours of impossible conversations and foolish deeds. It wasn't luck. We built it brick by brick with no blueprint, no template.

We're simply making it all up as we go along. Trying to learn from our mistakes and be true to our lights.

We started with Samhain, as one does, and it grew from there. Because my daughter had a silly experience in pre-school, I found myself with a regular gig when she got to public elementary school. (Her sweet pre-school teacher pulled me aside one day when I came to pick her up and explained that she had let the little one know that it wasn't nice to call mommy a witch.) I prepared a little pamphlet and gave it to each of her teachers, every year, until high school. And her kindergarten teacher asked me to come in and talk about what our family did for three holidays—Hallowe'en, Winter Solstice and May Day. I did that every year of her elementary years and continued it until her kindergarten teacher retired a few years ago.

Hallowe'en was The Turnip Show—I explained the Irish origins of the American holiday, taught the children how to count to ten in Gaeilge, and carved a turnip into a jack o'lantern. In December, I talked about the Solstice and how there are two of them and what they mean. And they learned some Latin and we danced a circle dance while singing "Deck the Halls." At the first of May, many of the teachers in that school put up Maypoles and I went to several classes. We talked about May baskets and leaving flowers hanging on friends' doorknobs. We'd go outside and wash our faces in May dew so that we'd be smart and good-looking forever. And then we'd dance the Maypole.

It really was that easy. There was one year that saw a bit of controversy—fueled by local media—but it was usually easy and fun. I still have some of those thank you cards, I think.

Maybe it was working with curious children that cemented my approach to Pagan leadership. I try to be careful with my language, to explain in a thoughtful way that isn't too complicated. I assume everything will be fine, until it isn't. And then I deal as calmly and reasonably as I can with the people or bureaucracies that are standing in the way of my community's full expression of its First Amendment rights.

This has helped me time and again in doing interfaith work. On two different occasions now, I have found myself the convener of a multi-faith group—the only Wiccan amongst the Abrahamics and Unitarians. If I had a dollar for every time I've used that umbrella metaphor to explain the family of spiritual systems that I'm representing, I'd have enough money to buy land for our new temple.

Our annual Samhain ritual was soon joined by an Imbolc one and a Beltane one and before long we were doing a public ritual—"open to the respectful public"—every six weeks. Half a dozen years ago, we added Earth Day as a public ritual on the Wheel because I was tired of it being another excuse for loud and bad bands to play in my town and close off the streets.

So, nine. A good number.

There are rabbis and preachers here—and pastors and priests—who will gladly tell you I am a leader in the Pagan community. They would happily tell you that I am a "faith leader" amongst the others. In fact, I sit on a committee for the county school board's superintendent. It has an awkward name—the Superintendent's Faith-Based Leaders Advisory Council—and it is sometimes an awkward situation. But we come together periodically, and we advise the superintendent on the delicate course settings between law and culture. That Wiccans are a visible part of the religion scene in our town is due to persistence and showing up when asked. It is a tribute to the interfaith work we've done together over the years. There are local politicians who will likewise confirm that I am a "Pagan leader." And the media here will sometimes call for a quote or comment. The one group that would hesitate to say I'm a "leader" is, in fact, the Pagan community.

And that's as it should be. We have three Pagan non-profits in this town and we have a food pantry and do Adopt-a-Highway and grow a community garden. We've tried "Pagan Pride Days" several times and they don't really work for us here. Too much trouble, too much red tape. Too much for a busy and growing Pagan community.

There aren't enough of us to do all the work that needs doing — political, religious, justice, outreach, rituals and classes. Things fall between the cracks and many of us teeter on the edge of burnout. I suspect all that sounds familiar to anyone who does the work of leading in an alternative community. I'm a big proponent of intersectionality and general bridge-building, and there is always another meeting to attend, another action to organize, another deliberately ignorant wastrel to educate.

There must be some lofty sentiment I can find about this notion of leadership. Something formal and pompous in which I cite studies and reproduce pie charts. Surely I could manage a Top Ten Dos and Don'ts list for those who think they want to do this.

But the simpler thing might be to tell you to be on your guard. If someone aims to be a leader, they probably aren't suitable for the job. They may have a quaint and Mosaic notion of bringing Their People together in commonality. Or an equally odd notion of guarding The Community from the predations of the dominant and dominating culture may be filling their little heads.

That's all rubbish, of course. Inspiring perhaps but not very practical. Do they know how to get a park permit? Can this aspiring leader actually communicate with Their People or is everything My Way or the Highway? Certainly a dictator may be able to get some things done but even a benevolent one is going to have trouble winning Hearts and Minds.

What does a real Pagan leader do? They're the ones that stay after the ritual to scrape the candle wax off the carpet in the rented space. They're the ones who field obnoxious and well-meaning questions from that new reporter during the month of October. They will be sitting by the bed of the dying, bringing food to the sick, helping new parents create a saining ritual.

There are certainly meetings and retreats and reams of good advice.

And, if they have worked hard and are lucky, they will stand in a circle under the full Moon with a circle of friends and co-religionists. They will feel their inner well refilling and their heart expanding and their shoulders relaxing, readying themselves to begin the cycle. Again.

Section 3
Leadership Models and Processes

The Traditions of Leadership in Stone Circle Wicca

Rev. Catharine Clarenbach

"Springtime the pilgrims will come back to the Land,
Bringing strength of numbers to what Landskeeper began.
And we'll all stand together, and we'll raise another Stone.
To the Seventh Generation and the children yet unknown."
("At the Center of Four Quarters" K. Stonesinger, S. Costanzo, P. Alexander)

In 1995, the first Standing Stone was raised at Four Quarters Interfaith Sanctuary on a hilltop beneath the branching embrace of oaks. In the twenty years following, Stones have gone up every year, and now the Ring comes close to the North Gate. Soon, soon—within a decade or so—a Ring of Stones nearly 200 feet in diameter will stand completed on a hilltop in southern Pennsylvania, USA. Stones as great as eight-and-a-half tons have been raise by people with rollers, ropes, sledges, and pulleys. Since 1995, the work has continued, Stone by Stone.

Four Quarters is and always has been a magical place. It is not only Stones that have appeared on the Land.100-some acres of gorgeous hills and creek are adorned by the work of human hands: Stone Circle, Fire Circle, Labyrinth, and several buildings for human habitation and activity.

In the mid-90's, those early days, ceremony after ceremony, ritual after ritual, we—the celebrants of ritual at Four Quarters—walked through the northeast entrance to the Stone Circle. We went through the smoke and beneath the cleansing, sprinkling water, past the fires that burned along the route around the North Altar. Summer to fall and winter to spring, we circled and spiraled within this holy place.

We walked Circle after Circle. Breathed the incense. Lit the torches. Adored the Divine Who we could come to know as One and Many—Male, Female, Both, and Neither. Stretched our arms out up to meet the arms of the oak grove where we walked, breathed, lit, called, danced, and sang.

In the fertile soil of Four Quarters Interfaith Sanctuary, this shared magic became a seed that took root in the relationships and leadership of a small group.

Circle after Circle. Aspect after Aspect. Stone after Stone. Ritual after ritual written, led, organized, given to hundreds of people at a time ...the seed began to grow.

Drums, dancing, fire and light, dark moon and full...the seed continued to grow.

This seed grew, ritual by ritual, ceremony by ceremony, into a sapling that would become the strong, living body of the Stone Circle Wicca (SCW). A Wiccan tradition within the larger interfaith traditions of Four Quarters, Stone Circle Wicca became a community of ceremonial expertise, teaching, personal and communal wisdom, and organizational tenacity.

All that said, let us begin at one place one might call the beginning —

Origins

The Stone Circle Tradition of Wicca appeared aboveground and opened its first leaves during an introductory "Wicca 101" class, taught in 1999 at Four Quarters Interfaith Sanctuary by Pamela Alexander. Ms. Alexander became our Craft Elder and first Initiator. Those who finished the class and desired initiation came together in the Stone Circle and initiated into the First Degree. (Degree of what, you might ask!)

We began, frankly not having any idea where our new knowledge and experience might lead us, nor into just what we had been Initiated. Some of us believed we were now Initiated into a Gardnerian lineage. But many of us were. The exclusively other-gender pairing of magical partners just didn't work for us, and Ms. Alexander had realized that. Some of us sensed already that we were something altogether new, a squalling babe in the woods, if you will.

What many of us would quickly learn is that we had been initiated into a path of leadership. Eventually, it became clear that no one would be initiated into any of the Three Degrees of Stone Circle Wicca without being some kind of leader.

From those early days, Ms. Alexander led by ritual example, as well as by formal teaching. She remains one of the foremost creators of ceremony at Four Quarters and is committed both to tradition and innovation. From a seven-foot, red chiffon-draped, ambisexual Aspect of the Divine alive before all creation, before the first rhythm, even before the Silence...from there to the Mud Mother, the wordless, adorned bulk of Earth, hidden and listening and speaking the language before language...from there to dancing for the orisha Yemaya, with arms full of watermelon...from there to ceremony replete with a wedding-cake altars of candles, mirrors, mangoes, cantaloupes, and more than enough fruit for the more-than-a-hundred celebrants...these are the gifts of Pamela Alexander. These are her leadership gifts, and they are gifts she passed on to those she initiated, the gifts we hold in trust.

The 2006 Charter and the Development of Responsibility

Still, who were we? Even into the early "aughts," we weren't sure. We made ceremony. We offered our gifts in leadership. But we didn't know what our leadership *meant*, or what it was we were becoming. After Ms. Alexander, in the Hands of the Divine, had initiated some to the Second Degree and then some to the Third, it was clear we had become something. Not the Gardnerian Tradition our Craft Elder had known long ago. Not even simple growth, straight up and out from that first "Wicca 101" class. We were something new.

After several years of various levels and styles of leadership, much informal ritual work, and notably irregular practice, the Tradition was formally confirmed in 2006: Degrees overseen by Ms. Alexander were affirmed, another iteration of a year-long "Wicca 101" curriculum began, and the Tradition became a recognized Circle of Four Quarters. Circles in this context are one way affinity groups at Four Quarters may take shape and be constituted institutionally. Furthermore, the work—spiritual, mental, and emotional—that went into creating the Charter began the process of institutional leadership *within* Stone Circle Wicca. The meetings, the ceremonies, the writing and editing and writing again...it was all part of the magic of the babe learning to walk. And while we have no official influence in the governance of Four Quarters, these early steps went towards a time when we participated at every level of the community.

Stone Circle Wicca was incorporated as a Circle of Four Quarters by way of formal Charter in the fall of 2006. The first article and section of the Charter, the Mission, reads as follows:
"The Stone Circle Tradition of Wicca is a Wiccan mystery tradition within the larger family of the Four Quarters Interfaith Sanctuary of Earth Religion, which exists to promote the spiritual development of Dedicants and Initiates; to encourage responsible fulfillment of diverse Wiccan vocations to priest/esshood; and to offer service to Four Quarters, to all in Earth's Household, and to the Divine Spirit of the Universe, One and Many, Male, Female, Both, and Neither."

Sustaining the Life of the Tradition

Stone Circle Wicca was blessed from the beginning with leadership tools that not all traditions have in such abundance. I list here some of the benefits and blessings Stone Circle Wicca has had in its leadership:

- It has been sustained not only by people who are called to public ritual and institutional leadership, but also by those with outstanding organizational skills and experience.

- It has the benefit of a formal Charter and *shared, overt* expectations for individuals Initiates and governance as a whole.

- Its Dedicants and Initiates are member of Four Quarters, a landed, liturgical, and spiritual home. Within the larger institution, they are also part of the Stone Circle Wicca tradition itself. These nested relationships may allow for a sense of commitment and rootedness that may otherwise be hard to maintain.

- In addition to their Four Quarters leadership, SCW leadership has included those with leadership experience and skills in nonprofit, private sector, collegiate, and federal sector, university teaching, labor organizing, clinical social work, and experience with other vowed religious communities.

- The nature of Dedicant work, particularly that toward the Second Degree. encourages personal growth and maturity.

- Stone Circle Wicca Initiates are dedicated to the practice of spirituality and religion in their personal lives, seeking in our various ways, knowledge of and communion with the Divine Spirit of the Universe Who Is One and Many, Male, Female, Both, and Neither.

- By virtue of the bulk of SCW-led rituals being in the context and for the benefit of the many members and visitors at Four Quarters, ritual skill and leadership blossomed.

Rich Times and Lean

Since the setting down of the Charter, the Tradition has ebbed and flowed in its public activity, the number of students in the First Degree Dedicant class, the number working toward their Second Degrees, and the number of those working for their Third. Sometimes many Initiates and Dedicants have taken leadership roles in Four Quarters ritual, sometimes there have been few. In some years, Dedicants to all Degrees have been studying in class or one-on-one, teachers have offered Advanced Wicca Seminars, there have been three sets of initiations, and groups of Initiates and Dedicants have conducted moon service ritual and festival ceremony consistently.

Those years felt full, rich, beautiful, even easy, though we worked very hard. We felt our gifts flower and bear fruit. We were like the youths dancing on Beltaine, exerting ourselves out of joy and love.

And then came the fallow times, the times when the harvest had been taken, and there were only gleanings to come to the storehouse and to feed the people. Leaves turned gorgeous, and then they fell.

In leaner times, in the "winter," when the larger community did not see much public activity, there were only a few — one priest and one priestess in particular — who kept the fires of teaching alive, and who blew on the ember of ritual leadership. They were superbly committed to keeping the Tradition alive and continuing the flow of Initiation. These two taught classes, made ceremony, and mentored others when much Tradition activity seemed to be underground. It was as if the organization itself was undergoing its own Second Degree journey. "I thought that was dead," a Four Quarters leader remarked, and yet mentoring had continued and thanks to the leadership of that dedicated pair, a class, along with its Dedications and Initiations, was continuing.

When Stone Circle Wicca has flourished publicly, it has fostered powerful moral, organizational, and ritual leadership at Four Quarters and beyond. Meetings have been helpful in maintaining cohesion and keeping the organizational aspects of the Tradition working. These gatherings have, like other waters of the Tradition's life, ebbed and flowed.

Happily, as of this writing, in the fall of 2014, over 20 prospective Dedicants came to the most recent Meet-and-Greet, and SCW teachers are working to teach a bumper crop of Dedicants this year. As of publication, 14 Dedicated students were initiated into First Degree priest/esshood. It seems that a new spring has come to the Tradition.

Leadership Beyond SCW and Four Quarters

"House of the Whispering Winds....[15]
House of the Warm Hearth...
House of the Ever-moving Stream...
House of Twisting Vines...
We call to the Household of Earth and hear Your Call.
We call to the Household of Earth and we know we are Your Children.
We call to the Household of Earth, and know You are our Ancestor."

Leadership in the larger Pagan community is something SCW Initiates have taken seriously throughout our time together, even

---

[15] Invocation courtesy of Dr. Jonathan White, 3rd Degree

before the Charter. Events like Sacred Spaces, Pantheacon, Crossroads, Starwood, various Pagan Pride Days, and District of Columbia, Baltimore, and Northern Virginia Interfaith Pride rituals have all benefited from the presence and expertise of Stone Circle Wicca Initiates. We have also participated in and led organizations like the Mid-Atlantic Pagan Leadership Conference, Pagan Leadership Skills Conference, National Capital Region Leadership Conference; Open Hearth Foundation, and Pagan Spirit Gathering. Whether teaching in conference settings, leading institutions, offering ritual in interfaith events, or teaching and preaching elsewhere, Initiates have been found at work throughout the mid-Atlantic region of the United States.

In addition to their internal, informal, Four Quarters, and Pagan community leadership, Initiates serve other parts of Earth's Household. By teaching, mentoring, counseling, community organizing, hospitality, activism, gardening, ministry outside SCW, and other works of service, Stone Circle Wicca Initiates acknowledge our family relations with all.

Leadership in Formal Governance

According to the Charter of 2006, Stone Circle Wicca is governed by two bodies: The Council of Thirds and the Gathering of Initiates. In this sense, the Tradition has both hierarchical and nearly consensus-based modes of leadership. That is to say, one person may not, for example, formally block a decision. Nonetheless, the Council strives for unanimity when possible. This Council of Thirds is responsible for the routine operation of the Tradition and its ongoing ritual responsibilities, as well as for approval of mentorship. The Council of Thirds may also agree to event or festival leadership, as well as to SCW representation at outside events, conferences, and the like.

Any matters of greater import, such as the ratification of the Charter or reorganization of leadership, must be discussed and decided through the Gathering of Initiates. The Gathering occurs once or twice a year, and extraordinary Gatherings may be called as necessary. Any matters of significance, such as amendment to the Charter, must be announced at least one full moon cycle in advance of the Gathering.

Responsibility in Practice

Leadership in Stone Circle Wicca has always been one in which authority comes with responsibility. Yes, priests and priestesses of the Third Degree, for example, certainly have influence — interpersonal power — within the communities of SCW and Four Quarters. They also have express responsibility for their actions and inactions and respective results.

Third Degree Initiates would never, as is done in some other traditions, insist on pride of place at dinner or expect to be served first. That is not the nature of our authority. Our responsibility may come with authority, but an Initiate must never let that authority devolve into a cult of personality or a basis for treatment above and beyond that owed to all beings of worth and dignity (which is to say, all). This responsibility is a personal, aspirational one, and goes along with the service delineated in the Charter Mission above.

Initiations are magical. Initiations happen in the Mysterious embrace of the Stone Circle, under Dark Moons and Bright. Initiations imprint new realities onto our souls. Initiations give and unleash power and leadership, both public and secret.

There are things and experiences within the Circle of Initiation of which one may not, indeed, *cannot* speak. Nonetheless, each Initiation has its own responsibilities of visible leadership. Each Degree comes with its own, separate set of leadership expectations.

Leadership by Degree: First Degree

People come to Dedication toward the First Degree because they want to learn ritual skill and develop the ability to make transformative, public ceremony. Dedication to the path of the First Degree largely concerns matters of skill and creativity, symbolic understanding, and a commitment to participate in the ritual life of the community.

Those seeking initiation into the First Degree must demonstrate their ability to craft, plan, organize, and lead a Moon Service as their "final exam." This "exam" follows a year and a day, at least, of formal learning with Mentor teachers in the Dedicant class.

Once initiated and given a dark green cord, First Degree priests and priestesses then enter into recognized, public ritual leadership at Four Quarters. They are initiated priests and priestesses. Initiates are expected to step into the Center, to facilitate at least one Moon Service a year, and to foster the ritual life of the community according to their gifts and skills.

Second Degree

Dedication to the path of the Second Degree is the Underworld Journey. It is the Hero's Journey. It is Inanna's trek to Her sister's realm and back again. For many, it involves powerful personal transformation over the course of two years or more. Indeed, those dedicated to Second Degree study are considered ready for Initiation only upon having demonstrated positive change in their lives. The one who walks this way is profoundly alone, and the path is recognized as fraught with personal peril. While there is no externally imposed danger, confrontation with one's Shadow — necessary for the work — is always difficult. Dedicants do "come up for air" periodically to connect with a Mentor, but the Work of the path is done alone. At Initiation, the Second Degree Initiate is given a black cord to be worn with the green.

The leadership of the Second Degree is more subtle than that of either the First or Third degree. It is leadership by the four Cardinal Virtues of Stone Circle Wicca: Authenticity, integrity, compassion, and wisdom. Second Degree leadership is a leadership of insight, self-awareness, and the development of a wise and discerning spirit.

Third Degree

Finally, Dedication on the path of the Third Degree moves toward active public leadership to the communities in which Stone Circle Wicca moves.

Leadership at the Third Degree — because it is public — is more like that of the First Degree than that of the Second. Third Degree leadership includes the skills, abilities, and commitments of the first two Degrees. Third Degree priests and priestesses both the inner wisdom of the Second, the ritual skill of the First, and a greater degree of integration and facility with each.

Upon initiation, Initiates to the Third Degree are given a violet cord, to be braided with the black and green. These Initiates must move fluidly between the brightest daylight of public service and the moonless dark of Mystery. We travel lightly on the sun-and moonbeams of personal and public practice, between attention to the individual and to the community, between ritual and non-ritual leadership.

Certainly, Third Degree priests and priestesses are expected to accept and fulfill great responsibility. For one, upon initiation, priests and priestesses of the Third Degree become part of the Council of Thirds, those most responsible for the ongoing life of the Tradition. For another, Third Degree Initiates are expected to have an intention to remain in rooted, committed relationship with the Land, Standing Stones, People, and overall life of Four Quarters.

Leadership in the Context of Our Mother Institution

The basic principles and responsibilities of leadership are delineated in the Charter of 2006. The Charter and the Confirmation Ceremony might be called sacramental, in that they were both affirmations of magic that had already happened, work that already been done, and systems that were already coming into place. The Charter was an expression of something we had sought since our beginnings: Clarity about who we were becoming and what we were doing. Magic had happened there and would continue.

In addition to our own personal and Tradition experiences, because we were all part of the landed community of Four Quarters, we learned some lessons about leadership in our context.

While Dedicants and Initiates of Stone Circle Wicca are *not*—nor should they be—the only ritual leaders at Four Quarters, we have nonetheless borne significant ritual responsibility. For example, SCW assumed responsibility for the development of Stones Rising 2007, a large, multi-day, multi-ceremony event. From the welcoming circle around the still-bedecked Maypole to the singing of traditional closing songs, SCW Dedicants and Initiates were responsible for making magic possible, the transformation possible, the psychological impact of ritual possible.

SCW Initiates led as they sang Moonsong each night and gathered around the fire circle with drumming hands, dancing feet, and magical pot-stirring skills. Others in the community planned the raising of the Stones, the pouring of the concrete, the rollers and the ropes, the engineering and the safety of the process of the Rising.

Again, let me emphasize that SCW Initiates and Dedicants did not do this work alone. Rather, we were responsible for leadership, for writing and coordinating ceremony for hundreds of celebrants. It was, however, those hundreds who made the magic by their presence, their transformation, their insights, and their participation.

Leadership in the Four Quarters community has looked different at different times. One Initiate managed the recruitment and scheduling of community ceremony at Full and New Moon Services for nearly three years. Others have been Members of the Board or Members Advocates to the Board. Two have been President of the Board. Four have directed the choir, each leading under different circumstances. Another runs the Four Quarters Meadery. Three of us have run the kitchen in various iterations. Others have been responsible for a yearly welcoming ceremony of festivity, finery, glitter and joy at Stones Rising. Some have lived on the Land of Four Quarters full-time, giving their lives and service to the People. None of these roles are internal to Stone Circle Wicca, but they express the responsibility that is inherent in the Tradition and to Four Quarters more generally.

Being children of the Land and People of Four Quarters, we know that if one wants to see something come into being, one has either to begin it oneself or find others excited and energetic enough to make it happen; we know that hard work and reliability are valued above almost all else; and we know that burnout looms for any committed volunteer. We have grown more and more aware that every single one of us is a volunteer with other significant responsibilities in our lives — families and other relationships, paid work, and other community involvement, for example — that we had to balance along with our SCW/Four Quarters commitments.

No Perfect People

That said, Four Quarters is not unfamiliar with chaos in leadership. It happens. There have been times leaders have overstepped the boundaries and responsibilities of leadership and used authority in irresponsible ways. Initiates of Stone Circle Wicca have become embroiled in community politics to the detriment of themselves and the Tradition. Initiates have stretched themselves too far and relationships have broken. Initiates have tried to lay conceit or arrogance aside, and sometimes we have failed.

More often than any of us would like to admit, we have taken on too much, failed to live up to our stated commitments with integrity, and have disappointed others and ourselves as a result. People have left the community; some have returned in various ways, and some have remained apart.

Thanks to the Cardinal Virtues of Authenticity, Integrity, Compassion, and Wisdom, as well as to our own commitments made in love to one another, our work has generally been fruitful. It is not that we have always lived up to our Virtues. Rather, we are called back to them again and again.

We have been able to seek mediation and live through brokenness. We have been able to recover from conflict. We have supported one another in the sacred acts of relinquishment as well as those of taking up of leadership. And we have returned to our work in love when strength, time, healing, and energy have allowed.

A Combination of Relationships

Stone Circle Wicca has both open and closed learning opportunities. Some just for Dedicants and Initiates, some for any who wish to come. For example, the Advanced Wicca Seminar, now on hiatus, was a regular, open class. The Seminar covered more theo/alogical concepts, theories of vocation, and questions of personal practice than do the materials of the First Degree class. Initiates, as well as those members of the larger Four Quarters community who are experienced ritualists, are particularly invited to attend and participate, but the Seminar is open to anyone.

The Stone Circle Tradition of Wicca is a combination of closed, protective, boundaried relationships and open, inclusive, and public ones. Many skills must come together to create this functional combination. The Tradition's Cardinal Virtues are meant to morally govern Initiates actions and concerns. Initiates need to comport themselves in such a way as to demonstrate striving for the Virtues' expression. This is personal leadership — leadership by example.

What Leadership Demands

Stone Circle Wicca is a Mystery Tradition, which means that all priests and priestesses are responsible for their own meditation, devotion, or other personal practice. Further, it means that the paths we walk and the initiations we experience are not merely private, but ritually secret.

Stone Circle Wicca is also a teaching tradition: Initiates who are called to lead through the twin vocations of organization and pedagogy come together to teach classes and mentor Dedicants to all Degrees.

Finally, Stone Circle Wicca is a ritual tradition. We know that ritual is vital to the life of Four Quarters. While the Four Quarters institution has become more and more deeply concerned with a secular focus on life in an age of environmental crisis, ceremony of all kinds still brings groups from ten to hundreds together on the Land over and over again each year.

Indeed, it is frankly breathtaking to see the pageantry and display of the Stones Rising event each August. It is awe inspiring to see dozens of people working ropes and rollers to raise multi-ton Stones into their positions in the larger Stone Circle. All this, while a choir sings; prayers are offered, drums play their soft, solid beat, and others witness the Rising for the first time.

It is astonishing to watch torchlit ceremony on Samhain, see the incense prayers rising for those who have died in the past year, hear the keening and the singing, and feel the invocations in one's bones.

It is humbling to see the tears on someone's face when a well-crafted, transformative ritual has touched them. Initiates of Stone Circle Wicca, together with others at Four Quarters, have been part of all of these. Initiates craft, plan, organize, and lead ceremony, rain or shine, in some frankly crazy weather, and with all our personal and collective transformation in mind.

Final Analysis

Both Four Quarters and its daughter tradition, Stone Circle Wicca, are human institutions, one part of the other, together comprising hundreds of individuals. These individuals are all striving to be happy, fulfilled, and well.

As in many organizations, it is easier to be a few steps away from leadership than to put your time, energy, heart, and reputation into something as fragile as a spiritual institution. But formal leadership exists to serve individuals and communities beyond the leaders themselves. This concept—often called "servant leadership" in Christian circles—is at the heart of Stone Circle Wicca's life. The Tradition exists to foster human gifts, as well as the *use* of those gifts in *service* to the larger community.

In the end, though Stone Circle Wicca's population, influence, and visibility have waxed and waned like the moon Herself, the Tradition is nonetheless vital to the life of Four Quarters and other communities. Initiates are committed to the moral search for leadership, accountability, and responsibility. My prayer is that Initiates of the Stone Circle Tradition of Wicca continue to strive to maintain authenticity, integrity, compassion, and wisdom, always in the service of those we love—others but not only others, ourselves but not only ourselves.

Blessings on all our paths.

Leader as Servant:
The Onus of Leadership
KaliSara

Leadership and respect are the hallmarks of reaching modern adulthood. They are the twin prizes that everyone wants to be given, the blue ribbons of success and power. And they aren't all they are cracked up to be. But grown-ups have responsibilities that go along with the respect: bills, jobs, time constraints, and obligations. These things are not always fun and adults can't just do whatever they want. At least, not without consequences.

I am currently looking at taking on additional leadership roles within my local and regional communities. For me, leadership roles are something that I accept with hesitation, not something that I pursue. Each role that I take comes with a series of requirements that I have to consider before accepting, because leadership is a burden of duty, obligation and responsibility, to one's own standards of behavior and to the community in which one becomes a leader.

The major onus of leadership is the idea of leader as servant, or Servant Leadership, which approaches the leader as one who puts those under them as a priority. The phrase "servant leadership" was coined by Robert K. Greenleaf in "The Servant as Leader" in 1970.[16] This type of leader is the decision-maker and law-giver, but not a dictator or tyrant. The power dynamic of a traditional leader places more power, resources and priority at the top of the hierarchy. A leader as servant puts the needs and ambitions of the lower levels of the hierarchy as the priority. The Servant Leader is the leader who serves the interests of their people first.

The leader as servant is a steward of the land (real or metaphorical) and a supporter of the people in their lives and in their growth, individually and as a whole. This leader celebrates that which helps others, even when it may hurt the leader. The leader as servant has been identified and recognized in the Tao

---

[16]   http://www.amazon.com/Servant-as-Leader-Robert-Greenleaf-ebook/dp/B008K5IPB8/ref=sr_1_1?s=digital-text&ie=UTF8&qid=1431883515&sr=1-1

te Ching, the Bible, and throughout history and the world[17].

This style is a way of leading that takes into account the thoughts, feelings and needs of all parties, particularly of those who are not the leader. But most leaders do not follow this path. Leaders are often given their roles as a reward or culmination of their work, and the leader as servant gains few rewards that are not solely altruistic in nature. At the extreme, servant leadership can even border on psycho-emotional masochism or martyrdom.

Challenges of Servant Leadership

The leader as servant focuses on their team, organization, or coven, and the growth of the members of that group, rather than on what they can get out of the role. They share information and resources freely, meaning they hold back nothing for their own advantage. The leader as servant can feel defenseless or exposed, taking on more of the risk for little to none of the gain. They, when necessary, sacrifice their own resources and benefits for the betterment of their group. While this makes sense when you take into account that leaders often have more resources available to them, it is still an uneven distribution of risk.

This means that the best type of leadership, for all those under that leader, is the type that is least likely to be immediately rewarding to the leader. Thus, the leader must be capable of working without immediate or tangible rewards, and even the rewards they do get may be less personal to them. They must have their own inner circle of support and confidence, because their leadership role is not about them, or their ego or feelings.

This is hard, even for those of us who actively work towards this spiritual attitude. It is hard putting others first all the time. It can, and often does, result in burnout for those leaders who do end up getting little or nothing back from the community that they work so hard for. We've all seen the group held together by a leader who suddenly quits or disappears, or suddenly becomes debilitated by a stress-induced illness.

In monetary terms, this is the basis of the debate on Pagan

---

[17] https://www.regent.edu/acad/global/publications/ijls/new/vol3iss2/IJLS_V3Is2_Winston_Ryan.pdf

teachers requiring payment for classes, readings, healing and other services. In organizational terms, this type of leadership can result in good leaders slowly transforming into bad leaders, as they try to reap some benefit for their work. To be a good leader, one must be willing to take on the task of serving the community, even after working for months, years, or decades to be recognized as a potential leader.

Benefits of Servant Leadership to Leaders and Communities

There are advantages to using this system of leadership, and not just getting to feel better than everyone because look at how self-sacrificing they are. Many of us are driven to help people, to be generous, and to spread kindness. The servant leadership model certainly has more of that than a dictatorial leadership model does. There is also the advantage of spiritual growth and satisfaction in placing the well-being and happiness of others above your own.

The leader as servant tends to be more ethical in dealing with their subordinates, which provides a spiritual satisfaction. This leadership model often results in more positive, long-term effects on the people under the leader and the society in which they live. This is often balanced by the years that it takes for a leader to put the techniques of servant leadership into place.

However, the most impressive advantage is that servant leaders tend to have more success leading their groups. Servant leaders often have fewer issues with subordinates being resistant or disgruntled. The behaviors of servant leaders, particularly in regards to paying attention to and validating the needs and feelings of those they lead, lend themselves to promoting a loyal and cohesive group dynamic, which translates to more efficient and effective action by the group. The group becomes more engaged in its own purpose.[18, 19]

Additionally, servant leaders tend to lift up or support the growth of the members of the lower rungs of the hierarchy. This can result in a cascade affect on all of the members of the group,

---

[18]   http://smallbusiness.chron.com/advantages-servant-leadership-style-11693.html

[19]http://www.regentuniversityonline.com/acad/global/publications/sl_procee dings/2007/wong-davey.pdf

with each member experiencing the support and growth as a part of the whole. Thus the servant leader gains an advantage indirectly due to the overall elevation and growth of the group. If the group is better off, then the person leading the group is better off. This big-picture method of leadership often leads to systemic, social changes and growth, which can affect people outside the servant leader's group.

Becoming a Servant Leader

Fortunately, leaders do not need to recreate this type of leadership on their own. There are classes and websites that discuss this leadership style and the techniques associated with it. Robert Greenleaf and others, such as Larry Spears, have created entire management systems based on this idea and based around these ten principles: Listening, Empathy, Healing, Awareness, Persuasion, Conceptualization, Foresight, Stewardship, Commitment to the growth of people, and Building community.[20] While many good leaders come to this idea on their own, it can help people solidify their leadership style by learning about these ideas and techniques.

We can also look at examples of servant leaders. Famous servant leaders include Dr. Martin Luther King, Jr. and Eleanor Roosevelt. Within our own community, we can find servant leaders such as Cat Chapin-Bishop and T. Thorn Coyle, two very different personalities who are both active in social protesting and vocal about ethics within Paganism. At the same time, both are extremely personable and often engage in one-on-one discussions. Peter Dybing is another, who most recently has helped head a relief organization for small, outlying villages affected by the earthquake in Nepal. Kerr Cuhulain spent much of his career as a law enforcement officer acting as a resource and liaison to bring understanding of Paganism and Pagan practices to law enforcement groups, yet his interactions with those who take his classes is friendly and attentive.

---

[20]http://www.regent.edu/acad/global/publications/jvl/vol1_iss1/Spears_Final.pdf

Personal Approach to Servant Leadership

I, personally, have used the practices of Servant Leadership in my own path. In leadership positions, I strive to achieve a consensus through discussion, only taking over the final decision if consensus cannot be reached. I have frequently prioritized discussing individual and group goals within regular meetings, and I actively work at bringing everyone's voice into each discussion.

This can be difficult. The urge to interrupt a bad idea still strikes. The desire to dismiss someone because of my personal feelings about them still rears up on occasion. Sometimes I want to stand up and say "Look at what I do for you... love me for it!" I spend a lot of time biting my tongue, then venting in private to my understanding husband. But, the very best technique I've found is to think how I would feel if someone did to me what I was thinking of doing to them.

Leadership is an onus, a burden, because when it is done right and done well, it is often hard on the leader. If it is not done well, it is harder on the group. To take on the responsibility of such a task is not a reward after much hard work, it is the beginning of a new and difficult journey. However, if we are to grow as Pagans and as people, we need to prioritize this leadership style in our spiritual groups. If we are to become an influential and rewarding community, we need to decide what type of leadership we will embody and embrace.

Resources for Further Study

The Case for Servant Leadership by Kent Keith. (http://www.amazon.com/Case-Servant-Leadership-Kent-Keith/dp/B001OU4H5E)

Greenleaf Center for Servant Leadership (https://greenleaf.org/)

"The Servant as Leader" by Robert Greenleaf. (http://www.amazon.com/Servant-as-Leader-Robert-Greenleaf-ebook/dp/B008K5IPB8/ref=sr_1_1?s=digital-text&ie=UTF8&qid=1431883515&sr=1-1)

The Seven Pillars of Servant Leadership by James Sipe and Don Frick. (http://www.amazon.com/Seven-Pillars-Servant-

Leadership-Practicing/dp/080914560X)
*The Three Levels of Leadership: How to Develop Your Leadership
Presence, Knowhow and Skill* by James Scouller.
(http://www.amazon.com/Three-Levels-Leadership-
Develop-Presence/dp/1852526815/ref=asap_bc?ie=UTF8)

Managing Multiple-Role Relationships in Pagan Communities
Christine Hoff Kraemer

Have you ever visited a massage therapist whom you also knew socially, dated a co-worker, or gone into business with a covenmate? If so, you have experienced a *multiple-role relationship*—a relationship where there are different sets of expectations and obligations operating simultaneously.

Community-oriented Pagans often love to create this kind of intimacy. It's not unusual for the same close-knit network of friends and lovers to engage in business relationships or live as roommates while also doing ritual together. These overlapping roles can turn explosive, however, when conflicts of interest between multiple roles are identified too late.

This article provides a model for doing risk assessments on various kinds of overlapping community roles and looks at ethical guidelines for decision-making around multiple-role relationships. Exercises for identifying, analyzing, and negotiating multiple-role relationships are included for individuals and groups.

Key Terms

Here is a list of key terms used in this article. Most of these terms come from a counseling context, but Pagans may find these concepts useful in a variety of community situations.

- **Boundary** -- A limit set in a relationship, concerning issues such as physical contact, emotional intimacy, financial dealings, etc.
- **Conflict of interest** -- A situation where a person has competing interests or loyalties, such as when a manager is tempted to hire their lover over other better-qualified applicants because of their personal connection.
- **Multiple-role relationship** (in therapeutic contexts, "dual relationship") -- A situation where two people

have more than one type of interaction or serve in more than one role for each other, especially when one such relationship is personal and the other professional.

- **Exploitation** -- An act that victimizes a person for another's benefit. An act that takes unfair advantage or uses another person as a means to an end.
- **Power differential** -- An imbalance in a relationship where one person has more power or authority than the other (or is perceived to have it) and may be able to use that power to influence or control the other person.
- **Self-care** -- Ensuring that one's own social, emotional, spiritual, physical, and other needs are thoroughly met so that one is not tempted to try to meet those needs in exploitative or otherwise unethical ways.
- **Transference and countertransference** -- Transference occurs when past experiences or relationship patterns are projected onto a current relationship. In a clinical setting, "transference" occurs when the client projects onto the therapist. "Countertransference" occurs when the therapist projects onto the client.

"Dual" Relationships for Therapists, Teachers, and Ministers

This article evolved out of a Cherry Hill Seminary intensive on negotiating multiple roles in the lives of Pagan leaders. We started by looking at the literature on what's called "dual" relationships for clergy of other religions and for therapists and counselors (some of these resources are included in the bibliography).

For professional therapists and counselors, any kind of dual relationship (such as client/friend or client/lover) has traditionally been considered unacceptable because of the potential to disrupt the counseling relationship. Therapists are generally advised to avoid seeing their clients socially; some set a boundary that if the therapist does run into a client at an event, the therapist will only greet the client if the client greets them.

The client's status as a client is completely confidential. Because the therapist knows so much personal information about the client, it can make the client feel or actually be vulnerable to the therapist in other contexts.

It is universally considered unethical for a therapist to have a sexual relationship with a client before treatment has been terminated (and usually for some years afterward, although some professional organizations require that therapists never have sex with former clients). Even if the therapist's intent is benign, the power imbalance created by the therapeutic relationship may cause the client to feel exploited. At worst, an unethical therapist can use a client's vulnerability to deliberately coerce them into sexual or other inappropriate activity.

Failure to recognize the power imbalance between counselor and client can have negative effects, even if the person initiating the dual relationship has nothing but good intentions. When I was in my early twenties, I went to a counselor to deal with issues around anxiety and depression. We worked together for about a year, and I found the sessions to be helpful. In the course of treatment, I talked a great deal about Pagan spirituality. This was an area of budding personal interest for my therapist as well, and he began to ask me for book recommendations and other resources. I suspect, because my counselor felt he was learning so much from me, he started to think of us as being in something like a peer relationship.

This was not the case from my perspective. One day, I mentioned a local Pagan event I was thinking of attending, and he (perhaps not realizing how small and intimate these events tended to be) expressed interest in attending as well. I immediately felt uneasy and clammed up. Afterward, I had a series of dreams about the counselor in which I felt threatened and violated. I made an excuse and terminated treatment.

My counselor, being a professional, should have known better than to initiate a dual relationship with a client. In religious communities, however, dual or multiple-role relationships are often inevitable. Their unavoidability, however, does not mean they are without risks. This is especially true if those who provide leadership also provide pastoral counseling or spiritual direction, as most leaders of churches and synagogues do. Imagine, for example, how it might be to have a church member confess to a minister that he is having an affair with another church member. Having this information can make it very awkward for the minister to relate to the members who are having the affair and their spouse(s), who may be in the dark. The stronger the ties of friendship with these members – yet another layer of relationship – the more awkward and painful it will be, until it may compromise the minister's ability to do their jobs.

Dual and multiple-role relationships can also be problematic in teaching relationships, especially when teachers become close friends or lovers with students. Close friendships in the classroom may lead the teacher to treat some students differently from others, singling them out for favoritism or negative attention and disrupting the classroom environment for other students. If the teacher gives grades, having a close relationship may interfere with their ability to accurately evaluate the student. If the teacher and student have a sexual relationship, the power dynamic between them may cause the student to feel manipulated into sexual activity. For these reasons, many universities prohibit instructors and students from having sexual relationships with each other.

Not all therapists, ministers, and teachers believe that multiple-role relationships are destructive, however. In fact, some therapists argue that dual relationships can benefit therapy. A number have made this argument about therapists working in LGBT communities. It is often much easier for a LGBT client to relate to a therapist who is also involved in the same subcultural community, as there is shared knowledge of the relevant issues and more shared experience. (Additionally, in small towns or small subcultural communities, it can be quite difficult to find a therapist whom one will never meet in a social context—that is, unless the therapist ceases to participate in the community she hopes to serve. Many LGBT therapists are advocating that professional organizations relax their rules around dual relationships for this reason.) Other therapists relate that close friends sometimes ask them to become their counselors specifically because they *are* close friends—their friends want a counselor who knows them well and whom they already trust.

These are just a few of the reasons that clients may want a

therapist whom they consider "one of their own." This can also be the case in religious communities and teaching relationships. Close and intimate ties between students and teachers, or between a ritual leader and a ritual participant, can enhance those communities by creating a sense of warmth, kinship, and trust. Knowing a community member or student well can better equip a clergyperson or teacher to work with them effectively and create a more joyful interaction.

Relationships with multiple roles are especially unavoidable for Pagan leaders. We are largely volunteers in communities that may or may not have any clear hierarchy and that are often quite small. These multiple-role relationships can be very satisfying, and at times they may be actively desirable. We like to do business with other Pagans to support our communities economically. We want to have close friends perform our weddings or act as our pastoral counselors, because we love and trust them. We want to be in small groups and covens with the people with whom we are most intimate, because strong emotional bonds often make ritual and magic more effective.

The problem in Pagan communities is that we often fail to acknowledge how these intertwined relationships are also risky. If we patronize a friend's business and their work isn't good, it can jeopardize the friendship. If a sexual relationship between two members of a small group goes sour, it can break up the group. Some multiple-role relationships, such as those inherent in being a coven leader, require a constant balancing act: a coven leader is often expected to both nurture and evaluate students, which puts them in the awkward position of having to both evaluate students for initiation, but also be their cheerleader. There's an inherent conflict of interest when the coach is also the judge!

Let's take a moment to sum up and clarify some of the main points from above.

What are the dangers of multiple-role relationships?

- **Exploitation in a power differential**: If there is a power differential in one area of the relationship, will it spill over into other aspects? If a student has sex with their teacher—even if they are no longer teacher and student—will that unequal power relationship persist unchallenged and un-negotiated?

- **Confusion of expectations**: What roles are the relevant ones right now? Are we acting as friends and peers, or are we acting as craftsperson and customer? What do we do if the expectations connected to these roles conflict?
- **Potential instability of the group**: When group members live, worship, and do business together, the potential for conflict to arise is enormous. When relationships are densely intertwined, how can other group members avoid being drawn in when there is conflict?
- **Contamination of other relationships**: If my lover becomes my business partner and then doesn't hold up their end of the business, what will happen to our personal relationship?
- **Potential to compromise confidentiality**: If a therapist becomes close friends with a client, then they have a fight, who can the therapist confide in without breaching client confidentiality?
- **Perceived or real unfair advantages**: If one of the members of a high priestess' coven is her daughter, how will other student members feel if the daughter always seems to get the best ritual roles, or never comes to circle prepared?

What are the benefits of multiple-role relationships?

- **Holistic approach/fuller information**: A relationship that is not compartmentalized allows both parties to see each other more clearly. In a traditional counselor/client relationship, the therapist only has clients' accounts of themselves and their relationships; in a multiple-role relationship, the counselor may have first-hand knowledge of the client's friends and loved ones and may be able to provide a more balanced perspective.
- **Expedites the process**: If two people already value and trust each other, the getting-to-know you process necessary for many working relationships is not needed.

Counselors can get to the heart of the problem immediately, teachers can skip the basics, and business partners can pool finances without fear.

- **Common vocabulary**: Isn't it a relief to go to a counselor who already understands what "transgender" means, or to hire an electrician who already knows not to put tools on your altar?
- **Deeper intimacy/potential for more deeply bonded group**: There is already a word for a social unit that lives, worships, and does business together: a family. Multiple-role relationships can be the basis of ties that last a lifetime.

Exercise: Identifying Conflicts of Interest

List the roles you play in your Pagan community and in your professional and personal lives. Here are a few of mine.

- parent
- spouse
- friend
- coven member
- nonprofit Board president
- employee
- supervisor
- mentor

By yourself or in a group, consider your list. Do any of your roles have expectations that conflict with each other? In case of a conflict, which role takes precedence? Do your partner(s) in these relationships share your priorities?

Exercise: Stories of Multiple-Role Relationship

By yourself or in a group, reflect on multiple-role relationships you have experienced. Can you think of both negative and positive examples? What did you learn from these experiences?

Here are two of mine.

Negative: I really liked my former teacher. After I was no longer her student, I asked her to tea, and we were friends for several years while she struggled with depression. I helped her throw social gatherings at her house, and we thought of each other as aunt and niece.

I moved away from the area for a few years, and when I returned, I was working as a massage therapist. Hoping for some relief and thinking to help me financially, she asked me to do massage for her in her home. Working on her, however, brought me face to face with how much her health had declined, to the point where she could hardly leave the house. I told her I wasn't comfortable working with her without her consulting a doctor, but she insisted that further medical care would be pointless. Her comments about mutual friends and acquaintances also became increasingly negative, making me uncomfortable.

When she decided to plan a party at her house, I offered to assist, hoping the social interaction would be good for her. As the date approached, however, she resisted talking about the event, and repeatedly rescheduled our plans to see each other. Shortly before the gathering, she pulled herself together; with some help from friends and a heroic effort on her own part, the event went off well. I had felt responsible for the event's success, and I was angry that she'd created such a stressful situation for herself and for me.

Finally, I wrote her a letter telling her how draining the friendship felt, expressing my concern about her unwillingness to seek health care, and conveying my discomfort at how negative she seemed to be about our mutual friends. She wrote me a long letter telling me how her behavior was justified and broke off contact.

Positive: Two friends offered to barter rent for massage therapy. I lived with them for a year, during which we often shared confidences and sometimes did magick together. I gave them each a weekly massage. I also started working for their religious organization on a contract basis, which helped my financial bottom line and gave me valuable skills.

Until they moved away, we socialized regularly; after their move, we visited occasionally, and for a time I helped manage a rental property for them. Although we are no longer in any kind of business relationship, we keep in touch online, and I am always happy to see them.

Risk Assessment in Multiple-Role Relationships

Once you are more aware of multiple-role relationships, it becomes easier to identify ones you are already in and anticipate the formation of new ones. With this awareness, you may have the opportunity to discuss the benefits and risks of adding roles to a relationship with the other person and/or get advice from thoughtful peers.

Here are some questions to ask to help you evaluate how likely conflicts are to arise in an existing or potential multiple-role relationship.

Expectations: What expectations does each person have about each role in the relationship? Have these expectations been explicitly discussed? If one of the relationship roles would normally involve a written contract, has this contract been made? Are there clear agreements around any payment or energy exchange that might be involved?

Social effects: Who else will be affected by adding roles to the relationship? Could conflict in this relationship affect mutual friends or a group both parties belong to?

Power differentials: Does one person have power over the other in one or more of their roles? Will adding a new role increase this power differential, balance it, or leave it unchanged?

Skills/needs match: If you are adding a role to a relationship that requires one or both parties to have particular skills (such as the ability to perform a wedding, provide therapy, or do business accounting), are these skills present and strong? Will each party's skills be sufficient to match the other's needs?

Transference/countertransference: Is either party aware of a past relationship, especially a traumatic one, that might influence how they experience the relationship? For instance, emotionally intimate small groups often bring up issues from the family of origin. Might your new covenmate start to drive you crazy because he reminds you of your deadbeat brother, or will you find yourself keeping secrets from your spiritual teacher because she reminds you of your nosy mother?

Resources: Do both parties have the time, energy, and emotional stability that the complexity of the relationship requires? Do both have good self-care skills? How well do they communicate when under stress? What other commitments and obligations are active in their lives?

Ethical issues: Are there legal or professional ethics issues to consider? Will the relationship involve client confidentiality that might be compromised by the existence of other relationship roles? Are both parties competent, mature, and otherwise fully able to give informed consent to the relationship? What motivates each party to enter into the relationship? Have all of these motives been openly discussed?

Support: If the relationship involves counseling, spiritual mentoring, or a close teaching relationship, is peer supervision or advising available? Do both people in the relationship have wise friends and family who will speak up if the relationship seems to be causing harm?

Alternatives: If the multiple-role relationship is being considered or exists to fill a specific need, are there alternatives (other religious leaders, teachers, contractors, counselors, healers, etc.)? Can the person filling the professional role refer the client to someone else?

Timeline: How long will the multiple-role relationship last? Is one of the roles of a limited duration?

Hot button issues: Does the multiple-role relationship involve sex or money? Is one or both parties struggling with mental illness or trauma? Are there cultural differences between the two parties with regards to what is considered polite or proper?

It is easy, when working in close community, to suddenly wake up and find ourselves in the midst of a complicated multiple-role relationship—especially one with tensions that have not been fully acknowledged. In these cases, using the questions above may help us talk things over with our friend, client, or loved one and find a way to shift or release roles that are likely to lead to conflict.

In some cases, becoming aware of how complex a relationship already is may help us to deliberately put off adding more roles. I once gave a version of this article as a presentation at a conference which I was attending with a friend. My friend was also my massage client and a student in the same witchcraft tradition that I practice, and at the time, she was also in a close relationship with a third person with whom I had a recent conflict.

During the presentation (with my permission), she stood up, described our relationship, and declared that our relationship should not acquire any new layers—it was clearly *already complicated enough!* I couldn't have agreed more.

A good rule of thumb when it comes to multiple-role relationships: *The more roles there are, the more risk of conflict!*

A Four-Step Process for Evaluating Multiple-Role Relationships

This evaluation process was designed for a multiple-role relationship that has a beginning and end date. However, it can also be used when finding oneself unexpectedly in the midst of a multiple-role relationship. The assessment stage can help to determine whether it may be best to withdraw from a role or roles, or it may identify aspects of the relationship that need to be carefully watched in case problems arise. Explicitly calling the other party's attention to the relationship can help to enlist them as your ally in being conscious about the relationship's complexity.

Additionally, this process could be used cyclically (perhaps once a year) to check on the health of an ongoing relationship. Committed romantic partners might find this checklist particularly useful, as marriages are inherently multiple-role relationships!

Step 1: Assess
1. Ask the risk assessment questions above and identify any hot button issues
2. Make a list of pros and cons
3. Consult with a peer
4. Meditate, do divination, or otherwise bring intuition to the situation
5. Generate a graceful exit strategy

Step 2: Negotiate
1. Purify, cleanse, and/or center oneself
2. Discuss risks and benefits with the other party or parties
3. Collaboratively define boundaries for all parties

4. Obtain informed consent (formal or informal)
5. If appropriate, ritually mark the beginning of the new role

Step 3: Monitor

1. Evaluate the relationship periodically for changes, especially increased power differentials or boundary violations (may include check-in with other party or parties)
2. Document the relationship (journaling or formal notes)
3. Consult with a peer periodically
4. Maintain self-care and cleansing/centering spiritual practice
5. Renegotiate if needed

Step 4: Revisit or Conclude

1. Celebrate successes
2. Apologize sincerely for mistakes
3. Consider how to replicate successes or make amends for errors
4. If appropriate, ritually end the role

Ethical Dilemmas

The following are a series of difficult situations involving multiple-role relationships. By yourself or in a group, practice your risk assessment skills by identifying the potential risks and charting out your decision-making process for each scenario. Are there details in the scenario that could be changed to reverse your verdict?

1. Starting a sexual relationship with a student

A Pagan teacher is teaching a workshop at a Pagan religious retreat. One of her students is a woman about the same age as the teacher. The student is new to Paganism, but of a similar level of spiritual and emotional maturity. The student propositions the teacher sexually. The teacher is available and feels attracted to the student.

2. Teaching your lover

A teacher has an upcoming six-week introductory class in Pagan belief and practice. Her new lover is interested in spirituality but has no background in Paganism. He asks if he can enroll in the class.

3. Performing your best friend's wedding

A Pagan priest's best friend is getting married, and they want a creative and elaborate wedding. They ask the priest to design and perform the ceremony and offer him a budget and a fee.

4. Initiating your partner

A priestess and her husband are members of the same coven. The priestess has recently been elevated to the highest degree the coven offers. She knows that her partner has also approached the High Priestess of a coven for elevation, but has been told he is not ready. Both partners, however, feel that some personal stress has recently been interfering with the High Priestess' judgment. Soon after, the High Priestess tells the coven that she has been diagnosed with cancer and will be stepping down from coven leadership. She asks the younger priestess to take her place as coven leader. The priestess' husband approaches his wife for elevation, assuming she will agree.

5. A friend who is not a good fit for your group

A coworker approaches a Pagan group facilitator about a small Pagan women's group she runs. The group has generally welcomed guests in the past, so the group facilitator invites the coworker to attend. When the coworker visits the group, however, she dominates the discussions and sharing sessions with anecdotes about her own idiosyncratic spiritual practice. When she indicates her intention to attend the group's next meeting, other group members approach the facilitator privately and ask her not to bring the coworker again.

6. Being a student in a former student's class

A student that a priestess taught and initiated into her tradition has recently moved back to town after an absence. The former student is offering a class on a spiritual practice that she trained in during her travels. The priestess is interested in learning the skill and on catching up with her former student, and she calls the student to ask about registering for the class. During the phone call, the student repeatedly defers to the priestess' authority.

7. Administrating a Pagan non-profit in which close friends participate

The administrator of a Pagan community center is in charge of renting the space to Pagan groups, organizing classes, and maintaining the finances. One of the administrator's close friends uses the space frequently to teach classes and lead rituals for the community. The rituals and classes are particularly popular. The friend is sometimes late with paying the rent for classes, and she tends to pay the administrator in personal contexts, like handing her a wad of cash when they go to dinner and telling her she'll drop off a check for the balance later.

8. Doing healing work on a former lover

A Pagan healer who practices Reiki, massage, and other healing arts is approached by a former lover who has been diagnosed with a painful auto-immune illness. The former lover's health is in decline, and he doesn't have much money, but he offers to pay her at her usual rate for a series of massage sessions and healing rituals. Although he hasn't spoken of it, the healer suspects that the former lover still has feelings for her.

9. Teaching a graded class in which another community leader is a student

A member of a teacher's religious community enrolls in a class that he teaches at a local community college. The student needs the class to complete his degree, and no other section of the class is easily available. The teacher and the student work together closely on the board of a religious nonprofit. The student assures the teacher that he does not want special treatment. The first homework assignment he turns in is carelessly done, as if in a rush.

10. Hearing secondhand that a community member was sexually inappropriate at an event

The members of a Pagan church, which is co-facilitated by a council of elders, attend a large regional Pagan festival together. Afterward, a group member approaches an elder of the group. She tells the elder that she saw one of the young men in the group repeatedly touching one of the young women in a sexual manner, and the young woman had seemed uncomfortable, pushed him away, and told him to stop, with little effect. The young man is the son of one of the most influential leaders in the group, and his mother is fiercely protective of him.

Divination and Ritual for Multiple-Role Relationships
Selina Rifkin

Tarot divination for multiple relationships

This reading is done for one of two people in the relationship, not both, but both are represented. The outer columns are for each person and each row is a relationship. If you have two role pairs – for example HP/covener and employee/employer – Card #1 is Person 1 in their role of HP, Card #2 is Person Two in their role of covener, Card #3 is Person 1 in their role of employee, and Card #4 is Person Two in their role of employer. If there is a third set of roles shared, set out another two cards.

The center column is for the mind, emotions, and spirit of the person being read. Lay out one card for each aspect. Read for the first role pairing in each aspect. How does the person relate mentally when in the role? How do they relate emotionally? Spiritually? Now do the same thing for the second role. If the other person is present for the reading, you can take up the Mind, Emotion, and Spirit cards, have them reshuffle the deck, and lay out three more cards without changing the cards laid out for the roles.

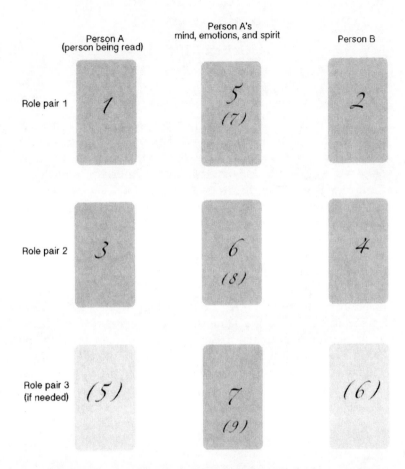

I have given an example (based on a real-life reading) below, and you can take out your deck and follow along.

Jeanette has invited her lover Allan to join her coven, and she is also thinking of going into business with him. She decides to do a tarot reading so she can be aware of potential pitfalls.

- *Card #1 represents Jeanette in her role as Allan's lover: the Fool reversed.*
- *Card #2 is Allan in his role as Jeanette's lover: the King of Pentacles.*
- *Card #3 is Jeanette in her role of HPS: the High*

134

Priestess.
- Card #4 is Allan in his role as covener: the Ace of Pentacles reversed.
- Card #5 is Jeanette in her role of business partner: the Five of Swords.
- Card #6 is Allan in his role of business partner: the Seven of Cups reversed.
- Card #7 is Jeanette's mind: the Six of Wands reversed.
- Card #8 is her emotions: the Hanged Man reversed.
- Card #9 is her spirit: the Eight of Swords reversed.

As a lover, Allan is a solid guy, but the reversal of the Fool card suggests that Jeanette hasn't really thought their relationship through.

The cards show Jeanette as a strong HPS, but the road may get a bit rough for Allan as a covener. The Ace of Pentacles reversed anticipates that fears and concerns will get in the way of his development.

The reversal of the Seven of Cups suggests that Allan's head is full of ideas about what the two of them could do as business partners, and none of those ideas are grounded. If Jeanette adds this business partnership to their relationship, it probably will not go well.

Looking at only these cards, it seems possible that these two might manage the first two relationships of being lovers and coveners. Allan is strong in one role (the love relationship), while Jeanette is strong in the other (the coven relationship). Their strengths might balance the other's weaknesses, although Jeanette would need to be careful about her authority as group HPS. Being HPS puts her in a role of power over Allan, and if he should start to resent that authority, the negative feelings might harm their love relationship. Adding the third role of business partners, however, looks like a clear disaster.

But let's look at the interaction cards in the center: all reversals. Fear of possible outcomes may mean that Jeanette will not be bringing her A game to the table. In addition, outside forces may cause delays that will put increased stress on the relationships.

Looking at this reading, Jeanette is forced to think twice

about her impulsiveness. If her role as Allan's lover is most important to her, she needs to say no to the business partnership and tell Allan that she made a mistake: it is too soon to bring him into her coven.

Of course, not all readings will be negative! If the reading is a positive one, then the next step is a ritual.

It's Just a Jump to Left: Ritual for the beginning of a multiple-role relationship

Ritual can be used to acknowledge the duality or multiplicity of a relationship and help limit any negative fallout. By marking beginnings and endings and providing opportunities to both celebrate and heal, ritual can act as a container and a safety net for multiple-role relationships.

Consider doing this ritual in the presence of physical witnesses, as with a wedding. Community support can be helpful in maintaining any relationship. Determine which roles each person will be working (at least two, but hopefully not more than three) and define the obligations of each role. Include the length of time each role is expected to last. Each party needs to agree on the obligations and duration of these roles before the ritual begins. If both people cannot agree, that is a good indicator that it is unwise to enter this dual- or multiple-role relationship.

For each role, cut a cardboard or paper circle at least 8 inches in diameter for each role. On each circle, write the name of a person's role. For example, if two covenmates are planning to also become business partners, make four circles: two that say "covenmate" and two that say "business partner." Place each pair of circles on the floor in front of an altar. One person's circles should be in a column on the left and the other's in a column on the right. The circle should be close enough to step from one to the next easily. Place a bell or chime in the center between the rows of circles.

Light candles as per your preference and call the directions. Specifically ask them to come as witness to your ritual. Cast a circle if that feels right to you. Call in the deities or ancestors of both people to act as witnesses. If none of these seem appropriate, invite Ma'at or invoke the energy of Justice. Offer some incense, a libation, or other appropriate gift.

Stand on the first set of circles and name your duties in those roles out loud. Promise to uphold these duties in the name of the deity or deities witnessing. When both people have spoken, ring the bell once and say "So mote it be!" in unison.

Step to the second set of circles and articulate the duties of those roles. Promise to uphold these duties in the name of the deity or deities witnessing. When both people have spoken, ring the bell and both say "So mote it be!" in unison.

Repeat a third time if necessary.

Speaking together say: "We ask the gods to bless our relationship. May it be fruitful, joyous, and productive! Blessed Be!" Hug, kiss, shake hands, or whatever is appropriate to the relationships involved and your comfort level.

Thank the gods, thank the directions, and close.

If possible, save the circles in a safe place. If at some point you decide to dissolve any aspect of the relationship, you can use them to ritualize that transition.

Our relationships are important to us not only as Pagans, but as humans. We need each other. If we have the skills to recognize when one part of a dual or multiple-role relationship is failing, then we may be able to keep the entire relationship from falling apart. Even more importantly, entering into multiple-role relationships with open eyes can help us make wise choices and sustain the close communities that we deeply value.

Copyright ©2012 by Selina Rifkin. Used with permission.

Conclusion

Multiple-role relationships form the foundation of intimate, lasting community. Successful multiple-role relationships, however, include the clear communication of expectations, the ability to set boundaries, good self-care, and the willingness to withdraw from aspects of relationships that are no longer working. I hope that this article will guide those in leadership positions in managing their relationships in Pagan community, as well as in providing advice and support about relationship issues to those around them.

Bibliography

Several of these articles were available electronically at the time of writing; I recommend a Google search for title and author in order to locate them, as web URLs tend to change periodically.

Breitman, B. "Foundations of Jewish Pastoral Care: Skills and Techniques." *Jewish Pastoral Care: A Practical Handbook from Traditional and Contemporary Sources.* 2nd ed. Ed. Dayle A. Friedman. Woodstock, VT: Jewish Lights Publishing, 2005. 95-124.

Elliott, D. and Lester, P. "When Is It OK to Invite a Student to Dinner?" *The Chronicle of Higher Education,* Career Network, October 8, 2001.

Friedman, E. "Psychotherapist and Wiccan Clergy: The Ethics of a Dual Relationship." *The Pomegranate: The International Journal of Pagan Studies* 14 (Nov. 2000): 16-25.

Harrow, J. "The Dual-Role Dilemma." *Counseling Basics for Wiccan/Pagan Clergy.* Ed. Judy Harrow, Marjorie Nelson-Brambir, and Gwyneth Harrow. Elders' Handbook No.2, October 1996 (Web version - May, 2001).

Kessler, L. and Waehler, C. "Addressing Multiple Relationships between Clients and Therapists in Lesbian, Gay, Bisexual, and Transgender Communities." *Professional Psychology: Research and Practice* 36:1 (Feb 2005), 66-72.

Montgomery, M. and DeBell, C. "Dual Relationships and Pastoral Counseling: Asset or Liability?" *Counseling and Values* 42:1 (Oct. 1997): 30–40.

Pope, K. and Keith-Spiegel, P. "A Practical Approach to Boundaries in Psychotherapy: Making Decisions, Bypassing Blunders, and Mending Fences." *The Journal of Clinical Psychology* 64:5 (May 2008): 638-52.

Zur, O. "In Celebration of Dual Relationships: How Prohibition of Non-Sexual Dual Relationships Increases the Chance of Exploitation and Harm." *The Independent Practitioner* 20:3 (2000): 97-100.

The Bigger They Are the Harder They Fall or, How to Avoid the Pedestal

Syren Nagakyrie

We are starved for good leadership. We seek individuals that are willing and able to lead, who are wise and knowledgeable, ethical, and passionate. Humans are social pack animals, and while we may not want to admit it, we look to our pack leaders to help guide us. Unfortunately, the model of leadership in our patriarchal, one-upmanship society has left us with many poor role models and a skewed vision of what good leadership really means.

So, when we encounter an individual who really seems to "get it," who leads by example and cares about their community, people start to flock to them. I call it the moth to the porch light effect; there is a bright light shining and we can't help but to be drawn to it. The people that are drawn to this bright light are "moths," beautiful individuals that perhaps haven't been appreciated or realized their beauty yet. This person, "the porch light" may or may not be willing or ready to take on the mantle of community leadership, but suddenly find themselves surrounded by individuals with a deep and crying need. This person, being who they are, has a difficult situation but an easy choice to make. When the Goddesses call, and the community cries out, you must answer.

This is when the pedestal begins to be built. Inevitably that pedestal must tumble, but in this phenomenon it is not due to any intentionally negligent actions of the leader. It is a pitfall I have seen many times, particularly in women's groups. Women have been socialized to accept power over them. We have come to expect it. We will hand our power to someone else and not even realize that we have done it. Yet we also have a deeper, instinctual knowledge that tells us that no one can or should have power over us.

When women start to awaken to the power that they inherently hold within themselves, they are suddenly thrust into a cognitive dissonance, recognizing the mixed messages they have been receiving from the outside world and their inner knowing their entire lives. This process is often catalyzed by a solid leader and guide. This leader, the person that they have trusted and often given some authority to, is now perceived as one of the people who have held power over her. They must be taken down.

This is not a conscious process. The "moths" have no real understanding of what they are going through, and need a place to release the rage and backlash from a lifetime of power and control. The leader (provided they are healthy) has not asked for nor taken any power from anyone they are leading. But they suddenly find themselves at the center of a coup.

Unfortunately, sometimes this process cannot be stopped. It is a part of the awakening of the people involved. It is healthy as long as they are guided through it and have enough self-awareness to recognize what is happening. So, it is extremely important for a leader to understand this phenomenon and do what they can to reduce the backlash and more gently and safely awaken people to the power they hold within.

Many of the ways to prevent the pedestal are, in essence, just good leadership skills. Honesty, humility, and accountability are all necessary traits for a spiritual leader. Here we will apply them to deeper discussions around power and control to create a model of leadership that, while perhaps not fully shared leadership, will resist the building of a top-down structure.

Forms of Power

There is nothing inherently wrong with power. We all possess it, but it is the wielding of it that can be harmful or beneficial. Reminding each other of the power that we possess, or what is referred to as empowering others, is essential to reclaiming our power and revisioning the world. Leaders are in a position to do this but it is important to remember that every form of power has its positive and negative side, its potential for benefit and its potential for harm. There are three types of power in groups, which have been written about thoroughly by Starhawk and the Reclaiming collective.

Power-over: This is the power structure we are most familiar with and in which we have all been indoctrinated. Power-over is essentially the power to make decisions and mete out punishment. When power-over is utilized in a corrupt system, as our society is structured, it becomes a way to subordinate and oppress the majority while the minority benefit from decision-making power that enables them to maintain control. In small groups, power-over looks like one individual with all of the decision-making power and none of the accountability, while the other group members are forced to abide by the decisions without the opportunity for input or feedback. When balanced by responsibility and mediated with input from people that decisions affect and accountability for those decisions, power-over may have a valid role. But we are all so deeply indoctrinated into the corrupt use of power-over that achieving this can be challenging in groups.

Power-with: This is a shared power structure. Power-with is the ability to influence, from a place of equality and shared respect among all group members. Power-with is the moment when one person claims power and suggests a decision or an action to a group of people who are all considered equals and each have the potential to claim that power in any moment. The group has the option to follow the suggestion or not. It often happens organically and in inspired moments. Power-with takes a turn to the harmful wielding of power when it turns into one person who frequently has the "best ideas" being followed without input or question, or one "elder" or other person of respect who is allowed to take action without accountability; both lead to one person holding authority over all others. Power-with can also be flipped, so that people who do not know how to access their inherent power will try to exert influence and authority over the group instead.

Power-from-within: This is the power that is inherent to us as beings. Power-from-within is the ability to see the value and resulting power of all things, and see the connections between one individual and the whole web of nature. Power-from-within is not competitive or influential, it does not oppress or exalt, it simply is and it sees the world for what it is – a system of interlocking connections. Power-from-within is the power you access when doing magic or ritual, when accessing the mystery, or when writing poetry or creating symbols. As such it can also be seen as the creative force. Recognizing the power within all beings is essential to being able to wield power to effect change, which is the purpose of power-with and power-over. When people don't recognize their own power, they will try to take the power of others which puts leaders at risk.

Have discussions about power and control

An important part of leading groups, especially women's groups, is to have an understanding about oppression, abuse, power, and control. We live in a patriarchal society and each of us has been brought up in a culture that values power and authority and demeans women and the egalitarian. We learn that the only way to be successful is to come out on top, and the only way to come out on top is to step on the backs of others on the way. This creates competition which perpetuates oppression.

Indeed, our societal structure depends upon classes of people remaining oppressed. We are all indoctrinated into this system, and unconsciously internalize the oppression. For some, this manifests as a greater desire for power so that they can feel a sense of control over their own lives. We use the tools that have been given to us through internalized oppression to perpetuate the system because it is the only thing we know.

In our groups, we have the opportunity to break this cycle. In every group I start I include a discussion about patriarchy, oppression and privilege, and power and control. We work together to unpack our experiences living in a patriarchal society. In a women's group this can begin with the women taking stock of the ways they feel discriminated against and objectified. Discrimination in the workplace, media images, and feelings of safety can be explored. In all groups, relationships with friends, family, and co-workers can be explored to discuss if the individual feels they hold the power in one relationship and feel subordinate in another, and how those dynamics play out.

To look at the bigger picture you can also explore how the need for control and superiority affects our interactions with the environment. If group members have a difficult time exploring personal relationships, their connection with the Earth may help them reveal how they try to maintain control in their lives and their resulting abuse of the environment. Questions about how they try to tame their lawns and gardens, the health of the water around them, and how they see wildlife, can all unveil internalized oppression and the drive for control.

You can then go into leadership styles and discuss alternatives. Consensus-building and shared leadership can be explored. At this stage it is appropriate to decide how the group will be organized, who will be the primary decision-maker, and how tasks will be shared, but it is important for everyone to remember that this can and likely will shift as the group changes.

Be honest about your personal life, challenges, and weaknesses. Set boundaries.

We've all heard it – no one is perfect. To try to maintain a façade that you are is to lie to yourself and everyone around you. Honesty is a paramount trait in a leader. You must be able to be honest with yourself before you try to lead others. This doesn't mean you have to make everything in your life align with some ultimate spiritual ideal. On the contrary, showing your humanity to others is the greatest model you can be.

I have sat in groups and felt like I couldn't share anything personal because I was the leader and couldn't be seen as weak or troubled. How would anyone trust me to lead them if they knew I was having trouble at home, or was struggling in my own spiritual practice, or felt completely inadequate in leading? So I would listen and support the other women in the group, nodding or offering advice when asked, but I would never truly open up to them.

I now know this is a huge disservice to them and me. It made me appear to have transcended personal challenges; to be someone enlightened with wisdom and without struggles. This only served to build the pedestal higher and secretly bred resentment that fed the dissonance in the mind of the group members and hastened the fall. None of this was intentional. I wasn't trying to look like I had 'risen above' the struggles of life; I was trapped in thinking I couldn't share these things and still be respected – it was the internalized sense of what holding power means and the fear of showing weakness in the competitiveness model. The women in the group weren't asking me to be an 'enlightened savior'; they were just eager to have someone actively listen to their problems and support them in their struggles.

Whether you are leading a small ritual group or are a public figure in your community, remaining open and honest about your humanity will be inspiring to others. Of course, you are your own authority in your life and you should use your own discretion and intuition when deciding what to share, when, and with whom. Balancing over and under sharing can be difficult. And of course, only share as much as you can safely share.

Setting boundaries from the beginning will help to avoid any confusion and group members later feeling like you weren't really there for them. Let the group know how much time you have to devote to group activities, when you are not available, and what kinds of things you are willing to do. Also be clear about what you expect in return, whether it is financial compensation or a certain level of engagement. This goes hand in hand with being honest about your life and your own struggles, so that no one has false expectations.

Empower Others

Leadership is as much about teaching leadership skills to others as it is leading. Shared leadership means not only sharing the power and responsibility of leadership, but empowering those who would like to lead. In a spiritual group, your ultimate goal should be to lead others to their own skills and wisdom within. "Empowerment" has become a bit of a buzzword, and as such much of its true meaning has been hard to define. The classic definition is to "give" someone power or "make" them exercise their power and authority.

Neither of these definitions includes the concept that individuals inherently have power; we cannot give power to them and making them exercise it places power over them.

So what does empowering others actually look like? To continue with the metaphor of the porch light, it is to guide others to their home, their sense of place and power within. It is to help them recognize the power they inherently hold. Recognizing systemic and internalized oppression is the first step to remembering the power that each person holds. Enabling

144

others to express their emotions, their anger and fear through allowing the space for the process is essential. Releasing a lifetime of oppression and emotion is the first step to remembering the power that each person holds. This process can be difficult and fraught with challenges that a leader-guide must be prepared for. The scope of those challenges goes beyond this article, but there are many resources available for clergy and lay counselors that have useful tools and techniques.

Once the dam is removed and the stymie of emotions has been released, a leader must be diligent in working with the individual to help them remember their power and allow the space for them to exercise it. If they have often turned to you to help them make decisions, now is the time to give that decision-making responsibility back to them. When counseling them, encourage them to ask themselves what they feel they should do, holding the space for them to tap into their own intuition. Reflect their feelings back to them and ask open-ended questions.

If you have been primarily responsible for coordinating events and conducting ritual, you should consider giving some of that responsibility to the group. In the case of teaching circles, every few weeks following teaching and practicing a certain skill, I set aside a meeting to encourage the group members to share their own insights into the practice and help teach each other. Another easy way to work this concept in is to designate the Sabbats, if you celebrate them, as group rituals in which everyone takes a piece and works together to develop the ritual. As the group continues to work together, begin sharing more ritual work with the rest of the group, until eventually rituals are being rotated or collaborated with everyone.

Recognize Red Flags

There are several red flag behaviors I have noticed that indicate that the individual is starting to struggle with feeling subordinated to power, and they will begin to tear down the person perceived to be at the top. At this point, it is perhaps too late to utilize some of the preemptive techniques discussed here. But you will still have the opportunity to discuss power and control, ask for feedback, and help them process what they are feeling. If appropriate, you can then share more responsibility and help them have more control in their own life.

Unfortunately, some people are just not self-aware enough to be able to recognize what they are experiencing and don't have the vocabulary and experience to truly grasp the effects of power and control in their lives. These individuals sometimes have their own dreams of power and want to be at the top themselves, and see tearing down a leader as the swiftest route. This is an issue we must address in the community as a whole and learn how to more effectively support good leadership.

Some Potential Red Flags I have noticed:

A person joins your group claiming to be completely new and is seeking guidance. They then begin to tell everyone in the group all about the things they have done and do not remain open to instruction or guidance. This can be a subtle way to breed distrust in your leadership and encourage others to uproot you and follow their lead. While they may cloak their actions with the claim that they are trying to help, encourage sharing, and provide their own point of view, the fact that they are not open to feedback is a clear indicator that their motives may not be pure.

There is a line between sharing leadership and letting someone else run the show. Don't let someone turn these techniques on you under the banner of shared leadership. If this happens, share your concerns, but be prepared if they say you are misinterpreting their actions or are just trying to maintain control of the group. If they do, I encourage you to have a conversation that perhaps this is not the right group for them and they should find a group that is working more with their apparent skillset.

You find the rest of the group members are meeting without you. Concurrently, behavior and the overall vibe of the group is changing. This can be a slippery situation. You should never ban anyone from doing anything. However, if the group is meeting behind your back and one person is secretly undermining you, this can be very unhealthy. My suggestion is to keep a close eye on the group dynamic. Do not begin to tighten your grip on the group to try to maintain control—this will only serve the purposes of the person undermining you. Encourage a group discussion about what the group wants and what direction they would like to go. Ask each group member to share a particular skill with the group and begin to incorporate those techniques into meetings to decentralize power and take some of the energy out of the sails of the person undermining you.

There is one individual who consistently blocks you in consensus-making or always has an idea that is "just a better solution" than yours. This is extremely uncomfortable and can be another way that someone uses shared leadership against you to gain attention and control. In this case, it is important to discuss the issue individually with the group members. If this person is blocking movement and decision-making, it is likely frustrating to the rest of the group as well. As a group, you should decide how to handle the situation. You could adjust decision-making for a while or decide to remove the person entirely if they are being obstructive.

These few examples can take any number of permutations but have the same end game, to (whether consciously or unconsciously) undermine and tear down the group leader.

In my own experiences, by not addressing these issues preemptively, our group relationship shifted to me being perceived as the untouchable leader who had all the answers and the group members feeling unvalued and like they needed "fixing." This is not healthy and enables and perpetuates power-over, whether you actively utilize that power or not.

As a leader it is essential to have an objective third party as a sounding board. A mentor or peer that you trust can be the most valuable tool you have. Share your ideas about leadership with this person, explain the dynamics of your group, and ask for their feedback. They can help you decipher behaviors and look at the group dynamic from the outside to determine if there is a power struggle happening.

Changing the way we interact with others at the grassroots, in our groups and micro-communities, will have the greatest impact upon our culture as a whole. As the power shifts and equality gains momentum we can reach critical mass. Soon these discussions will be common and people will be more willing to unpack their own patriarchal tendencies and shift group dynamics. Abuse of power is rampant, but we also hold the power to shift culture. This is the work we are here to do. And it starts with you in your own community.

Resources

Starhawk. (1987). *Truth or dare: Encounters with power, authority, and mystery.* San Francisco, CA: Harper & Row.

Starhawk. (1997). *Dreaming the dark: Magic, sex, and politics.* Boston, MA: Beacon Press.

Harrow, Judy. (2002). *Spiritual mentoring: A pagan guide.* Toronto, ON: ECW Press.

Mountainwater, Shekhinah. (1991). *Ariadne's Thread: A workbook of goddess magic.* Freedom, CA: The Crossing Press.

Three Leadership Tools and a Mystery
Shauna Aura Knight

There are three tools that I frequently teach in my leadership workshops, and they also pop up a lot when I'm fielding email questions from Pagan leaders. While they won't solve all your problems, they are some solid foundations for building healthy group structures and can resolve many conflicts before they escalate into a community-wide explosion. The most common questions I get are about how to deal with group drama and conflicts.

One of the secrets is that many conflicts can be prevented with the right structures in place. And beneath even that is a deeper mystery of leadership that we'll get to as well.

Tool #1: Structures, Group Agreements, Bylaws, and Mission Statements

I know. It sounds so unmagical. Mission statements? Bylaws? Not every coven or grove wants to be structured like a corporation...I get it. However, some basic group structure, and a focus, is actually a fairly potent magical act.

I ask this question almost every time I teach. "How many of you have an actual set of agreements for your group for what behavior is acceptable and what isn't? How about bylaws? How about any agreements for how decisions are made, for how power moves in your group?" I see more hands go up these days than I did a decade ago, but most groups don't have any formal agreements in place. Most groups or events also never go through the process of establishing a mission and vision statement, or high level goals, strategies, and even shared values. Heck, most groups never even have a conversation about what the group is about.

Why is this important?

You can't hold water without a bowl or a cauldron. And you can't heat water without a fire. Imagine the cauldron as your group's structure; the water is the group. And imagine the fire as your mission and vision statement, your statement of purpose, your group's focus and intention. Without the cauldron, there's no boundary between what's in the group and what isn't. You have to have a line somewhere about who can be a member and who can't, about what behavior is appropriate or inappropriate, about what the group is there to do (and isn't there to do). And your group has to have some kind of binding energetic focus — the fire that heats the water — otherwise it'll just fizzle and stagnate.

Here's a pro tip: Many conflicts within a group begin because group members have vastly different ideas about what the group is about, except nobody ever talked about their expectations. Is it a private coven? Is it a teaching coven offering public workshops? Is it a group that puts on a local Pagan Pride? Those are very different focuses, very different intentions. Is your group offering rituals where children are welcome, are your rituals skyclad, or is your group a sex temple? All of these involve *vastly* different agreements for what behavior is acceptable during rituals and among your group members. Is your group about hosting open discussion nights, or are you focused on one specific Pagan religious tradition and offering rituals in that tradition? Again, different intentions.

Pagans often talk about spells and magic, but so often we forget that words themselves have power. Establishing a mission statement is an act of magic; it declares your group's focus. Establishing your group agreements, or bylaws if you want to go that formal, describes the edge of your circle, the edge of your cauldron. Whether you work with a spiritual tradition that casts a circle or not, the circle is still a pretty useful geometrical metaphor. In this case, what we're talking about are group boundaries vs. individual boundaries.

Group agreements — or group boundaries — as well as group mission and intention — are important for so many different reasons, but one is that most of the conflicts I hear about causing drama within a group come from groups that had nothing established.

- What happens when a group has no leadership or power structure established?
- What happens when a group has no idea what to do when a group member has done something harmful to another member?

- What happens when half the members of a group think the group is about ABC, and half think the group is about DEF?

Simple Agreements

It's really amazing what happens when a group actually establishes a few agreements. I once talked to a woman who ran a healing circle for Reiki practitioners. You'd think that this would be a healing, positive experience. "It's the worst night of my week, every week," she said. She was obviously stressed. I asked her what happened at the Reiki share that made it so frustrating. "People come in late. And we talk first, we have a sharing circle, and some folks just go on and on. Some people go off topic, they interrupt each other. The energy's all over the place. Some people are just openly disrespectful of others."

I suggested a few quick group agreements that I use when facilitating workshops and rituals. Here's how I might introduce those to a group of people. Imagine we're sitting in a circle together and it's time to begin.

I might say, "Hi, I'm Shauna, and this workshop/ritual/session is about ABC intention. We'll be starting out with some time for checking in with one another before we move on to some more hands-on exercises. Before we get into that, I'd like to ask for a few agreements from each of you so that we all can come together and do this work in the spirit of mutual respect. One is that I see there are about twenty of us, and we only have an hour here together, so when you're checking in, try to just keep it to a few sentences so that each person has time to speak. Please also keep in mind the focus of our work here together, which is on ABC, so let's keep things on topic. I'd also like to ask that we each focus on listening to the person who is speaking, and that only one person speak at a time. I'm asking that you don't interrupt that person, offer advice, or have side conversations. Also, since we only have an hour together each week, I ask that each of you commit to being here on time."

Typically I offer a few other agreements about I-referencing and self-responsibility, but these were the ones that were relevant for this scenario. After a few weeks of using those agreements with her Reiki share, and having a quick one-on-one conversation with the folks who were often showing up late, the woman running the healing circle reported that this was now her favorite night of the week.

What I've found is that we can assume that each person comes to a healing circle (or other group) in the spirit of mutual respect...but we actually have to spell out what that looks like. People don't necessarily notice that their behavior is not respectful. Or at least, not respectful in that context. People who are habitually late, who habitually interrupt others, who habitually tease, or who habitually ramble on and on and take up a lot of the group's time talking about their personal life may have no idea the impact of their actions on the group.

This is why establishing group agreements is crucial; it's the obvious stuff that isn't always obvious. They are useful whether you're running a one-off workshop, a ritual, or a long-running group.

Group Agreements and Power Structure

What I mean by a power structure is just that—how does power move in your group? Do you have a hierarchy with a high priest/ess, or an elected president? Do you make decisions by consensus? Do you have twelve members and each month the power rotates to the next person in line and they run the ritual or teach the class? The answer is not, "We don't have anyone in charge." Or, "We have a leaderless group." Or, "Let's just not have any power dynamics in the group."

Power just means energy. Power is the ability to take an action. If you don't structure your power, it's like electricity; it goes to ground via the easiest route. If you don't have a power structure for how decisions are made in your group, then the power goes to the person who is bossiest, or who speaks first, or the person who is the most charismatic, or the most manipulative, or even the whiniest person.

The other issue that happens when a specific power structure isn't established is that there's a frustration when someone's trying to get the group to make a decision, but not everyone responds. In that situation, who makes the decision?

I've been on email planning lists where one person was

always the one to say, "Ok, let's plan the next sabbat. There's liturgy A, liturgy B, or liturgy C. What do you guys want to do?" And they'd get maybe one or two responses, and a couple of "Whatever you like" responses...and most people not messaging back. Who makes the decision about what liturgy to offer, and what date to offer the event, when not everyone responds? That's what a power structure is for, even if it's just establishing someone in the role of an administrator who is empowered to make things happen and bug people.

I've also been part of event organizing teams where we had no formal leader, so each decision had to be discussed by all participants, and when one participant took days to respond, or never responded, everyone got really mad. And when two people disagreed about how to do XYZ, there was no method established for the team to make a decision about what to do. This comes up more frequently with teams that plan events, but it comes up in covens and other small groups as well.

When there's no power structure established, conflicts and frustration are inevitable and these often lead to the group exploding or imploding.

Mission, Focus and Intention

This is where a lot of inadvertent conflicts happen. You know that axiom about the word assume? It's pretty true. Assumptions and expectations—at least, unspoken ones—are the root of a lot of tension within a group.

Here's an example I wrote about on my Pagan Leadership blog on Witches and Pagans.

> Many group conflicts arise because everyone assumed they were all on the same page about the purpose of the group...except it turned out that Jane wanted an intimate coven, Barb wanted the group to start offering public rituals, and Fred wanted the group to begin teaching introductory workshops to the broader community.
>
> When Jane reluctantly agrees to help support the public rituals but gets burned out, and Barb gets upset at Jane,

it's not as simple as "Jane dropped the ball." *Jane and Barb had fundamentally different ideas about the intention of the group and what type of work they were signing on to do.* When Fred starts teaching workshops, he gets ticked off because no one else in the group is attending or helping.

Jane, Barb, and Fred aren't bad people, they just never articulated their expectations.

What can you do instead? Maybe your group has a meeting and talk about your goals and intentions first. While it's not fun to realize that these people you thought were all on the same page with you had very different ideas about the focus of the group, it's far better to realize that before you try to organize an event together, or two years down the road when several people are increasingly frustrated with the group and tensions have risen.

Group Agreements and Safety Policies

Sometimes these get as formal as bylaws, and that's not a bad idea, though I know the idea of creating a set of bylaws can sound intimidating. In general, you want to have an idea about what behaviors are acceptable and what aren't. After some of the recent sex scandals within the Pagan community, and as it's become obvious that Pagan communities are not free of racism, homophobia, and other discrimination and harassment, more events and groups have begun adopting anti-harassment policies or safety policies. It's beyond the scope of this article to go into those specifically, but if you're looking for policies to use as a template feel free to message me and I can send you to the current ones that I'm aware of.

Sexual harassment is a useful example of why you want to have group agreements. What do you do if one of your attendees is sexually harassing members of your group? What counts as sexual harassment? How do you take the complaint? How does your group decide whether or not to ban this person from your events? Who makes the decision? Is there one hierarchical leader who must make the decision? Is consensus required? Is a two thirds majority required? Who counts as a member and can participate in the decision-making?

You can see how one problem unravels a lot of questions and — if you have no answers to those questions — this can break a group. There are lots of different ways to structure a group, lots of different power structures, lots of different agreements you might have, but the point is that you've had those conversations and you have agreed on a structure so that when something comes up (and it eventually will) you have some idea how to proceed.

The time to figure out how your group makes a decision about membership isn't when you're dealing with a sexual predator.

It's worth it to figure out who is a member and who isn't, what's in scope for your group and what isn't. I once was part of a group in St. Louis, and our primary mission was offering public and semi-public events in St. Louis. However, we were also connected to a larger organization that had members in Kansas City, and we had agreed that it would be within the scope of our group's work to support some of the Kansas City events. You want to have clear conversations about what your group is and does, and what members are signing up to be a part of. Don't rely on assumptions; these are things you want to talk about before you expect the other members of your group to be on board.

Tool #2: Boundaries

Group agreements are the boundaries of a group, and boundaries are also a common reference to you, the individual, and your personal edges. I write a lot about boundaries because it's one of those core concepts that most people manage to forget. Here are boundaries in a nutshell: My wants and desires end at the edges of me — of my skin. Just because I want to touch someone doesn't mean it's ok to, and just because I want someone to think something or feel something doesn't mean they're going to. Boundaries are both our physical edges and also our mental/emotional/psychic edges.

When we talk about poor boundaries, we're talking about assumptions again. A lot of conflicts begin with unspoken assumptions. And honestly, this happens all the time and it isn't necessarily about evil intent; we humans are often operating on autopilot.

Boundaries are very much about our ego, our identity. You can think of that as psychic skin. Just as the edge of your body is your skin, the edge of your mind/body/spirit is your ego identity. People also sometimes use the word boundary when what they mean is a limit. A limit is when we enforce a boundary, usually by saying "no."

In fact, the word "no" is probably the easiest way to understand boundaries. Think of a number of different scenarios where you have the option to say yes or no.

- Are you willing to drive me to the airport at 3am?
- Do you want to go out on a date?
- Can I hug you?
- Will you organize the programming for this event?
- Will you work for twelve hours as a volunteer for Pagan Pride?

Now — very often, these types of questions aren't actually framed that way. *It would be healthier if they were.* The problem with boundaries is that people who want something are usually afraid to frame their request as a question where you can say no, so they say, "You'll volunteer for Pride, right?" or, "Yeah, I'll have you run the registration table." We usually aren't asked for our consent for a hug, either.

Our culture is a culture of yes and we are pressured to say yes often through teasing and shaming. What are reasons you say yes when you didn't perhaps want to? You felt obligated, you didn't want to hurt someone's feelings, you felt you should even though you didn't have time...the list can go on. The point is that many problems within groups occur because of poor boundaries, assumptions, and the pressure to say yes, because "no" is perceived not just as, "No, I don't have time to help, sorry," it's perceived as a total rejection...not just a rejection of the person's idea, but of that person. Why? Because that person doesn't have a boundary between their ego/identity of themselves as a person, and themselves as an event planner, and the event itself.

And this is why people often don't ask for things if they can help it; *they don't want to risk the rejection of being told no.* Part of the problem of poor boundaries is sourced in the larger problem of poor self image and poor self esteem. If I ask you to do ABC for me, and you say no, it means that you don't like me, because nobody likes me, nobody has ever liked me. Poor self esteem is a trigger for a massive number of conflicts not just in the Pagan community but in the broader world around us.

Dropping the Ball

Here's a common scenario in the Pagan community. Visionary Event Planner comes up with an idea. They're really excited about it! And then they start "voluntolding" people into supporting roles. Maybe they do a good job and get people to volunteer for things where they have the appropriate skills and talents. Person A is good at graphic design, Person B is a good greeter/registration table person, Person C is good at working with presenters. And maybe the event team is also excited about the event at the meeting....

But then they get home and they think of all the other stuff they are committed to. Or they try to carve out the time to do the planning work, but the planning emails get overwhelming, or they aren't able to make the planning meetings. This gets worse is when the task is a bad fit. I like organizing event programming, but I'm not the best person to email and follow up with potential presenters because the communication volume overwhelms me. I can work well in tandem with someone else who is better at the communication part of things, but if being the communication point person is my job, I'm almost guaranteed to blow the deadline or drop the ball entirely.

So the Visionary Event Planner (VEP) is sending out emails asking for updates about the event, and Person C isn't responding, and VEP is getting more and more frustrated and Person C is starting to panic because they just don't have time to do it, but they felt that they had to say yes, and now they know that VEP and the team is going to hate them for failing. Nobody ever hears from Person C again as they slink away in shame.

You see where this becomes a problem? Have you been the VEP? Have you been Person C? *I've been both.* I've been the person with the Big Idea who wanted everyone to be as excited about the event as I was. Guess what? Rarely are the other team members as excited as I am. I'm willing to put in the 12 hour days to make the event happen; not everyone else is so motivated. I've also been Person C; I was excited about the proposed event and I knew I had the skills to help, but I also was already overwhelmed by all the other things I'd agreed to.

The idea with understanding boundaries is that if Person C isn't going to have time to help, you'd probably rather they say "no" right at the beginning. Instead, the scenario often plays out so that they are pressured to say yes…and then they eventually say "no" (without saying it) by dropping the ball several months later when it'll be almost impossible to get their job done in time.

Poor Boundaries: New Moon and Full Moon

There are two core types of poor boundaries and with a little self-exploration, you can get an idea of where you're at. Pro tip: You can be both types at the same time.

One of my mentors, Dr. L Carol Scott, once referred to these as Full Moon and New Moon. I've taken her concept and taken it a little further. Full Moon is the person who is so full of the idea/thought/desire that it's spilling out their edges. It doesn't occur to the Full Moon person (like the Visionary Event Planner) that everyone else in the group isn't thrilled about kicking in ten, twenty, forty hours a week for six months to pull off the event. *Their boundaries don't end at their skin—they are assuming that you, the volunteer, wants this event as much as they do.* So they get offended when you don't put in the time and effort that they feel you "should." The word "should" is a pretty solid red flag in a lot of situations to let you know that there's a problem.

The Full Moon VEP, particularly one with really poor self-esteem, is also likely to get offended at any number of things related to the event including:

- People on the team who disagree with them
- People who offer up a different way of doing things
- People who don't do a good job
- People who complain about the event

Why? Because the event itself, and the planning process around the event, *has become like an extension of their own ego, their own self identity*. The VEP often has no perceived boundaries between themselves, their team, the planning, and the event.

I'll tell you the truth—I sometimes do that. I'm an artist, and my paintings become an extension of myself. When I write a book or run an event, it becomes an extension of myself too. And when I'm part of a team, they become a part of me. It's somewhat a natural function and can happen with any creative effort or with any group collaboration.

The issue with this habit-itis, are you aware of the places where your boundaries are overlapping someone else's? And are you respecting their personal sovereignty, their edges, their limits? It's ok to be an excited, motivated event planner, but you have to know when you're pressuring people to say yes, and that the consequence of that is that they're likely to drop the ball on you later. If you work to respect people's space and actually ask them if they want to be volunteers—and respect them if they say no—*you can keep yourself from engaging in the unhealthy Full Moon dynamic.*

New Moon is the opposite. It's the person in the group who never has an opinion, or who feels so pressured by the expectations of others that they go with what they think other people want of them. A common example of New Moon at work is five people sitting around and someone says, "Let's go out to eat. Where do you guys want to go?" "I don't know, wherever." "Yeah, wherever." "Whatever you want." New Moon often looks like someone not caring enough to make a decision or having an opinion, but the more damaging aspects of this dynamic is the tendency to cave to someone else's expectations.

You can also sometimes see if you have New Moon tendencies by looking at your emotions. One red flag for it is if you easily emotionally dissociate, or you perhaps you aren't quite sure what you feel or think until someone else demonstrates it that emotion. I'm sometimes New Moon about emotions; it's hard for me to feel an emotion or understand what I'm feeling, and then someone sitting next to me breaks down into tears and I do to because I realize that's what I'm feeling.

Noticing your Full Moon and New Moon tendencies isn't necessarily about "fixing" them or changing yourself; it's being aware of your tendencies so you don't get stuck on autopilot in a way that fuels a group conflict.

Recipe for Conflict

Full Moon and New Moon are especially complicated when they interact. Someone who is New Moon about the event that our Full Moon VEP wants to run is perhaps more easily pressured into going with the flow, but is also more likely to drop the ball. Their excitement for the event comes directly from the Full Moon's "light," their energy, their excitement. Once the New Moon volunteer goes home, their energy for the event evaporates.

The New Moon is guaranteed to frustrate the Full Moon VEP. What our Visionary Event Planner almost always wants, during the planning process, is feedback from the team. The VEP will put out an email to the team asking what people think about bringing in XYZ presenter, or having several vendors, or using ABC venue, and when the New Moons don't respond back, the VEP will get more and more frustrated.

What the VEP wants is for the team to care, and when they don't hear anything back, the VEP feels very alone. That feeling of being alone is what leads many leaders (many of them Full Moons like this) to the dreaded burnout that so many Pagan leaders face. The New Moon is vulnerable to the Full Moon in that New Moons will often say "yes" because they fear the social consequences of saying "no."

Again—this stuff is usually on autopilot. Most people don't wake up intending to cause a kerfuffle in the group.

Unraveling Boundaries

The trick to unraveling this dynamic is to be aware of it, and to talk about it. If you're a Visionary Event Planner type, cool. Own that, and learn how to do it better. Understand that just because you want the event, doesn't mean everyone else does. Learn that you end at your skin, and just because you want your volunteers to be excited and willing to put in all that extra time, doesn't mean they'll be willing to do so. Respect their space, their bodies, and their sovereignty. Give them an out, a safe way to say "no" that doesn't involve any social consequences for them with you or the group.

If you're a New Moon and you don't have much of an

opinion about an event, or how the group is run, learn to at least give feedback and say, "I think either way is fine." Also notice if you tend to say yes a lot and then drop the ball later, or if you constantly fear saying no to people. Do you say yes to help people out because you are afraid they won't like you if you say no? Are you afraid to offer negative feedback because people might get mad at you? *Those are some significant red flags for poor boundaries.*

The New Moon is often looking to fulfill their self-identity and self-esteem by the approval of others.

Don't feel bad about your Full Moon or New Moon tendencies, or anything related to poor boundaries. There's no shame in it because it's pretty darn common. The key to all of this is knowing yourself, knowing your patterns, and working to engage in a healthier dynamic going forward. Even better if you can talk about some of these patterns in your group and work out those dynamics together, particularly if your group has been frustrated by some of these dynamics.

Often establishing healthy boundaries involves being willing to hear "no" and be ok with someone saying it...and being willing to say "no" instead of just agreeing and going with the flow. Most people are raised to be very avoidant of conflict— and we are shamed for saying "no." In fact, saying "no" can lead to some short-term conflicts in groups, however, if you're willing to work through them, they can prevent some of the longer-term conflicts that break groups apart.

Tool #3: Four Levels of Reality and Conflict Resolution

There's one tool that I teach a lot for conflict resolution. And— seriously—if people actually used this tool, so many petty conflicts wouldn't ever erupt into decades-long bitterness and blown-up groups. *It's really simple—you first have to determine if there was a conflict at all, or if you yourself were making it up in your head.*

See, we perceive the world through our own filters. And many of us in the Pagan community (and in the broader world, for that matter) have endured bullying, abuse, shaming, rejection in our lives...all of which colors how we see the actions of others. The culture I was raised in certainly doesn't raise children with good self-esteem. We're given endless opportunities to see how we are not as beautiful, as handsome, as smart, as worthy as we "should" be. Remember, the word "should" is almost always a red flag.

A lack of healthy self-esteem, though, leads directly to conflict.

The four levels of reality are a framework for how we humans experience things. This tool set was developed at the Diana's Grove Mystery School, and they adapted it from some of the work in Jean Houston's Mystery School.

Physical Reality is what actually happened in the physical world. Mythic Reality is the story our brain instantly writes where we assign motivations to people's actions. That Mythic Reality instantly generates an Emotional Reality, which is how we feel about that story. Beneath it all is Essential Reality, which is how we perceive the world. It's our self-identity and our perception of how things work. Your Essential Reality is going to be really different if you're naturally trusting of others and have good self-esteem and a lot of confidence...vs. if you are naturally very shy, untrusting, and have poor self-esteem. Essential reality is the lens we view the world with, and our Essential Reality is driving when our brain picks a Mythic Reality for something we experienced.

Example: But They're Glaring At Me

Let's say you're in a group with someone, and they consistently glare at you from across the room. You get pretty ticked off at them. Because, they obviously hate you. In fact, you start to suspect that they are psychically attacking you.

But, how do you know you're being psychically attacked? How do you know this person hates you? This is Mythic Reality, unless you have concrete proof. But that's the point of this tool is that our brains are wired to instantly fill in data, to create a story, where there is missing information. We instantly assign a motivation to people based on our assumptions.

What if the person across the room isn't glaring, they just need glasses and they are squinting? This is why it's crucial to understand what's actual Physical Reality (actually happened) and what's Mythic Reality (your story and assumptions of what happened).

Let's work through the Four Levels of Reality to frame, and then reframe, an experience.

Physical Reality

What actually physically happened.

Example: I'm leading a workshop and one attendee sits with their arms crossed, their brow furrowed, and eventually leaves the room noisily, scraping their chair across the floor and shutting the door loudly.

Mythic Reality

The story we instantly tell about our experience filling in the data we don't have with assumptions, such as about what people are thinking and feeling.

Example: One of the workshop attendees is glaring at me, then storms out of my workshop. He must think I'm a horrible presenter, he must have hated my workshop!

Emotional Reality

How we feel about that story.

Example: I'm embarrassed, my cheeks are flushed. I know that this person probably hated my workshop, but everyone else sitting there probably hates it too. I'm hurt and I'm angry and I know that everyone sitting there in my workshop is privately laughing at me.

Essential Reality

Your filters. If you have poor self-esteem that can flavor how you see the actions of everyone around you. If people early in your life bullied and abused you, you'll come to expect that. You might mistrust people or perceive them as a threat.

Example: Of course this person hated my workshop. Everyone in my life has always hated me, people have always been out to get me. My peers in grade school rejected me, people laughed at me. I'll always be a failure and this is just proof.

The Drivers: Emotion and Story

The challenge is that our brains are wired for emotion. Emotion is the fuel of our memories, and intense emotions drop a bigger memory anchor than other times in our life where we don't have a peak emotion. Our Emotional Reality, though, comes out of Mythic Reality, which isn't necessarily what truly happened. Why did this participant leave the workshop? Why would I assume he hated me, was disgusted with what I was teaching, or just thought I was a crummy presenter? *Why wouldn't I assume he got an emergency text message instead?*

One community conflict I'm aware of erupted because Group Leader A was convinced that Group Leader B was trying to take over her group. Their conflict formed a rift in the local community for over a decade, and it was all based over Group Leader A making an assumption that Group Leader B was "after her" because Group Leader B offered to help out with something. She perceived him as a threat, but she seemed to perceive most people as a threat.

Often we become convinced someone is angry at us, or someone has a particular intention, but we don't ever actually talk to them about it. We just get passive aggressive about it.

I had one member of my group say, "I know that Person B hates me." I asked him why? He said, "Because she was sitting down in the back room of the store during the meet and greet, and when I came in, she left." No amount of convincing on my part could get him to understand that this was all potentially projection on his part, and that he'd never know if he didn't actually ask Person B if she had an issue with him.

For whatever reason, our brains like a complete story, and if we don't have adequate data, we fill in the blanks and make something up. And the flavor of that story is based on our filters. If we have poor self-esteem, then we're more likely to assume that someone else hates us, is psychically attacking us, is undermining us.

Essential Reality and Self Esteem

Let's reframe the Four Levels example with the person leaving the workshop. This time, we're going to operate from an Essential Reality of someone who has strong self-esteem, strong self-confidence. Same physical reality—someone leaving the workshop noisily.

In this scenario, the mythic reality might be concern instead of defensiveness. I might think, "I hope he's ok. Maybe he's ill or got an emergency call. Or maybe my workshop topic wasn't of interest to him."

Thus, my emotional reality is a lot less charged. I might be irked about the disruption, but I'm not worried that the classroom full of folks that hate me, I'm more concerned with refocusing the group and continuing the workshop.

Whenever you are facing a potential conflict, or helping someone else deal with a potential conflict, if you can walk and talk through these Four Levels and get down to the actual Physical Reality, and if you can also articulate the Essential Reality that's fueling the Mythic Reality, you can defuse the emotion and get to the bottom of things. Often, there's no conflict at all, there's just our own self esteem issues rearing their heads.

Do you tend to think everyone's out to get you? Or do you generally give people the benefit of the doubt? Keep in mind, I'm not suggesting that you keep giving people a pass for rude (or worse, abusive) behavior. This tool is more about being able to discern the difference between what you know about someone's motivations, and what you assume, as well as how your assumptions are flavored by your own worldview.

There are a few ways out of the Mythic Reality trap. The first is just to be aware that we do this. Take a look at yourself and your own thoughts and assumptions. If you know that you tend to make assumptions about others, if you tend to get defensive and you often think that people are out to get you, great! *Now you know you do that, and you can begin to work on your own self confidence and self-esteem.*

If you do that work, then when you do have an actual conflict come up, you'll have better tools of discernment around it. A lot of scenarios are just in our heads, but in the Pagan community, we do have situations where Person A actively sabotages Leader B. Perhaps they try to steal Leader B's group, or perhaps they just try to blow up the group so that it's not competing with their group. We also have abusive dynamics that occur as well.

However, it's hard to discern if someone's actually targeting you, or if you're in an abusive dynamic, if your autopilot is to assume people are out to get you.

Doing your own personal work is a part of getting out of this trap, but there are further steps. One is to recognize every time you are projecting an emotion, thought, or intention onto someone else. Despite the fact that psychic development is a part of many Pagan paths, *never* assume that you can actually read someone else's mind and know their intentions. You can observe a consistent pattern of behavior, such as rude or abusive behavior, but you can't just assume someone's motivations.

Direct Communication

The next phase of this tool is pretty simple, pretty direct, and if people actually did this, most of the group conflicts would be resolved without blowups. Go to the person you have an issue with (or that you think has an issue with you) and actually have a conversation with them. The problem is, we live in a really conflict avoidant culture, so we go passive aggressive. We avoid the shorter-term potential conflict of bringing up something uncomfortable...until we reach overload and lose our temper, thus causing a larger conflict that could have been circumvented.

Here's how it might look if, instead, I were to talk directly to the person who left my workshop loudly.

"Hi wolf, I noticed that you left the workshop I was offering kind of quickly. Was something wrong? Or were you angry at something I said?"

And maybe Wolf says, "Oh, I got an urgent text message." And then I might say, "I hope everything is ok. Next time if you can leave a little more quietly that would be great, you were a little disruptive."

Here's another scenario.

"Hey Raven, I noticed that at the last meet and greet you left the room when I came in. Are you angry at me? Or did you just need to leave?"

And maybe Raven says, "Well, yeah…at the last event you said something about transgender people that I found to be really offensive, and I don't really want to be around people who say things like that."

This is why the direct communication thing is hard, because we are trained over and over to avoid conflict, to avoid offending anyone. We learn to be passive aggressive, to not say anything bad…until we blow up at someone. We avoid having any uncomfortable conversations, unless we're angry enough to not care.

Conflict and Self Identity

Getting back to the self-identity thing, if you have poor self-esteem, your ego's going to work overdrive to make sure you never hear anything bad about yourself. It's one of ego's core jobs — to make sure you feel basically good about yourself, even if it has to stick your head in the sand or lie to you. So when you ask someone a direct question and they offer you negative feedback, it can really sting.

I'm not going to lie, I avoid these direct conversations too sometimes because I'm human, I screw up, and I have a life-long struggle with my own self esteem. I've gotten better about having these conversations and what has helped me the most is growing my actual confidence and healing some of my self-image.

What also has helped me, particularly in working to have direct communication with people in a way that didn't make assumptions for their motivations, are techniques taught in the book *Nonviolent Communication* by Marshall Rosenberg. I-referencing is a popular communication technique, but it really works best in context of the other techniques offered in the NVC book, or at an NVC group. The essence is trying to not project your own issues and assumptions onto someone else.

Dealing with Abusers

One thing that NVC isn't great for is when you're dealing with someone who is, genuinely, a bully or abuser. These techniques don't work well on sociopaths, narcissists, and a few other related personality disorders, but it's not important to have a diagnosis, more that if you're aware of some of those behavioral red flags you can better discern when it's time to stop trying to resolve the conflict and instead it's time to just remove someone from the group, or leave the group.

What you're looking for are people who repeatedly act poorly and then lie when you directly address them. A classic pattern with an abuser is that, when confronted, they get genuinely contrite and apologize. "I'll never do that again," they say. "I promise." They aren't even necessarily intending to lie— they're lying to themselves as much as they are lying to you.

With the Four Levels tool, I'm not saying to just trust everyone's intentions and word for everything. But, it's really hard to discern what's going on if you're always projecting your own issues. It's a lot easier to figure out what's happening in a conflict when you have good basic confidence, or at least, when you know some of your own issues and shame triggers. If you are on autopilot thinking that nobody likes you and Person B is out to steal your group because people have always been out to get you, that's more problematic.

Generally, I try to operate from a place of giving people the benefit of the doubt. I check out my own projections and how my Essential Reality might have informed my Mythic Reality. I work to get back to the Physical Reality. Sometimes, there's genuinely someone out there trying to undermine me…it happens. Often, it's just my own issues and insecurities.

However, the only way I can discern between those is to understand my own core issues.

Tool #4: Inner Mysteries of Leadership

I promised three tools and a mystery. The secret to all these tools is discernment and exploration, it's going past assumptions. And, in most cases, it's going deeper into your own baggage, it's doing your own personal growth work as a leader. It's looking into the mirror and facing your own fears, understanding your own shadows, and being willing to look at the places where your own behavior is causing some of your group's problems or your problems with other leaders.

In fact, you can use all three of these tools above, but your group will still blow up if you aren't doing your personal work.

I have watched (or heard about) a lot of groups exploding. I've heard stories about "witchwars" and conflicts lasting decades. And I've seen groups that are still standing, and yet their leaders eventually drive off the best people. I see many great people who hang in there trying to make things better but they eventually throw in the towel. These "I'm going solitary," they say. "I don't have time for this crap."

So many of the Pagan leaders I encounter are causing their own problems. Pro tip: I cause a lot of my own problems too. We all do it, and if we can get out of the shame spiral and look in the mirror, many of these tendencies are things we can work with so we aren't self-destructing our groups.

Many Pagan elders are stubborn to a point of fault, some even veering toward being abusive. And it's worth pointing out that stubbornness is probably why they are still out there leading, and why they still have a group when other groups folded...but this isn't what we want for our future. And most of those super-stubborn types of leaders that I meet aren't ever going to change. They're never going to be self-reflective enough to acknowledge that they themselves are harming the people around them.

I do a lot of shadow work, and I still cause a lot of my own problems.

Here's a secret of my own; within me, I have the seeds to become a stubborn, intractable, bullying leader. I have that visionary, entrepreneurial personality. We visionaries can be an obstinate lot—we have to be, else we'd never build a group or run an event or create a tradition out of nothing. But that stubbornness, coupled with a dash of control freak and a smidge of perfectionism, plus a healthy heaping of arrogance (and that's usually a gilded frosting to cover our own insecurities, shame, and poor self-esteem), can become the difference between a successful leader who makes things happen, and that person that drives everyone away because they are so unpleasant to work with.

There's a saying, "What got you here won't get you there." The Pagan community as it currently exists is a field that was ploughed by the stubborn. We wouldn't be here today without

Shauna Aura Knight

the fortitude of our elders. But that kind of stubbornness (and in many cases, arrogance) won't take us where we want to go from here. There's one way around this, and that's doing our own personal work. It's doing shadow work in ritual, it's doing therapy, it's becoming self aware.

There's another axiom, "Know thyself." You can't change a behavior unless you know you do it.

I fight my own tendencies toward perfectionism and being a control freak all the time. I also struggle with anxiety and depression. While I've healed a lot of old wounds, and I've grown a lot of true self confidence, I still have those fears deep within me from my past, the fears that people will hate me and reject me like they did when I was a kid. Those fears linger; our younger selves are still there within us.

Like a lot of Pagan leaders, I say yes to too many projects because I want these resources to be available for our community. I know the mystery of service—that only through service, through work, can we build a better community, and if I say no, there may be nobody else to say yes and get the work done. But—like so many other leaders—I take on too many volunteer projects, and then stress out, burnout, drop the ball, and that doesn't serve anyone either.

The mystery beneath any leadership tool you'll learn typically comes back to self-knowledge and personal growth. It's not divorcing ourselves from our shadows, it's understanding our fears, our assumptions, our way we view the world, so that we can process through it. So that we have the discernment to make a different choice next time. It's not saying, "I don't have any fears," it's working to become the person that isn't ruled by those fears.

And that's the work of a lifetime, but it's worth it. It's worth looking into the dark mirror at the places we cause our own problems, as leaders. It's worth learning about groups and group dynamics and how to work with (instead of avoiding) conflict. Only then can we build healthier communities, and to leave something lasting (and healthy) for the generations to come.

Resources:

http://witchesandpagans.com/pagan-culture-blogs/pagan-leadership/paganism-and-problem-solving.html

Knight, Shauna Aura. *The Leader Within: Articles on Community Building, Leadership, and Personal Growth.* 2014

http://witchesandpagans.com/pagan-culture-blogs/pagan-leadership/what-are-boundaries.html

https://shaunaaura.wordpress.com/2014/03/15/assumptions-expectations-and-boundaries/

Section 4
Group Structure, Agreements and Bylaws

Creating Conscious Community:
Avalon as Metaphor
Jhenah Telyndru

The Three Foundations of Spirituality:
Hearth as altar, work as worship, and service as sacrament.
– Celtic Triad

Ynys Afallon. Island of Apples. The Blessed Isle.

Avalon

When I founded the Sisterhood of Avalon in 1995, I had so many ideas about Avalon in my mind and my heart. I felt called to a service that took this multifaceted concept of Avalon and applied it to the spiritual journey of today's seeker, making this path of Women's Mysteries – and indeed the path of all who are called to seek the Divine Feminine in their lives – into a relevant, accessible tradition which encouraged women to enter into balanced, healing, and soul nourishing relationships with themselves, their sisters, and with the Goddesses of Avalon.

Though the Sisterhood of Avalon was created as a women's group, our ethical framework may provide some guidance for other leaders and other groups.

The very name Avalon evokes the sense of serenity and wholeness one would expect for a place revered as an Island of Healing and a resting place for the beloved dead. Known to us from the pages of legends and through the transmission of folklore, Avalon today holds a special place in the heart of Neo-Pagans, especially those who draw spiritual inspiration from Brythonic Celtic lore, Arthurian tradition, and Welsh mythology. For some, she is the Summerland, where the souls of the dead abide in joy as they await rebirth and where a healed King Arthur sleeps, anticipating Britain's need. For others she is the British iteration of the cloistered women's communities which can be found dotting the historic and folkloric landscape across the Celtic world; the women of these Ninefold Sisterhoods were renowned as healers, shape-shifters, augers, and priestesses. For still others, the Holy Isle of Avalon is a symbol – an archetype for the whole and empowered person, who is complete unto themselves, having feasted upon the fruits of their own inner wisdom and found the Goddess dwelling there within.

Self-actualization, reclaiming one's sovereignty, and acknowledging one's connection to Source are the three chains which uphold the Cauldron of Transformation sought by those who work in the Avalonian Tradition. We are inspired by the vision of Avalon as a template for spiritual wholeness, and the journey to Avalon – in the tradition of Celtic Wonder Voyage tales which require journeys over water to reach the islands of the Otherworld – has much to teach us. The path one must travel to reach the Holy Isle is itself a metaphor for the process of self-actualization, and in undertaking this quest, we learn to hear and trust our inherent wisdoms as we work to become conscious in our connection to the Divine.

To begin, we must first call the barge – to verbalize that which we need as we announce to the Universe our intention to seek transformation. Then, we must undertake our journey across the lake, whose waters represent the depths of the unconscious. Through this process, we see that the path to wholeness requires that we look within, and part of what we will see reflected in those inner waters are the Shadow aspects of the self – the illusions we have come to believe about who we are, the wounds that keep us from being whole, and the emotional baggage which weighs us down and prevents us from moving forward to birth forth our full potential.

These challenges manifest as the veil of mists which keep us from seeing ourselves and the world around us with clarity, and which keep us disconnected from the Source of wisdom which lies within us. Parting these mists reveals the mirrored surface of the lake, upon whose surface the truth of who we are is reflected; it is from these maternal waters of rebirth that we, like King Arthur, receive the sacred sword of Avalon from the hand of the Lady of the Lake. This is the weapon which allows us to see with clarity and act with truth, for by confronting our Shadow, we have earned the sword of Sovereignty – empowering us to act in the world with conscious self-determination.

With the way made clear, we reach the Holy Isle of Avalon

175

at last, and find ourselves standing on the shores of the place which Geoffrey of Monmouth describes thus, in the *Vita Merlini*:

The island of apples which men call 'The Fortunate Isle' gets its name from the fact that it produces all things of itself; the fields there have no need of the ploughs of the farmers and all cultivation is lacking except what nature provides. Of its own accord it produces grain and grapes, and apple trees grow in its wood from the close-clipped grass. The ground of its own accord produces everything instead of merely grass, and people live there a hundred years or more.

Here, we are presented with a vision of a self-sufficient community, which – after outlining its purpose, thoroughly examining its weaknesses, and embracing its strengths – is able to meet its own needs and provide a safe and sacred home base for those who have come to dwell there. This sense of being complete in and of one's self is one of the goals of those who walk the path of the Avalonian Tradition, and while much of our work is focused on that which is within us in order to seek a way to meet one's own needs on a personal level, we also work to apply this ideal to the ways in which we choose to be in community with others.

The Sisterhood of Avalon actively engages our membership – The Sisterhood of Avalon is comprised of members from literally all over the world; some sisters are blessed to gather in person to form local hearth groups, while others engage in their practice alone at their personal altars. Whatever the circumstance, we all gather together to participate in our vibrant online community, where we actively engage in a co-creative space where we collectively work to hold space for each other, guided by a set of principles we call the Nine Keys of Community.

These keys provide an ethical framework for community standards which encourages pluralism, honors the spiritual process of each individual sister, and creates a safe haven within which ideas, goals, and passages can be birthed and celebrated. This concept of a peer-supported and collectively maintained cooperative has served the Sisterhood of Avalon well, and reminds us that there are other ways of being in community than those most commonly seen in the mainstream. Each of us is an equally important stitch in the greater tapestry of our community, and our actions affect both ourselves and those with whom we choose to share space with – physically, emotionally, and spiritually.

It is a powerful exercise to meditate on the ways that the women of Avalon and the other examples of the Celtic Ninefold Sisterhoods – be they the Breton Korrigan, dancing by moonlight around holy wells, or the Gallisenae dwelling on their sacred island off the coast of France, or the cloistered women of Cill Dara tending the flame of Brigid in Her fire temple – may have built thriving and enduring communities which were perhaps founded on principles of communal self-sufficiency, collective interdependency, and interpersonal balance. Drawing from the wisdoms of this Ninefold template, a pattern emerged which inspired a code of Nine Keys which we have used to help create, support, and maintain community.

These are the community guidelines of the Sisterhood of Avalon, revised somewhat to be more broadly applicable. I share them with you here in the hope that they catalyze similarly honoring ways of entering into conscious community for those seeking alternative paradigms of leadership and collective responsibility for the whole.

The Nine Keys of Community

Key One – Establishing Sacred Center: The foundation of any spiritual community should include the establishment of a solid center that uplifts and empowers each member. The community should be a soul home and haven; a nurturing support system based in mutual respect and trust. Like the vision of Avalon as an enclave of holy women maintaining a temple and living in sacred service, the Divine – rather than any person or dogma -- must be the center around which the bonds of community are woven. If the call to walk a collective spiritual path is what draws the group together, then service to the Divine must be foremost in the heart of the community.

Key Two – Supporting Creativity and Growth: A powerful characteristic of the Priestess Isle was the idea that it functioned as a self-sufficient community, providing all that it required in and of itself. As such, everything the women of Avalon would have needed was created on the island, or else gotten in trade for what they produced. In the same way, it is important to support the work of the members of our spiritual community, especially those who are reclaiming culturally significant folk crafts and who express the sacred through the arts and music. An especially powerful way to manifest this collective support is to incorporate the reclamation of female systems of exchange, as with the gift economy and through bartering.

Key Three - Maintaining Safe Space: Just as the primary archetypal image of Avalon is that it was a marshy island ringed by water and cloaked by mists, it is important to protect the community by establishing and honoring collective boundaries, especially when it comes to emotions. There must be safe space for the group as a whole as well as existing between individuals. The honoring of oaths and the sanctity of silence - that is, to keep the soul sharings of our community members in confidence, except in situations where safety is a concern - are essential to building trust and safeguarding the community against negative influences. This also requires that we hold each other accountable to the ethical guidelines by which our community functions.

Key Four - Healthy Functioning: Renowned as a legendary Island of Healing, the women of Avalon were famously gifted in the arts of restoring and maintaining health. Any community is like a body, with each of its members comprising a vital part of its functioning. It is critical, therefore, that healthy relationships and balanced group dynamics be maintained. Periodic reflection on the group shadow is important, as is mediating any interpersonal difficulties, in order to keep the group energy clear. Any system, however, is only as efficient as each of its parts. Therefore, it is important that the group take an active role in the healthy and honest support of the process and growth of its members and of the community as a whole. Trust must exist in order to meet these challenges.

Key Five - Clarity of Vision: Exercising the gift of Sight for which they were renowned, it is easy to envision the women of Avalon seeking the guidance of the Cauldron in pursuit of sacred knowledge. Every person is a reflection of the Divine, and the innate wisdoms and intuition of the self and others should therefore be respected and consulted with discernment. It is important to establish clear group goals and a unified mission so that, in the event that the collective vision should become cloudy, the community will already have a pre-established and agreed-upon focus with which to come back into alignment.

Key Six – Keeping the Sacred Order: Just as we can imagine these Ninefold Priestesses – a lunar number – honoring the tides of the Moon and the cycles of the Earth, a spiritual community should concern itself with maintaining order and establishing rhythm. It is empowering to step outside of the mundane to honor the sacred that resides within each of us. A community is unified through enacting rites of passage, performing rituals of celebration and release, and fanning the flames of spirit by keeping the Holy Days and gathering in Lunar communion.

Key Seven – Establishing Strong Connections: Though Avalon was an Island Sanctuary, it was likely not entirely cloistered from the rest of the world. As with many of the other Ninefold Sisterhoods who chose to dwell apart, these women nevertheless served their communities when their people had need – sharing their gifts, their insights, and their wisdoms in many ways. Today, community awareness and responsibility, through such avenues as activism and volunteerism, are powerful ways of serving the Divine in the outer world. Keeping open channels within the community itself is just as important, and can be accomplished through communicating needs with honesty and clarity of expression.

Key Eight – Establishing Ethical Guidelines: Like many of those who follow the ancient ways, harkening back to a time where humanity was subject to the tides of the seasons and the abundance of the Earth, it may be that Celtic priestesses and wise women spent a great deal of time learning to work with the guiding principles of the Universe, seeking to understand and utilize the mechanism of the Great Pattern. In keeping with the guiding importance of this pattern, gatherings of spiritual seekers should strive to create clear and fair community guidelines, set a standard for ethical behavior, and encourage each of its members to act with integrity in all things.

Maintaining a centered position by expecting the only the best, yet understanding when members fall short of these ideals is important. Steps should be taken to ensure that the balance is restored, but as in all things, the swing to the right must equal the amplitude of the swing to the left. Any correction, therefore, must be in keeping with the energy and severity of the error.

Key Nine – Preserving Wisdoms: Transmitted orally from person to person and from one generation to the next, the Celts took great care to preserve their traditions, and it is believed that the bards memorized vast amounts of history and lore. Much has been lost down the stream of time, but some wisdoms have remained which can be remembered, reclaimed and renewed. It is of great importance, therefore, to actively research the peoples and cultures from which spiritual inspiration is drawn, and to honor the ancestors by keeping true to the patterns they have established as best we can, even with incomplete information. In the same way, we have an obligation to our future generations, and it is equally vital to keep new histories, to create new stories, and to pass on hard-won wisdoms to those who are to come.

We have found that a balance of these nine elements play an important role in the creation and maintenance of a healthy community. When each of Nine Keys is present, they have the ability to catalyze the growth and evolution of the group while supporting similar positive transformations in its members. For those of us who are dedicated to the Avalonian Tradition, we believe that the path of Avalon directs us to look within, and that even when we gather in community, we are individuals walking solitary, yet parallel, paths with our Sisters.

When all is said and done, only we alone can make the changes and obtain the wisdoms that will unlock the doors to manifesting our authentic, Sovereign selves. Yet the support, love, and soul-connections which are the fruits born of a balanced and centered community make the journey very sweet indeed.

Resources

Telyndru, Jhenah. *Avalon Within: A Sacred Journey of Myth, Mystery, and Inner Wisdom.* Minnesota: Llewellyn Worldwide, 2010. Print.

How to Create Your Very Own Pagan Community

Taylor Ellwood

I've always wanted to belong to a community. Actually I've always wanted to belong to a family, and that desire in turn had bloomed into wanting to belong to a community. When I was going to college I joined the Pagan college group at each university I went to, but I found that each group was fairly fractured. There wasn't a sense of unity or community, so much as there was a gathering space where a meeting was held.

I also spent a fair amount of time exploring other Pagan communities, but what I discovered was that I didn't fit any of them. I didn't relate to most of the people attending them and I wasn't really sure how to connect. Part of that was due to poor social skills on my part, but part of it, I eventually realized was also due to the fact that there really wasn't a group out there which embodied what I wanted from a community.

When I moved to Seattle in 2006, what stood out to me, once again, was how fractured the Pagan community was. There were lots of Pagan and occult groups around, but not much was happening with them. I hated living in Seattle, so my ex-wife and I moved down to Portland. Once again, in Portland, I found the same fractured scene, lots of groups, none of them doing much and none of them doing anything I was interested in. It became pretty clear to me that if I wanted to find a community that I could belong to, I would need to actually create that community.

My first attempt at creating community involved inviting people I knew over to my home and teaching them about magic. Once a week, each week, I'd have people come over and I'd teach a lesson about magic. However, I quickly realized that this wasn't the community I wanted to create. In fact, it wasn't a community at all. It was a class, and I was getting burned out.

It also didn't help that I didn't have the support at home for what I was doing. My ex-wife didn't like doing gatherings like I did, which created a real clash of values, but also taught me a valuable lesson: If you want to create anything, make sure you have the right people in place to support what you're doing. I eventually disbanded the class and spent some time thinking about what it was that I really wanted to create.

In 2009, a couple of years after I'd disbanded the class, I finally figured out how to create the community I was looking for. I started up a new group which I called Magical Experiments and I asked a couple of friends if we could host the event in their home once a month, as my ex-wife didn't want people coming over to our place for such a gathering. They were open to hosting it and so I invited some people I knew, but this time I changed a few things.

First, I decided that if we were going to do an event like this, we needed to schedule it around a meal. A meal is a social event. It brings people together as a community. When you break bread with people, you are engaged in an act of intimacy. We asked that everyone bring a type of food or beverage to the meeting. Those meals really helped us connect with each other socially, which helped create that sense of community I was looking for.

The second thing we decided was that everyone had to take a turn presenting. This way it wasn't always on me to present a class or experiment. Other people also had to present a workshop or share an experiment they were working on, so we could all learn together and no one person was the authority. At first it was hard for some people to come up with ideas, but as different people presented, everyone became more interested in presenting. Now when I post the dates for the magical experiments meet up, they get filled quickly by people who want to present and even newcomers feel comfortable with the idea of presenting.

From 2009 through the first quarter of 2010, the magical experiments group met at the place of my friends, but those friends decided to move up to Seattle in the spring of 2010. I'd gotten divorced from my ex-wife, but still lived with her. I was worried I'd have to discontinue the group, and for a period of a few months I did because we had no place to meet.

However, I also met my wife Kat in February of 2010. When I told her about the magical experiments meet up, she loved the idea and told me that she thought we should host it. She believed in what magical experiments was about and fully supported it. My ex-wife moved out in June of that year, and Kat moved in. Shortly after that we re-started the group and everyone who had been in it and still lived in Portland was thrilled at the idea of it happening again.

We did create a new rule when we started hosting it in our home. Kat suggested that we make it a private event. In other words, the only way you'd know about the event is if you were invited to it by someone already going to it. I thought that was a good idea overall, so we instituted it, though I did make sure I could mention the group in my e-newsletter that I send out twice a month, because I wanted to provide people who liked my books the opportunity to meet and have a meal with me if they were in town visiting when Magical Experiments was happening.

Since that time, our group has met almost every month of the year. The only time we don't meet is in February, because it's the height of the Winter Pagan convention season and Kat and I are usually out of town. Otherwise we meet once a month, have a potluck, and learn from one of the people attending. And through those meetings we've created a community, because we don't just meet once a month, but also meet at other times. Sometimes we host a movie night or party, and we also host a game night every week that some of our community members come to. What we've created is a community and for the most part we've been able to do it in a hands-off manner.

Guidelines for Building Your Own Community

If you want to create your own Pagan community, to create a social and spiritual group that can meet up, the following tips can be useful.

First, pick a dedicated space to meet. It's a lot easier to organize events when you have a dedicated space where people can meet each month. In the case of magical experiments, we meet at my home. It's centrally located for everyone else, so it's actually easier for everyone to meet there. By having that dedicated space, people know where to go each month for each event that is happening. You don't necessarily need to meet in a home, but having a dedicated space makes a huge difference.

Second, have a dedicated online space where members can

post as well. We have an e-group we use through Google groups so that we can coordinate events. People can also post their own announcements. You can use Yahoo, Google, Facebook, or something, but you should make it accessible only to members of the group.

Third, I recommend figuring out if your group will be a public or private group. There are advantages and disadvantages to both. A public group is openly public, which means that anyone can come to the event, and members are knowingly being open about the fact that they are Pagan. Such a group will advertise where they are meeting, when they are meeting, etc., on places such as Facebook. A private group is only open to people who are members of the group. Guests can be invited, but they can't join until they've been vetted by people. The group won't advertise its meetings online. It's easier to grow a public group, but a private group is likely much more focused than a public group will be.

Fourth, your group ideally has some type of theme that brings people together. For example, in Portland there is a Hermetics group where people attend, who are interested in classical magic. And there is also the Magical Experiments group, where people who are interested in experimenting with magic go. Groups that don't have a coherent focus tend to be groups that don't last or are unified. I'll share, further down, a useful exercise you can do to help identify the core values of your group.

Fifth, if you want the group to claim ownership, it's important to take a hands-off approach to leading it. What this means is you lead by facilitation as opposed to leading in a manner that allows for little input from other people. You don't handle all the details, you delegate, and you also recognize the strengths of different people. For example, if you have someone who likes to cook and help out in the kitchen, then let that person do that. With that said, it's also important to help the members of the group stretch themselves. What I mean is that you want to challenge them to step up.

Sixth, if you want members to step up, provide them a forum to step up. In the Magical Experiments group we have one rule, which is that anyone who joins the group is expected to present on a topic of their choosing. It can be an experiment, or a classic topic, but they have to present to the rest. By putting this stricture into place, what we do is challenge members to not only learn magic, but also learn how to teach it. We also give feedback to the people presenting, which helps them become better at it. The result has been quite nice. When we announce dates, people are eager to get their name on the calendar so they can present workshops. People want to step up, provided you provide them a way to step up and make it mandatory to do so.

Seventh, make your meeting a social meeting. While you want to do ritual or teach a workshop, it's also important to make part of your event a social event. When people first arrive, give them time to catch up and chat and help out. After the presentation is done, leave some time open for further socialization. Whether its people chatting or playing a game, keep the space available in such a way that it actually can be a community space. By allowing for social time, what you enable is bonding behavior that helps the people really connect with each other.

Eighth, don't tolerate people who are unhealthy for your group. Not every person belongs in your group. If a person joins who is passive aggressive or gossipy or undermining, it's really important that you recognize it for what it is and talk with the person. Give the person a chance to change, but if the behavior continues, ask them to leave. It's also important to be clear about what behavior your group won't tolerate. For example, if a person is creepy and hitting on every one left and right, you don't want that person in your group. Don't tolerate behavior you don't want.

How Does Leadership Apply to Building a Community?

When you want to build a community, leadership skills are an essential part of that process. What's also important is that what you build is a healthy community as opposed to a cult. One resource, which can be useful for evaluating your group is Isaac Bonewits' Cult Evaluation form, which can be found here: http://www.neopagan.net/ABCDEF.html. Obviously you don't want your group to become a cult. Using this tool can help you and the members of your group evaluate if that's even a possibility.

However, an exercise that I have found valuable, both in business and for community activities, involves defining what the core values and ideology of your group are. Your core values describe what your group is about and explain why the group is important. By defining them, you develop clarity about what the purpose of the group is and why people have joined the group. For example we have the following core values in the magical experiments group:

- We want to provide a safe space for magicians and Pagans who want to experiment with magic or want to explore and share their spiritual paths with others.
- We don't value a given spiritual tradition or practice over any other spiritual tradition or practice, but are accepting of all of them.
- We want our community to be welcoming to newcomers, and we want people who to join who want to contribute to our group.
- We are open to new perspectives and want our members to be open-minded
- Anyone who joins needs to respect the anonymity of other members as some have day jobs or other situations where they need to be in the closet.

By having that clarity around our core values we're able to evaluate the actions of our group and make sure those actions are in alignment with those values. This is important for the solidarity of the group and for the creation of a culture that supports the community. It's also important because it provides each member with a sense of purpose in relationship to the group and how they want to contribute to it. When you meet with your own group, spend a meeting brainstorming about the values of your group. Why is your group in existence? What is its purpose? How do you support each other? These are good questions to ask that will help you define the core values and ideology of your group.

Being the leader of a group involves leading for the right reasons. If you are leading because you want peoples' approval or you enjoy having a sense of power, those are the wrong reasons to lead and will cause you to sabotage your group. If, on the other hand, you feel a genuine desire to serve your community, to better it in whatever way you can and you're willing to put the needs of that community above your own, then you could be a good leader.

However, to be a great leader involves not just putting the needs of the community above your own, but empowering them to become leaders in their own right. If you are consistently the decision maker for most or every decision, you are doing both yourself and your community a disservice, because you are micromanaging the community. Your ideal goal should be to empower the other people to make decisions as well by delegating authority or setting your group in such a way that people are making some of the decisions.

In Magical Experiments, Kat and I host the meeting, so we do make decisions about the date and usually provide a menu item. But other people decide what food they'll bring and each person gets the opportunity to come up with a presentation of their own choosing. We provide enough structure to support our group, but enough freedom so people can step up and be leaders.

Obviously if your group is more structured or does rituals, this can change the dynamic, but I don't think it needs to be changed much. For example if you do rituals, you might require members to rotate so that different people take on ritual roles, instead of just select people doing the roles. By making it mandatory that they step up, what you set up is a culture where people are expected to participate. Eventually they become eager to participate because they feel empowered to do so.

If you've always wanted a Pagan community to belong to, but never felt like you fit in with the ones already existing, why not create your own. Figure out what the focus of the group is and then start telling people about it. You'll find some like-minded people relatively quickly and then start meeting up. Whether you meet once a month or more, as long as you keep it consistent, you'll soon have the Pagan community you've wanted, with people you like.

A Few Leadership Stories about Bylaws[21]
Sam Wagar

Over thirty years of being involved in Pagan communities, much of it as an active group organizer and community builder, I have overcome any fear that I once had of formal organization. I now consider bylaws, policies and procedures, and democratic congregational self-government to be essential to the future growth and service of the Pagan communities, to protecting seekers and young Pagans from abuse, and to checking the frequent abuses of power in the community. And I'll give a few examples here of where those things were not in place, and a couple where they were. Because the specific examples are only examples, and stand in for far too many cases that I do not have personal knowledge of, I'm going to change names and locations.

I will make a formal disclaimer here: although I have been affiliated over the years with a variety of groups, political parties, and religious organizations, none of them had any say in the writing of this chapter and any opinions expressed in here are my own, in no way representative of the prevailing opinion of any group.

There was a painful period, twenty years ago, a major Witchwar which shaped a Pagan community, whose effects linger because the underlying issues have never been dealt with. It resulted from the decision to go public with my coven's concern that the community around a bookstore was developing into a Wicca-based cult. This bookstore had opened up in 1991 and the Priestess who started the store met with various local Elders, including me, to talk about books she might want to stock and to publicize her store as a community meeting space. At that point she informed me she was a Gardnerian 1st degree although she hadn't been practicing with her teachers for some time. I later referred a fellow to her store. He had just moved to town and was looking for a place to do psychic readings. They became a couple and began to run the store as a joint enterprise.

---

[21] Large parts of this chapter were adapted from my memoir "I Know Where the Bodies are Buried" (Obscure Pagan Press/Createspace, 2014)

The fellow claimed an "honorary Gardnerian Third" and she became an overnight Third degree.

They began Wicca 101 classes and charged fees for them. Then, when people had completed one series of classes, they came up with "102" classes, also at a fee, and required those. All events of the community around them had to happen at the store, and pay rent for the space. Students earned their Second Degrees by working for free in the bookstore.

They also conferred a whole mass of degrees on people in the community that they wanted as allies and began plagiarizing others' work as "Traditional Craft Teachings" and selling this as their own work. They formed covens by gathering groups of students together, having them swear an Oath to the HPS and assigning them a Priestess. Coven meetings could only be called with prior permission from these two. Three or more coven members together was classified as an implied meeting and forbidden without prior permission. Shunning techniques were employed to maintain control and obedience over a very quickly growing community.

A three page manifesto was produced (for private circulation) announcing that as High Priestess of the Tradition, this Priestess had absolute control over the community. All coven members were to swear a personal oath to her. From their "Community Statement of Principles": "The First among Equals in the community is Lady R. In any dispute, hers is the final word. When she chooses to leave the post, she alone will appoint her successor. In this way we honour ... the tradition of the Priestess who represents the Goddess.

The response to what most people knew about this bookstore was to not have anything to do with them and to concentrate on their own spiritual work. However, some people involved in their group visited with my Trad's Sabbat circle and told us about the deepening cultishness and some of the issues mentioned above. It was alarming enough that a council of our Elders got together and pulled together a document outlining what they had learned and sounded the alarm. It was sent out to other groups in the area for the purpose of warning people.

At this point the merde hit the fan. Although the document was written and endorsed by a group of Elders and backed up by letters from several people that had been involved in the bookstore community, the spokesperson for the group of Elders became the public face of the controversy and immediately went onto the permanent shit-list of the groups descended from the bookstore. Projecting the blame onto the whistleblowers was easier for the larger community than dealing with its lack of response, or their responsibility to now help people heal from the experience.

This was another occasion where keeping our mouths shut and continuing to be cowards would have saved us from a great deal of trouble, although it would also result in more people being exploited, our religion being distorted and perverted, and little issues like that. But certainly a better thing than annoying the "un-named Elders" again, who wrote the whistle-blower nasty letters (pre-Internet so no death-threats as there were during Gamergate).

My largest take-away lesson from that whole experience was that the bookstore group had no member control or governance – it was centred on the arbitrary action and whim of the HPS and her consort, and on unethical practices such as charging money for training toward Initiation, and unpaid labour. The "Statement of Principles" was imposed by fiat, Oaths were required of people arbitrarily. It was a mess as it disintegrated.

How Not to Do a Church

A little time after the bookstore mess there was another personality cult issue. There was a legally established pan-Pagan church that grew out of the Pagan Student's Club at a university, which also had a bookstore owner involved. It was set up to be a self-governing and multi-tradition Temple spiritually guided by three founding High Priestesses. Its founding HPSes quickly had a falling out over how much democracy and how much direction the group should have and various other things. In particular there was the problem that decisions about money were being made without consultation by one person, husband of one of the Guardian HPSes who came from a wealthy family and was using his money to control the group.

Shortly after the group was set up they committed the Temple to purchasing a parcel of land for a retreat centre using "money from an anonymous donor" who would only talk to him. So there was a poorly considered rush to legally incorporate in order to own this land. By the end of their first year the church was in deep trouble. Two of the unhappy founders had applied to the Registrar of Societies to dissolve it.

The faction that wanted to keep things going secured the contact list and called a special Annual General Meeting (AGM) and invited a neutral "friend of the Temple", and friend of prominent figures in both factions, to chair it. That AGM managed to prevent the disgruntled HPSes from legally dissolving the organization, but little more.

Two years later, there were two attempts to get quorum to hold an AGM, both of which failed. So, the "friend of the Temple" suggested that the little group of members outside of the founding Temple should host an AGM and adopt changes to the bylaws to make it work better, including a bylaw governing choosing clergy. So, they gathered, including the remaining Guardian HPS and her husband, and had an AGM and after thorough discussion adopted some changes to the bylaws and constitution to make it more democratic and member-run, as well as adopting a clergy authorization process.

The "friend of the Temple" was elected Secretary and started a Temple, a newsletter for members and friends, as well as filing all of the required paperwork with the province – the Temple had received a "Notice of Dissolution" because no paperwork had been filed since it was founded and so it was urgent to get that done. Almost immediately the remaining High Priestess, who no longer had the authority to 'guide' the church, objected that the new bylaws were nothing that had been agreed to and that the proposed clergy rules were undemocratic.

At the next AGM the former Guardian HPS and her husband called together a by-invitation only meeting the night before to plan how to throw "the friend" out. He was blindsided, arriving at the AGM to be informed, by the Membership Secretary, without notice, or any kind of due process, that he was going to be thrown out based on unspecified accusations by unspecified people. He protested in shock that due process and the bylaws must be followed or he'd have to go to the provincial government agency and have the organization investigated. A process of sorts, with a carefully-stacked investigating committee with a specific mandate, was agreed to.

Instead of attending his son's 7th birthday party the now "former friend" was at a Special General Meeting of the Members getting thrown out of the group. He had expected to be thrown out, but was determined that these guys and their unethical sycophants would have to fight it all the way through to remove him.

The church did remove the "former friend" and continued as a snakepit of takeover attempts and the clash of massive egos until it collapsed amid mutual recriminations about five years later. It was run on the basis of membership meetings, open membership, and the whim of the HPS. I don't believe that the paperwork was ever filed to legally wind it down.

I must say that the church was a marvellous series of lessons in what didn't work and what kinds of things to avoid. The clergy authorization bylaw of the Congregationalist Wiccan Association (CWA), founded ten years later—both BC and Alberta branches—is basically the same one as the all-knowing HPS rejected. It seems to be working pretty well for us.

The takeaway here is that bylaws and structures must apply to everyone, particularly including the founders and leaders of the group, and that member control cannot operate without fully legitimate oversight. And that spiritual growth and community cannot flourish amidst chaos and arbitrariness.

Something That Works

Several years after the collapse and meltdown of the pan-Pagan Temple group, there was a lengthy online discussion of how "Somebody" should start a Pagan community centre which segued into starting a Temple. I had often experienced that this meant, "Somebody else, probably Sam, should start up this thing which I could use and benefit from without doing any work." Well, just this once, I decided to decline. Except that the wife of a man in the Pagan community died suddenly and there was a need for someone to perform a funeral. A small group of his friends gathered together at the chapel in the hospital, and I was called to be the Priest because that's who I am.

I knew then that I had been thinking about this Temple thing all wrong - it wasn't about weddings and babies and

The Pagan Leadership Anthology

celebrating the joyful turning of the seasons, it was about sharing the pain, healing the hurts, loving and caring for those who suffer. This man was able to find the community to care for him in this horrible time, someone to say the words and ease the pain of his wife's death. If he had not been well-connected to the Pagan community already he would have been alone to suffer.

So, I talked to my coven-mates and the Priestess of another coven and we all got together and went through a set of the bylaws I had written, line by line, at first through email discussion and then in person – six naked Witches sitting in circle discussing bylaws, life doesn't get much stranger than that! That's how we founded a church with two Temples in March of 2004, as the provincial branch of the national CWA, which had existed on paper for thirteen years.

I was the Secretary (I usually am, because I like and understand bureaucracy) and so I applied to BC Vital Statistics and we had our marrying credentials as of September 2004, me and the HPS of the other coven. This was the realization of a goal of mine of many years standing. The HPS disagreed with the church setting down conditions for the clergy credential (which applied to all clergy, including her) which meant that she could not go exactly her own way and was gone by the end of that month. She resigned (at the firm suggestion of the Chair) in a huff because she thought that she was personally awarded her marrying credential because of all that she knew and had done, rather than being granted it in trust by the church, and so she didn't have to do things the way we had all agreed to do them. We were, and are, serious about congregationalism in CWA – it is not an ego trip or client cult.

I wrote a set of expectations for marriages to be performed by our church which were adopted by our Board. This is still the set which is used for our Temples in both BC and Alberta, and I believe they have been proven to be workable.

In mid-January 2005 Congregationalist Wiccan Association of British Columbia, at this point just my tiny Temple meeting up at Simon Fraser University--where we could get free meeting space by booking it through the student Pagan club--was contacted by a couple of groups in other parts of the province. I went out to Penticton to visit a friend but while I was visiting her she hosted a local Pagan coffee meet-and-greet. There I met a

193

Priestess from Vernon, and a Druid / Wiccan Priest in Penticton. I agreed to work with these folk toward getting groups going in the Okanagan, if my travelling expenses were met. I later had the pleasure of writing an ordination ritual as well.

Then later that year, a Priest contacted me from Nanaimo and I went over and met his group. So, our church's Board adopted another policy written by me on authorizing the formation of Temples from non-members and the training and ordination of clergy.

Every month for a year I travelled to Vernon (8 hours) and then Penticton (another two hours) on the bus, spending a weekend in the Okanagan working with the clergy of these two Temples, co-authoring and performing the open public rituals, assigning reading and discussing it with the clergy candidates. I did the same thing in Nanaimo, although the ferry ride was a lot more comfortable and quicker than the bus. I supervised, trained and Initiated the clergy in both Temples. My friend and co-founder Deb was able to help out with Nanaimo and she Initiated those clergy.

Then I had the great pleasure of overseeing the joint Ordination ceremony for the three Okanagan clergy on 15th of April 2006, which made their Temples the second and third in our church. We combined this visit with a very productive clergy retreat. The Nanaimo Ordinations for three clergy, happened on Saturday the 12th of August 2006. We combined the visit with the church's Annual General Meeting.

CWABC adopted some sensible policies – we required our clergy to get Criminal Record checks done, established periodic reviews of clergy and formal procedures for disciplining them and firing them. In 2007, after power struggles around various issues, the founding Priest of one Temple refused to get a Criminal Record Check done and refused to acknowledge the authority of the church over him. He resigned from the Board (June 7th), then as a clergy person, effective the 16th of July, and the Board was required to suspend his clergy credential (unfortunately interfering with a wedding that he was scheduled to do) and remove him as a member on the 15th of July.

He was a classic Antagonist,[22] contesting the authority of the Board to establish regulations to govern members, or to discipline clergy (or perhaps only him). He rescinded his resignation as clergy and appealed his membership suspension to the August 11th 2007 AGM, and we upheld his expulsion. A neutral 'friend of the church' was recruited to chair the membership appeal, which was two tough hours.

The Temple happened to be short of its full year probationary period at the AGM so we continued its probation. Although this Priest had been running the Temple as his private fief and had been the teacher of all of the clergy and mentor to other active members, CWABC only lost a small number of members when he went and the Temple continued to be involved in CWABC. Our attitude was that they needed us more than we needed them, because the church as a whole owns all of the legal prerogatives, such as being able to license Ministers to perform weddings.

The Temple in Penticton split in half peacefully in February 2008 because of differences in approach between the HPS and HP. When it split the PS's proto-Temple fell apart almost immediately and the other staggered along for another year or so until the HP and his family moved to Saskatchewan. Differences in the Nanaimo Temple resulted in it splitting in three with one faction recruited to another Wiccan church in BC at the same time as the Temple in Nanaimo was peacefully dividing over differences in approach in October 2011. The two Nanaimo Temples are both successful and collaborate together – the bylaws were set up to enable friendly splits like that, and a variety of approaches to our common religion in a congregationalist framework.

As Secretary and founder and generally knowledgeable guy I assisted the CWA of Alberta, CWABC's sister church, to get established in 2007. A friend who was a Priest with a coven in Edmonton came to me asking about CWABC and how to get something going in his province. So I connected up with the HPS of the project, Ali Hammington, a woman I'd met a couple of

[22] Kenneth C. Haugk *Antagonists in the Church: How to Identify and Deal with Destructive Conflict* (Minneapolis: Augsburg Fortress Publishing, 1988)- this book is worth its weight in palladium as far as dealing with the specific types of destructive people who are attracted to religious bodies.

times through my visits to Edmonton but didn't know well, and offered a great deal of advice on procedures, bylaws and the like.

I offered her support when she broke with my (former) friend around the issue of Great Rite initiation of Priestesses into CWAA (which he favoured and she didn't) and general obstruction. He had been pushing to get as many Priestesses in training as possible, and had stated directly that our church required Great Rite in clergy training (which we do not). But, by using the bylaws, and her authority as Board of Directors Chair, plus the support of the rest of her Board, he was removed with a minimum of disruption, and with no public scandal.

Our bylaws, in brief, set our church up as a congregationalist association of Temples, each of which runs its own affairs, subject to oversight by the Annual General Meeting of the members, which has the authority, by a super-majority, to dissolve a Temple. Voting membership is restricted to adults who have been involved in the church for a year, agreed in writing to our common statement of beliefs and ethics, and paid a membership fee. Only members can vote, be elected to Temple or Provincial Boards of Directors, or train for clergy. Clergy candidates must be second degree Wiccans (or equivalent – some Wiccan trads do not have a three degree Initiation structure), and must work under the supervision of a clergy person for a minimum of a year before being examined by a committee of clergy and approved. The decision about which clergy will be awarded marrying credentials is in the hands of the members of each Temple – clergy must be associated with a particular Temple to hold the credential. Clergy have no particular authority in running the church – they are in charge of the ritual and religious education, but the Temple Boards need not have clergy as members. And there is a specific procedure for stripping people of their memberships, and disciplining or removing clergy.

Because bylaws must be amended by the members at AGM, and amendments require a super-majority of 66%, the organization is stable, and the members all know where things stand.

We have been successful in building a small church, now with three provincial sister churches (Saskatchewan established 2014), nine Temples, and hundreds of members. Our bylaws have enabled us to fire obstructive clergy without blowing our organization apart, to divide Temples peacefully and co-operatively, to train clergy and lay leadership with agreed standards, to gain legitimacy with governments and the general public, and to successfully transfer our leadership from the founding members to elected successors.

Thank you to my lifelong Patron, Ares, the God of War – struggling with you, against you, and in partnership with you has made much that I have accomplished possible. "I will not cease from mental fight / nor shall my sword sleep in my hand / 'til we have built Jerusalem"[23]

---

[23] From *Jerusalem* by William Blake (part of the epic poem *Milton*, 1810)

Just Breathe
Melanie A. Howard

Underneath a sage candle, inside the cupboard of a small mahogany altar, sleeps a journal sewn with rhinestones; that was our first charter. We laid the cards and asked the East, South, West, and North what gifts would be needed for our spirituality group to serve our community and to succeed. Faithfully recorded there is every gift that surfaced, and one we did not understand at the time. The North bestowed on us permission...to fail.

Our intent was simple, we felt: to turn a monthly Women's Gathering into a self-sustaining spirituality center for women. We had a steady group of interested women and we, the founding members, had a multitude of gifts between us and the drive to make it happen. By the end of the first year, the Blessings and Breathing Center was a registered LLC with its own website, newsletter, events, classes, devoted charitable giving team, and a table at several conferences and fairs. At the core, the monthly Women's Gathering fanned the flame of purpose. We were the only openly multi-denominational spirituality center in a superstitious town of 20,000 people—the only place that would talk about Tarot cards, chakras, and healing touch in the same breath as God, saints, and angels without cringing as though lightning would strike. We regularly joked about whether or not the locals would shun us after this event or another.

All of us certain that any threat would come from *outside* the group.

In the early months of innocence, we thought little of the North's gift. A member of the group, the wife of a successful local businessman, gave us a small endowment that more than covered our first-year costs. Food and a guest teacher were provided at every Women's Gathering with free-will donation defraying some of the costs, while the Center took care of the rest. The women loved these gatherings and we loved hosting them. The endowment quickly dwindled.

It was during the dwindling that we began to have a crisis of leadership. They say every married couple will fight about money. The founding members of a spiritual group, no matter how well-intentioned, will do the same. Our situation was very unique; the founding members who did most of the day-to-day running of the Center were family: my aunt, my cousin, and myself. Center funds were kept in a checking account belonging to my aunt, with my cousin and I as signatories.

Strain on the Center created strain on the family, and also highlighted how an organization will take on the personality traits of its leaders. Specifically, we were raised to be generous, well-intentioned, kind, loving, helpful, understanding, and meek. We fell all over ourselves to avoid anything approaching conflict in action and in speech. Still, being Minnesotan, imagined slights, behind-the-back chatter, and passive-aggressive behavior managed to thrive. *Did you know you haven't updated the website for such-and-such event?* - and - *No, I'm not planning on taking anything home - we need to cover the cost of the table.* - and - *Maybe I should just take care of that.* - became hallmarks of our daily conversations. We smiled so hard our teeth hurt and grumbled quietly when one of us was away. The language between us was carefully polite, and one by one, in one way or another, we began to disengage.

As things got more tense, my aunt began to loudly deny the idea that she was the leader of the Center—that it was a group effort. Privately, she expressed exasperation at being responsible for *everything*. My cousin, by far the youngest of the founding members, buried herself in her phone when manning the table at conferences and complained that no one treated her as an equal, as a grown up. I stopped updating the website and put out the newsletter later and later, and finally not at all, convinced it was a waste of time to keep the momentum going, but never saying a word.

Meanwhile, there were some not-so-behind-the-scenes problems emerging with the Center. Aside from the touchy issue of finances, we also found it difficult to ask for other kinds of help and support. In our family, help is given without asking — or rather, without asking *directly*. Naturally, the running the Center became an endless knot of people willing to help, but given nothing to do, and help needed, but not asked for. An easy point of connection with the spirituality center was left severed due to a sawing back and forth of taking too much control, and too little.

Our undefined leadership led to situations that were awkward, painful, infuriating, and downright scary at times for the founders and for the members of the Center. We had a handshake contract with a belly dance instructor to give classes, only to have her keep the Center's percentage. We had several private practitioners come in to give readings or massage, past life regressions or energy work, and took no percentage—in one case, we paid a practitioner to come, and members then paid for private sessions later.

One memorable evening, I was the only founding member able to attend a Women's Gathering, and the presenter unexpectedly spat on one of our members to excise evil. I had no personal frame of reference from which to effectively handle the situation, and the Center had no written rules for me to enforce. I just stared open-mouthed. That member never came to another gathering.

My grandfather wisely once said, "People don't change until they have to." The same happens with groups. After the spitting incident, we had our very first founders meeting on the topic of rules and regulations. We determined we were responsible for the safety of our members while they were in our space or at one of our events, and that it was important any future presenters had an idea of our group's culture, and also its rules, *and that those rules had to be abided by.* With extensive input from the other founders, and the oversight of an attorney, I penned several documents, two examples of which follow this essay

Just having these documents made us feel more secure both in our mission and in our ability to carry it out with the right intentions and with the proper support. We had a real discussion about who we were, where we were going, and the people we served and wanted to serve.

In our endeavor, we failed many times. We didn't properly protect our members, we didn't handle finances gracefully, and we didn't always treat each other, as founding members, with the respect we deserved. But after this meeting, we fell on our faces a lot less, and we were able to continue forward with the Center with renewed faith in its future. When we dissolved the Center last year, it was not because we didn't know what we were about. It was because strong leaders are hard to find, and especially hard to replace.

Resources

These following documents can be adapted and used for your own group.

Resource Document: Pamphlet with Mission, Rules, and Agreements for the Blessings and Breathing Center

The Peer Group of the Blessings and Breathing Center, LLC is delighted that you have agreed to provide a service for the Blessings and Breathing Center. We recognize you as an authority in your field, a gifted speaker, a great teacher, and a caring practitioner and are honored to have you.

You may have met one of us, a handful of us, or all of us at a Blessings and Breathing Center event, or at our booth at one of the many expos and conferences we attend during the year. That you are reading this packet shows that we were very impressed with you. But we realize that a one-time contact, class, or event might not prepare you for what to expect at the Blessings and Breathing Center, or what the Blessings and Breathing Center may expect of you, so we have prepared this welcome packet to explain more about the Center and its mission. We would also encourage you to go to www.blessingsandbreathing.com and peruse our website for more information about what the Center is and what we do.

History

A small group of women started meeting in support of one another, and learning about each individual's journey through life. We came to know that each of us was searching for ways to re-connect with our self, to know and experience who and what we are meant to be, to celebrate our uniqueness, and to bring this reality of love of self out to others.

This led us to begin having monthly Women's Gatherings, celebrations, sharing and learning experiences. What started out with 4-6 women attending, has steadily grown to include more than 40 women. As we re-connect with ourselves and connect with each other, we are finding there is a need for more options and opportunities to enhance our spiritual journey.

The Blessings and Breathing Center, LLC was founded in 2008 to provide a safe and sacred space for women to come to know their true selves. We have grown to include Tarot Readings, Spiritual Healing and Counseling, Education, Spiritual Library, Labyrinth Walks, and more.

We continue to seek ways and the means to offer women a chance to explore and experience who they are.

Mission

The Blessings and Breathing Center, LLC is committed to serving and supporting women on their journeys of self-discovery. This has always been the core, heart, and soul of the Blessings and Breathing Center's mission. In order to fulfill this sacred contract we have with our clients and members, we adhere to these principles:

Safe and Sacred Space

Our number one top priority is that our members and clients feel safe and supported. How can a woman comfortably explore her inner being if she doesn't feel physically safe? To that end, we at the Blessings and Breathing Center, LLC do everything in our power to ensure that the physical space in which an event is held is comfortable; that the atmosphere of the space is always relaxed and welcoming; and that personal boundaries are respected by all members, outside practitioners, and clients.

The hard and fast rule is that "no" means "no." Touching, hugging, and other shows of affection are anticipated and even encouraged, as long as a member or client is receptive. However, we have in the past had some practitioners get a little overzealous and participate in unacceptable behaviors such as spitting on a client to "get the evil out." If a client agrees to have a private exorcism, then by all means the two of you should arrange a time and place and have at it. However, the culture of Hastings, MN is rather conservative, as are many of our members, so any private acts of this kind, or any service performed before the group that becomes overly personal/focused on a single group member, should be removed to a private setting at a later date. This keeps things comfortable for everyone.

At this time, we do not allow men or male practitioners at the Blessings and Breathing Center, LLC. The sad but true fact is that many women do not feel comfortable being themselves around men, and we have made the executive decision to keep men out of the mix for the time being.

It should also be mentioned that the Blessings and Breathing Center, LLC is a spirituality center. All faiths are welcomed and respected. We do not recruit our members to any specific faith, and would appreciate it if you didn't either.

Education

The Blessings and Breathing Center, LLC is a learning environment. While we quite often contract outside practitioners to come do private readings, we do this with the understanding that the practitioner will also teach something to the group. This could be as simple as your personal journey/a little background of your profession, or it could be something more hands-on such as card-making or how to use a pendulum. Your presentation need not exceed half an hour if you are there to do private readings. We realize your time is valuable.

If the Blessings and Breathing Center, LLC has sought you out as a presenter, it is our hope that you can fill at least an hour of time. We lean more toward the experiential – it is all about self-exploration, after all – and if you are trying to choose between giving a long talk or providing something hands-on, we would recommend that you go with a hands-on presentation.

The ultimate goal of having someone outside come in is to provide our clients and members with a wide variety of tools and ways to explore their inner landscapes and to strengthen their connection with the Divine, whatever the Divine is to any individual member. Creativity, passion, and individuality are strongly encouraged.

Community Action

As a spirituality center devoted to serving the spiritual and creative needs of women, the Blessings and Breathing Center, LLC will quite often sponsor, support, and/or actively participate in community and charity events. You might have even met us at one. We will probably discuss opportunities to participate in charity and community events at our Gatherings.

If you have a charity or organization you support, we would love to hear about it *before* the event you are scheduled to attend. Please realize if you as someone we've contracted to have in mentions an event or organization that the Blessings and Breathing Center would not or does not support, it puts us in a very sticky situation. If we like your charity, and it meets our mission, we will most likely be more than ecstatic for you to talk about it at our event. We just need to be given the opportunity to review your charity or organization beforehand to ensure that it is in line with the tenets of the Blessings and Breathing Center.

Peer Group

The Blessings and Breathing Center, LLC is currently run out of the home of _____, who is a co-founder and the inspiration behind the Center. The governing body of the Blessings and Breathing Center is made up of six core members called the Peer Group. The members are:

Melanie Howard – Co-founder and Marketing and Media Specialist for the Blessings and Breathing Center, LLC. Melanie is also an author and Tarot reader.

(List the rest of your staffers with brief info here)

*Please note that if you have a friend or colleague in mind who you would also like to recommend as a presenter or practitioner at the Center, that Peer Group members are chosen first in their field. We would be very unlikely, for instance, to accept another massage therapist as a presenter at one of our events. If you do have a friend or colleague you believe would make a good presenter at the Center, please have them contact **center@blessingsandbreathing.com**.

We hope this Welcome Packet has provided you with more insight into the Center, and we look forward to working with you in the future.

Resource Document: Contract for Multiple Event Practitioners

I _____ certify that I received, read, and understand the policies and procedures laid out in the Blessings and Breathing Center, LLC Welcome Packet on this day _____, 2010. I agree to abide by these guidelines as listed below:

1. I will respect the rule of Safe and Sacred Space at the Blessings and Breathing Center, LLC and/or at any location at which the Blessings and Breathing Center is hosting me. To this end, I will not perform any one-on-one service or ritual on any of the Blessings and Breathing Center clients or members without first having their express written or verbal permission from both the potential client and the Blessings and Breathing Center.

2. I recognize the time and effort the Blessings and Breathing Center has put into hosting and marketing these events or classes. To this end, I agree that 15% of the proceeds obtained from the services I provide between _____, 2010 and _____, 2010 to take place on _____ at _____ PM at _____ will be donated to the Blessings and Breathing Center, provided that the Blessings and Breathing Center has provided me with the minimum number of _____ clients who will participate in paid sessions and/or pay for all sessions ahead of time whether they are present or not.

   a. I recognize that the Blessings and Breathing Center, LLC will be physically and financially responsible for arranging space for my event or class. If I have concerns about the space provided, I will bring them to the authorized Peer Group representative(s) of the Blessings and Breathing Center, LLC and not attempt to negotiate with any outside parties in any capacity in any aspect that pertains to this particular event or class. I realize that the Blessings and Breathing Center may have a contract with the space provider and will not enter into any agreements with the space provider that will violate the terms of the contract that the Blessings and Breathing Center has with the space provider. I certify that the Blessings and Breathing Center, LLC has provided me with a clear set of written guidelines for use of the space and that I will abide by these rules.

Signature_____ Print Name_____ Date_____

Before Peer Group Member _____ Signature_____

Thirty Years and 3,500 members
Jade

In 1976 I made a statement to several friends that I thought I knew how to work for the Goddess. My exact declaration was "If I just had a little money, I think I know how to organize for the Goddess." Little did I know I was making a prophetic statement. Now, 38 years later I am one of the founders of the Re-formed Congregation of the Goddess—International (RCG-I), which is, as far as I am aware, the oldest and largest legally tax-exempt religion serving the women's community.

What Has the Congregation Accomplished?

We've just celebrated the Congregation's thirtieth anniversary. Over 3600 women from all over the world are members. Almost 100 women have graduated from the Women's Thealogical Institute (WTI,) a multidimensional school and seminary for women who wish to further their understanding of the Goddess, women's spirituality, and/or women's witchcraft. Forty-one of the women who completed the rigorous WTI six-year course of study, participated in a community service project outside the Congregation, and completed an internship at the RCG-I Mother House have been ordained as Priestesses.

RCG-I has produced fifty-eight large Gatherings, chartered 11 Circles and published 112 issues of two newspapers. The Congregation owns its own "Mother House" and I have been given a stipend for my work as a Priestess for the last 26 years. I'm not listing these accomplishments to boast, but to provide an example of what an organization can accomplish with judicious stewardship.

How Did All This Happen?

I did get a little bit of money. It turned out to be a couple of thousand dollars in inheritance from my Grandmother, which came in the form of a 2.5-carat diamond ring, a mink coat, and some nuclear power plant stock. I moved from Kentucky to Madison, Wisconsin. Madison has a large Pagan community which I hoped could support an organizing effort. I then began to keep my promise to organize for the Goddess.

This was before the internet. I had heard a quote from Gandhi which was something like "If you want to build a movement, you need to have a press." So, I started looking for women who could help me accomplish this goal. I thought I would need several women, but instead I found Lynnie Levy who became the other co-founder of RCG-I. This turned out to be one of the most significant elements in the formation of the Congregation. There were two of us. Lynnie and I went to work and RCG-I sprang to life.

Non-Profit Administration

In the first few years after the formation of the Congregation, I worked a "straight" job as an executive director of a non-profit organization. This turned out to be an invaluable training ground for working with a religious non-profit. I became informed about budgets, volunteers, bylaws, mission statements, fundraising, and what the IRS cares about.

I learned that "non-profit" did not mean a group/organization could not make money or have salaried staff. I became aware that one of the most important elements of any legally recognized non-profit is its board of directors. I also learned the steps in creating a non-profit organization and vital information about how one is run.

Recommendation: If you want to start a non-profit group/organization, learn about non-profit administration. Consider volunteering to be on the Board of a local non-profit, or do some other kind of volunteer work which will give you insight into how non-profits operate.

Decide How Decisions Will Be Made

The very first thing to decide in beginning a group/organization is to choose a decision-making method. There are many ways to make decisions. All of them have strengths and weaknesses. Before you invite your first member or have your first meeting, decide how you're going to make decisions. Will your group/organization be using consensus, majority rule, a modified majority rule system, or will you be leading and making decisions for the group/organization?

No matter what decision-making structure you decide to use, let people know what it will be before they join your group/organization. Then, at one of the first meetings, train your members about how that structure works. Many people have misconceptions and/or are uncomfortable with different decision-making styles. Providing information about how a specific decision-making style functions can reduce this discomfort and insure that everyone engaged in decision-making is functioning with the same information.

RCG-I uses consensus. I am often surprised what women think consensus is. The same is true for groups/organizations that are using Robert's Rules or a modified majority process. If you are sharing decision-making responsibility with the members of a group/organization, make sure everyone knows what decision-making system is being used and how it functions.

Recommendation: Decide how you're going to decide before you do anything else.

Decide What You Want To Do

Before my involvement with RCG-I, I had been in several Pagan and feminist groups which had short lifespans. One of the things which was common among many of these failed groups was their amorphous purpose. People would have the desire to gather with others of a like mind, but after six-months or, in the best cases a couple of years, most of them dissolved.

The beginning of each of these groups was similar. Someone would bring people together and ask what it was they wanted to do. The members would dialogue about their interests, which many times, were divergent. Some in attendance found connection to spirit in scholarship, some in ritual, some in drumming, some in divination, etc. Each person came thinking the others in the group would have similar interests. Occasionally, this was true, but often it wasn't. For a time, the group members might be able to move among the interests of the people in the group, but after a few months most of the members would feel there was not enough focus on what inspired them and the group would disband.

I learned an important lesson from being a member of these groups. Decide what you want to do before you start. If, for example, you want to begin a group/organization focused on ritual, tell people before they agree to participate what the emphasis of the group/organization will be. There are many choices for spiritual groups/organizations. Book groups, a choir, a drumming circle, a dream group or many more things can be the center of a spiritual group/organization. Choose the focus of the group/organization you want to begin and tell people what the emphasis will be when you ask them to participate.

Recommendation: Decide what you want your group/organization to do/be before you start. Tell people what the group's/organization's focus will be before they join.

Delegation

Delegation requires trust that the persons with whom you share tasks will accomplish them in a way that meets the expectations of the group/organization. Sometimes I attend events where I find a struggling Pagan leader who has already been there for hours setting up. This same person is now trying to greet people at the door, finish the altar, and brew a large pot of coffee while other members of the group have nothing to do. What I often see is people who are willing to help, but are not given a chance to do so.

When I'm looking for volunteers to whom things could be delegated, I try to assess their interests and skills. I consider tasks that need to be done and ask volunteers if they would be willing to do something that falls within their skill set. For example, many people make more beautiful altars than I. So, if I'm aware someone is drawn to do that work, I ask her if she would be responsible for creating an altar. I share with her whatever guidelines the group has established for this activity. I'm always available to answer questions, but I empower her to do the work herself.

I have found most people who volunteer to do an activity will complete what they have agreed to do. However, I have observed that often they will not do it as I would have. Delegation requires I accept the way projects are done and the outcome of the work. If the end result of a project fulfills the goals envisioned for it, I have learned to deem it a success. Sometimes the results don't look like what I would have done, but what has been accomplished is another way to complete the task. When a project is over, I find ways to acknowledge and appreciate the volunteers for the work they have done.

Recommendation: *Watch for the skills and interests of the people in your group/organization and match them to tasks that need to be done. Be willing to accept that volunteers may complete a project differently than you would have, but if the outcome serves the purpose consider it a success.*

Following

Step forward when leadership is required, but also learn to be a good follower. When geese fly in a "V" formation, the lead goose provides "upwind" for the other geese flying behind. This supports all the birds that follow. But, the position of lead goose rotates regularly because flying out front causes fatigue. I think this example from nature is a good analogy for leadership.

If a volunteer agrees to take responsibility for an event or activity, I may become a follower. Following is an art and can require patience, perspective and keeping silence. If your goal is to empower the members of your group/organization, don't be afraid to let someone else take the lead.

Recommendation: *Don't be afraid to lead, and be willing to follow when needed.*

Turning Over Power

In addition to many other activities, every RCG-I Priestess has at least six years of training in Administration, Organization and Leadership. As a consequence, these Priestesses step into leadership roles with knowledge and confidence. This also means the organization can infer that the Priestesses who comprise the Congregation's committees and councils will have an understanding of what it means to hold power.

Each time a group within the Congregation establishes a stable structure, we have turned over decision-making about that group to its members. For example, when twenty-five RCG-

I Priestesses had been ordained, they began to meet together in what we call the "Priestess Assembly." In a few years the Assembly coalesced into a solid body. At that time decision-making for Priestesses was turned over to the Priestesses themselves. After several more years when the Assembly had created a structure and developed a system for administration of its funds, fiscal responsibility for the Assembly was turned over to its members.

Recommendation: Assist the people in your group/organization in learning leadership skills. As the group/organization grows, share leadership functions with others in your group/organization.

Don't Gamble

I know of a Pagan group that decided to organize a conference. They borrowed money from their credit cards and put out publicity. The members of the group were not well connected and they did not have a good understanding of how to reach the Pagan community. As a result, virtually no one attended. Now, fifteen years later, one of the leaders of that group still pays on the debt she incurred from that event.

I think many of us have dreams of what it would be like to have our own gathering, magazine or seminary. The first step in planning any undertaking is to make sure you have people that will utilize the activity/product you are envisioning. And, if you don't have the money for your undertaking, or a plan about how to raise funds, don't do it.

Recommendation: Be certain your group/organization has a way to financially underwrite whatever activities it undertakes. If what you're considering looks like an unfounded gamble, don't do it.

Remember It's Not About You

People step into leadership for various reasons, many of which will not sustain a group/organization. If you Google "Jade River" you'll find a river in China and some take-out restaurants, but you won't find much about me. But, if you look for the Re-formed Congregation of the Goddess—International you'll find pages and pages of information. If you're looking for recognition or adoration, it would be better to try another venue. The women's and Pagan communities hold their leaders to standards that are exacting and often conflicting. Being a Pagan leader should not be about finding personal friends, inspiring veneration or a cult of personality. Paganism should not be about getting others to love you, but about learning to love yourself.

Recommendation: Don't begin working as a leader in a Pagan group/organization for personal recognition.

Be Prepared To Say No

No one individual or group can meet the needs of every Pagan. Significant numbers of people who are involved in Pagan activities have many challenges. Some are marginalized and need help with basic living skills. Others have psychological issues or may be recovering from severe trauma or addiction. Unless your group's/organization's specific purpose is to work with individuals who are challenged, assess if your group/organization can sustain problematic members.

One of the most difficult, but most important things I have learned to say is "I'm sorry, we can't meet your needs." People have asked for ongoing pastoral counseling for severe mental health issues, for us to provide open-ended housing in our Mother House or to participate in all activities we provide without offering any support to the organization.

Although we have a "community support fund" which offers emergency assistance and do at times provide emergency housing to Congregation members, we are not able to offer the type of ongoing assistance offered by many mainstream religions. All RCG-I Priestesses are asked to develop a list of referrals for individuals who approach them with requests beyond our means. So, although we may need to say, "I'm sorry, we can't meet your needs." We also try to say, "Let's see if I can help you find someone who can."

Recommendation: Evaluate the amount of energy you can devote to marginalized individual/s. It's okay to tell someone that you or your group/organization cannot meet their needs. Knowing how to make referrals to community organizations and keeping these resources on hand can be useful.

Keep Your Perspective

Many times our work within the Pagan community is so engaging that we allow it to take up all of our time. Despite Pagan leaders good intentions, being solely focused on a group/organization can be detrimental. When there is a conflict or a disturbance within the group/organization, if it is your only social outlet, it can be devastating.

Doing activities and having friends that are not involved in your group/organization is a good idea. It allows one to keep perspective and remember that, in addition to Pagan leadership, there are other things of importance. Make it a priority to take a class, work on a project, volunteer, get some exercise or simply spend time with people outside your group/organization.

These activities can help support you as a leader. Having outside interests and friends is what has allowed me to keep functioning in difficult times. Some Pagan leaders burn out and retreat into solitary practice. Keeping perspective about the work you do, and the people with whom you do it, with is an important part of being a leader.

Recommendation: *Do not have your entire focus be your group/organization. Maintain some friends, interests or activities outside your group/organization.*

Being a leader in the Pagan community has been rewarding, fulfilling, and challenging and has brought with it many opportunities for growth. I have been exhilarated and also filled with deep sorrow by people and/or events in my organization. I am often asked how I've been able to keep functioning as a Pagan leader for thirty years. The answer is simple. I made a promise to do Her work. It has taken perseverance and commitment to keep my promise, but I have never regretted that this is the path to which I was called.

Section 5
Delegation and Volunteers

Pagan Volunteers:
How I Got 100 Pagan Volunteers to Show Up On Time, and Leave Happy
Diana Rajchel

Here's the main problem with the herding cats metaphor for Pagans: it's a blame shifter. By labeling a group "impossible," it divorces the person that makes such a claim from responsibility for the ensuing chaos. It also ignores the problem that usually underpins the disasters often blamed on Pagans being Pagan. Organization takes teaching, practice, and frequent updates. The skills necessary to organize any group change as culture changes. The truth is that Pagans, as a group, are no more or less difficult than any other group. Pagans in general respond well to clear communication, and most need to commit to causes that make them feel valued. These basic requirements can cross to any type of group. I suspected this truth for most of the 1990s, and when I joined the Twin Cities Pagan Pride board, I tested the theory.

In 2003, I agreed to serve as the volunteer coordinator for Twin Cities Pagan Pride. I happened to work for a nonprofit that trained other nonprofits in improving their volunteer forces. I used the tricks I learned at this job on the local Pagan community to good effect. Most of my methods still work.

It took some time, more than it should have since I often had to skip board meetings because of my job, but I made sure I got a clear and detailed description from the rest of the coordinators about their tasks. I nodded a lot. I listened carefully. I assessed who did and did not consider delegation a blow to the ego. I took advantage of my status as a community newbie: gossip has little meaning when you are still just learning names.

During my intensive questioning, I recognized two trends immediately: first, these people relied on a very small core of volunteers to do the bulk of the work, often calling on family and friends at the last minute. This made burnout and physical breakdowns a normal part of the process. Second, the more a community compares its Pagans to intractable cats, the deeper the community's mutual mistrust.

Feeling inadequate but at least able to cover the burnout problem, I cobbled together a signup list that I brought to a university-area Pagan group meeting and a few area Pagan-related events. The signup sheet stated the job, a time slot of no more than two hours, and a promise of pizza on the day of Pagan Pride. I made sure to fill the cleanup slots first. Only one slot went empty so I filled it myself.

On the day of 2004 Pagan Pride, some volunteers showed up, and some didn't, to my chagrin. Rather than rail about unreliability, I paid attention to those who did show. For them, I handwrote thank you notes, did check-ins and brought beverages, and made it a point to introduce them to each other, providing conversation starters when I could. I also put out a sign-up sheet for those who wished to volunteer at the event the following year, including a sheet for smaller fundraisers that led up to the big day. At one point, I took a nap, and I encouraged two or three other people to take naps, too.

I considered my success mediocre with a turnout around 45%, I ended up having 15 volunteers showing up that day. The nonprofit organization I worked for considered 80% the acceptable minimum. I had no idea I'd set a record for this Pagan Pride.

During post mortem, the other board members kept repeating comments about the impressive volunteer turnout. This stunned me. No one before me had employed the simple maneuvers of clear schedules, pre-identified tasks, and the promise of small rewards.

Like most Pagans my age, I'd spent most of the 90s hearing how impossible Pagans are too organize, how squirrely and over-sensitive we are, how we will follow our bliss into a burning building while leaving. While that happened a little bit during my days as a college Pagan group organizer, I always assumed we experienced less flakiness than average because we were Midwestern, my co-founder converted to Paganism long after working for the university itself, and we welcomed sympathetic and sensibly grounding Christians to our membership. The bouts of flaky often had more to do with college than they did with Paganism. Keeping consistent about our meeting place and time usually allowed all the growth needed.

Perhaps my post-collegiate attitude gave me room for the forgiveness needed to run any such group. In 2005, the Pagan Pride board enthusiastically reinstated me as the volunteer coordinator and decided to level up with the board's decision to make it a bigger event. My own ambitious goal was to recruit 100 volunteers for Pagan Pride Day.

I did it.

On that day of September, 2005, 100 Pagans showed up to volunteer, did what they agreed to do, and went on their merry ways. Many even signed up to volunteer the following year.

While going to meetings and presenting on Pagan Pride day did take a chunk of my free time, it was not the source of my success. The reason what I did worked was because I put as much time and energy as I could into continuing communication with the people that signed up.

Organizing isn't rocket science. It is labor, sometimes tedious, and sometimes fun.

Fortunately, especially for those of us comfortable with technology, we have a host of tools to automate some of the repetitive tasks. These seemingly minor, annoying activities all build a stronger core community.

Outreach

Let's say you have an event that no one knows about yet. You must do all the work: outreach, marketing, and volunteer enlistment. Even with a different person assigned to each aforementioned sector, work overlaps. You need to put together a package of tools that help you get word out about your event, and word out that you need volunteers.

Unless Witchvox.com (Witch's Voice) gets a serious update, your best bet is to use what you have at hand: your own core of friends, these days usually congregated on Facebook. For close friends, you may need to text a small group. Ask everyone working with you to do the same, and to repeat the requests every few weeks. The same laws that apply to job seeking also apply to any type of voluntarism: people find out about and join new causes after hearing about them from friends of friends much more often than they do in response to a call on a mailing list.

After you send out those first personal, word of mouth calls, follow up with the mailing lists, Facebook groups, and WitchVox listings. This will likely reach the same audience — but this way you keep their commitment in their consciousness.

Communication

The first and by far most important rule of community organizing — any community — is communication. This is not the same thing as an open forum for discussion. For event organization, clear, regular updates that keep the event in people's consciousness ensures a better volunteer turnout. Open forums can impede communication because important information gets buried under argumentative threads. Set up one-way channels that get important information such as where, when, how, why to your volunteers. Establish a second channel that allows them to chat, bond, and argue.

The following tools help you establish one way and two-way communication channels:

- Announcement email lists — rather than discussion lists
- Post cards — reminders for the analog inclined
- Bulletin board announcements
- Blog posts closed to comments
- Text message groups, especially those synched with Google calendar

Connect volunteers to these communication channels within 24 hours of signing up. Save text blasts for the seven days leading up to the event.

There's more to proper communication than knowing when and where to attend meetings. In volunteer work, it's important to make sure that the people you work with know exactly what to do before they arrive at your event. Have a list of jobs open before anyone signs up; if possible let people sign up for specific tasks. When people sign up, also let them know exactly how long they will work and at what times. It's one thing to take two hours out of a fun day, but another altogether to give it all up for the greater good. Volunteers come back when they still get to party.

Orientation

Even if you do communicate regularly beforehand, hold a special meeting just for event volunteers before the big day. This orientation session runs through rules of conduct, regulations from the government, and lets people get to know each other before the event starts. This sense of comfort and familiarity makes the anxious more likely to show up. Many people volunteer so that they can meet people, so offering small social events satisfies that desire and reaffirms the idea that they made the right choice by volunteering.

Finding the Right People

There are two approaches to finding volunteers when you operate from a specific list of jobs to do: the open invite, where anyone can sign up for any position, and the specific invite when you ask a person with unique qualifications to fill a specific role. Both approaches have their place: in specialized work, such as bookkeeping, I try to find the exact right person for the job.

For example, one year an organization I worked with needed an accountant - so I asked someone I knew personally who had a bookkeeping background. On the other hand, I take anyone willing to help with cleanup: it's the hardest position to fill and often enough the most necessary.

Add a Buffer

Always recruit a few more people than you actually need unless redundancy causes problems. You can't recruit more than one website designer—but having some extra people on table staffing or door checking shifts leaves room for error when a few volunteers inevitably have a last minute emergency. I've found that recruiting about 20% more people than I actually need evens out to the exact right amount of people I need on the day of the event. So far there has never been a situation where all the volunteers that signed up show up. If it should happen someday, there is sure to be a shortfall of volunteers elsewhere that they can fill.

Playing to Strengths

Every time you meet someone who wants to volunteer for your event, ask "What are you good at?" Follow this question with "What do you enjoy doing?" Sometimes the best place for that person isn't apparent. Often, if a person volunteers in a generic role one year, it gives you a chance to get a sense of that person and what activities best suit him or her. When the next round of volunteer assignments comes up, contact that person with a role in mind.

Offer Perks

Few people volunteer just because it's a good thing to do. That's true of any cause—from Habitat to Humanity to Goodwill, volunteers engage in the work because of something that benefits them. Sometimes that's meeting people, whether for dating or for friendship. Sometimes it serves other needs: in college, I hovered around the theater department and often helped break set at the end of a play's run because the volunteers got a meal out of it, and back then, I had no money for food. Some do it to build job skills. Others volunteer if it gives them a sense of achievement.

One area of difficulty for people in Pagan volunteer positions: they develop valid job skills in the course of their work with a Pagan organization but then can't report how they learned those skills or call on references built during that time. However, they can still benefit from references given by the people they have worked with.

There are those who believe no one deserves thanks for doing their job, and that voluntarism is its own reward, or that karma will take care of it. I think that's wrong in paid work and that outlook is dead wrong when it comes to volunteers. The average volunteer's work is valued at around $23.00 in 2014[24].

---

[24] "Independent Sector: Value of Volunteer's Time Per State." 2013. Web. August 25 2014.

Voluntarism is not organizers getting something for nothing. Repeat volunteers return when they receive a reward. The more repeat volunteers you get, the less work you need do in the following year.

There are several small things—low cost or no cost—that can reward volunteers. Discounts to the events are good motivators; often, however, festivals can't afford this. Providing meals works; having a lounge area just for volunteers also builds community while it rewards. Free tarot readings (be sure to compensate the reader!) often have specific appeal, as do small goody bags with toys or stress relievers, and hosting an after-party just for the volunteers often does much to encourage volunteering again for the next event.

Make it Cyclical

One thing that event organizers forget to do that drives me crazy: bring signup sheets to every related event you attend. If you have a table at Gay Pride, bring a volunteer signup sheet. If you give a lecture to a local Pagan group, bring a volunteer signup sheet. If you are running an annual event that you plan on happening again the following year, have sign ups available *at the event*.

A lot of people that will look at this recommendation and say, "Wow, a year is a long time."

When it comes to event planning, it's not. Organizers must book venues for events a year or even two years in advance. Competition for events and meeting space is intense, especially in heavily populated areas. A long time frame makes sudden changes much less sudden and stressful. You have an opportunity to make plans A, B, and C in case weather, life, or law forces a change in plans.

Tools to Help the Journey

There are still Pagan organizers that function best in analog, but they are unusual. Most people have some degree of Internet access and rely heavily on their own phones. Save phone conversations for night-before reminders; most people communicate by text or email because it does not take up a chunk of time the way a live conversation does.

This list of recommended organizer tools is not exhaustive: it just gives you a place to start.

Google Products

The **Google Drive** software suite now has means for publishing to the web and for embedding spreadsheets and documents on web pages. This makes it much easier to share information, such as volunteer contacts, with your other board members.

It can also make volunteer signs ups easier. If you need to post a volunteer schedule to a web page or let people access it via email, you can do so and let current volunteers check their information themselves.

Gmail itself has a feature called **"Canned Emails."** This helps with repetitive emails — such as answers to requests for how to volunteer, or a volunteer welcome email with information about staying in touch and upcoming orientations.

A plugin for Gmail called **Boomerang** lets you write emails and send them out at scheduled times. This is useful for when you have an email that must go out a few days before the event, and you can schedule these communications well in advance, leaving you free to focus on other details.

Google Calendar can be shared on and off platform, embedded in websites, and can send automated reminders to your phone. You can also send these reminders and calendar invites to a small group of people via email. For larger groups, a mailing list is still more effective.

Yahoogroups is still the most effective and affordable email group list feature. While not as popular as it once was, most people still have Yahoo IDs and understand the basics of how the listserv system works. It is possible to set up a Yahoogroup that sends announcements only; as long as the text remains the same you can use it to schedule routine reminders and messages.

All this is just a small amount of practical details that any volunteer manager can use. Often organizers end up overwhelmed — and even lost — in the personalities and conflicts, frustrated that people just won't do what you've asked them to do. Yes, this will happen in every group. In a well-organized

Diana Rajchel

group, you can reduce moments of conflict because the first point of anxiety, understanding expectations, is reduced. Pagans have these problems as much as anyone, and Pagans can equally benefit from these best practices and tools.

Sharing Leadership
Melissa Hill

Leading a Pagan group is an amazing experience. People look to you, admire you, and listen to you. The feeling that comes when someone hugs you or shakes your hand and tells you that you helped them in their life can fill you with joy for days. There is a deep satisfaction that comes from building something real that will help change our culture and our children's future.

Leadership will change you. Each experience that a person has shapes them. Each choice we make alters who we are in tiny ways. This can build over time to shape us as better individuals. We can become the best version of ourselves that we can be. There are many lessons that Pagan leadership can teach: compassion, strength, love, perseverance, public speaking, and self-confidence are just a few. At its best, Pagan leadership should be a process of transformation both for the community that you serve as well as for yourself.

Even at its best, group leadership is hard, messy and frustrating. Most likely it will be exhausting and will need to fit in around the rest of your busy life. You will still have work, kids, or significant others that need you. You may feel badgered, attacked, nagged, let down, or just plain angry.

That's part of why leadership is a medicine that is best shared with others.

Leadership is a potent transformational magic that needs to flow through a group. But how does that work? I've seen so many groups where the leader can't seem to get others to do anything. Members of the same group are frustrated with the leader because things aren't going how they want. I've seen leaders stagnate and fail, get exhausted and fail, burn out and fail. Recently I've been going through burnout myself, after being an officer in my grove for over seven years I've needed to change my relationship with the group. I didn't want to leave, but I did want to have more time for my writing and my art. So I've been working on transitioning leadership for about three years now.

I was the Chief Liturgist. In Cedarsong Grove that position is about making sure that our public high days get done. As a

Chartered ADF Grove, we are required to host eight public high days a year in order to keep our charter and church status with the IRS. So you can't mess up with this one. If you can't find someone else to lead that ritual, it's your job to plan it, find people for the parts, organize the offerings and props, make sure all the sacred items are in their places, and perform the rite.

I call this process the Six Week Countdown because there are about six weeks between each high day rite. Four years into the Six Week Countdown, my Grove voted to remove term limits in our bylaws specifically so I could keep doing the job. No one else wanted it.

I realized at that point that I needed to more actively work to help the transition occur if I wanted to eventually move on from that position. I started trying to get people more involved and discovered that some things worked better than others. Here's a short list of some of the essential processes that emerged:

- Break it down into smaller jobs.
- Let go of unnecessary expectations.
- Accept that the job will be done differently than you would do it.
- Be a mentor.
- Be aware of people's skills and needs.
- Be friendly and welcoming to new people in your group.
- Expect that the process will take a while.

Breaking it down into smaller jobs

In my case, that meant looking at our liturgical structure and finding ways to make complicated ritual pieces simpler. We have a moment called "Opening the Gates" where we use our three sacred things to create an opening to the Otherworlds. We do this so that our offerings and our voices can easily reach the ears of all the spirits and gods. It's a big thing. The magical act of creating it while simultaneously voicing the connection to the fire, well, and tree can be intense. It was one of the things no one else wanted to do. So I broke it down. One person for each sacred item, and one person to do the actual gate opening part.

Then we would rotate through so that by four rituals, one person could try each part and get the necessary experience to do the whole thing.

Letting go of unnecessary expectations

In anything we do, there are some things we're really good at and some things we're not good at. One thing I've noticed about leadership transitions is that the outgoing individual wants the new person to be able to succeed in the ways they succeeded. Most likely, that's not going to happen. When you're letting leadership go, be really brutally honest with yourself about what truly *needs* to happen versus what you would *like* to happen. They're going to have different abilities and might not want to record how many people came to every event in color coded Excel document format if they don't really have to do that. If all they need is to know how many people came to each high day they should be comfortable doing just that. Knowing what minimum expectations are can help someone feel like the job is manageable.

Accepting that the job will be done differently than you would do it

This is similar to the last idea, but is less about minimum expectations and more about getting excited about new ideas. People bring their own vision and hopes to a job. In volunteer organizations it's really important that people enjoy the job they're doing on some level, because they're not getting paid to do this stuff. By getting enthusiastically behind some of their ideas you can help to make sure they are inspired and take ownership of the job.

Be a mentor

Always think about how you can help others to gain the skills they would need to do your job. Then offer to teach them. Keep offering. There are lots of reasons they might not want to. This offering must be balanced with allowing people to say no and accepting that fully. However, sometimes people don't realize that without their help the leader will burn out and the group will eventually fail. It's important to express your own needs without whining or nagging.

When someone does want to learn a skill or take on a task, think about what you wish someone had told you before you started. Give them the leg up that you might not have had. Do your best to prepare them for the job by thinking about what challenged you and what you wish you had done better. Take some time to share that knowledge one on one. You've already put a lot of time and love into this position. It's worth it to go that extra mile and share what you've learned.

Be aware of people's skills and needs

I keep track of people. It's like baseball cards. Each person has certain stats that I observe and note, so that when a task is to be done, I have an idea of how much time they have available, what their skills are, what their emotional state is, generally how much stress is in their life, who they work well with, if they are an extrovert or an introvert, or if they respond to a logical argument or prefer an emotional one. By observing these things and keeping track of them I have a running list of likely candidates for any task that I can approach. By knowing more than one person who is a possibility, I then can stress less if someone lets me know they can't do the thing I'm asking.

Be friendly and welcoming to new people in your group

As Pagans we are often outsiders. We have felt strange and alone in a sea of conformity. It is easy to get lost in the idea of being the Outsider. It is easy to push people away because you were pushed away before. As members of a community we now are in the position where we can choose to be the outsider or be included. We have the choice to reach out to others. Remember that each new person is a potential leader. Each individual has their own gifts to offer and their own vision. It takes work to be welcoming when you have not found welcome in the past. Don't expect that it will come naturally. Do know that you can learn how to lead, and that it's worth it to do so. Be interested. Ask questions, and listen to the answers. By doing so, not only will you potentially meet some really wonderful people, you will also learn about what they may have to offer to your group.

Expect that the process will take a while

Pagan leaders work hard. The rewards are not often tangible, and the community we hope to build may take many decades to evolve. We are in the work of paradigm shifting, and we have to accept that moving mountains takes time. Be patient with the members of your group and be patient with yourself. Imagine that you are oak trees setting roots that will last for centuries. Build slowly and share what you learn. Every time you pass on skills and knowledge you have succeeded. This process of sharing skills can take time. It takes time to figure out what you have to teach. It takes time to figure out how to teach it. This process can take years.

Once you have found people who want to support their community, encouraged them, taught them your skills, and listened to their wisdom, and once they are ready to become leaders in your community, then make sure you celebrate the passing of leadership. Mark it in your rituals and honor the work that has been done and that will be done by future leaders. Take the time to thank those that come after you, and practice accepting it when others thank you. We are all pioneers, who are experimenting with ideas, and exploring new ways of thinking. Our leadership models will evolve out of our traditions and our values. By sharing leadership we can help our vision survive to be shared with future generations.

In my tradition we say, "A gift for a gift." By this we don't mean that when someone gives you something you must give something back. We mean that by giving of yourself there is an opportunity created for someone to give back to you. This openness to reciprocity is one of our sacred mysteries. Everything exists in relationship to every other thing. This relationship is called *ghosti*, which is the proto-Indo-European word that both guest and host are descended from. (Serith) The idea of *ghosti* is incredibly ancient; we don't have any records of it even existing. The asterisk in front of the word indicates that it was created by linguists comparing all the Indo-European languages, which includes English, Gaelic, Greek and even

Sanskrit. In my modern practice *ghosti* has led me to a practice of compassion and attention to both my needs and the needs of others.

So in my tradition, to share is to give someone an opportunity to be gifted to as well as to gift. To share leadership is to share a gift with your community and with the future. It is an opportunity to be vulnerable, to be wise, and to come to know yourself and those around you.

Works Cited

Hill, Rev. Melissa. "*Ghosti a Weird Word for Relationships" http://dandelionladyseeds.blogspot.com/2015/07/ghosti -weird-word-for-relationships.html

Serith, Ceisiwr. "Sacrifice, the Indo-Europeans, and ADF" https://www.adf.org/articles/cosmology/sacrifice-ie-adf.html

Serith, Ceisiwr. *Deep Ancestors: Practicing the Religion of the Proto-Indo-Europeans*. Tuscon: ADF Publishing. 2007.

A Few Good Betas
Cat

Confession time: I'm not a leader. At least, I'm not a leader in the "Alpha-Big-Name-Pagan" sense, which in truth is how most of our community sees leadership. What I am is an awesome beta leader. And it is from the perspective of being a dedicated beta that I write this article. You yourself might be a beta if you've ever said something like:

"No one volunteered to be liturgist again? Let me get out my pen."

"The rite needs a flaming spear for Lugh? Hold on, there's some papier mache, duct tape, and extra fabric around here somewhere. Oh, and a fire extinguisher."

"Joe Pagan is making you feel uncomfortable? Would you tell me about it and I'll make sure it's handled appropriately."

"Let me support you in your vision, let me help you create something magical, wonderful, grand."

Hel, we can even delegate on good days.

A healthy population of empowered betas, in my experience, makes the difference between success and failure in a group. Actually, I'd go so far as to say that what the Pagan and Polytheistic communities need are *fewer* alpha leaders—that we actually suffer from too many people grasping after Big Name Pagan status or setting themselves up as the rulers of their own very small kingdoms. The problem is not that we need newer, better, more alpha leaders (with frickin' laser beams!). The problem is that we need to support the ones we do have. This is where betas come in.

For those not familiar with the alpha/beta terminology, it arose out of the studies of animal behavioralists. Wolves are probably the most famous examples of this sort of hierarchy, but the alpha/beta/omega dynamic has been applied to other species as well, including chickens, chimps, and yes, even to humans.

We're all pretty familiar with the stereotypical alpha (or worse, wannabe alpha) in the Pagan and Polytheistic communities. Now, don't get me wrong, good alphas are definitely needed. They act as the public face of a group—having a single point of contact is a proven way to interact effectively with the broader culture. With any luck, Pagan/Polytheist leaders will also converse with heads from other spiritual traditions and with the government as necessary. Alphas spearhead events, found publishing houses, and raise temples. They have tough, tough jobs, and frankly, I don't envy them. Still, we have plenty of people queued up for alpha leadership roles.

Betas, by their very nature, are a bit more difficult to pin down. Betas aren't flashy. There's little name recognition for them. They know the rules of the group, and will enforce them equally across the board. Bearing these underlying qualities in mind, here is a quick field guide to a few of the different flavors of beta that I've encountered in my Paganistan travels.

The Second-in-Command: Often called right-hands (or left-hands if you're a Thelemite), these highly visible betas act as both assistant to and conscience for our alpha leaders. Part of that support includes calling our beloved elders on their shit—a task often easier said than done. Standing up to a misguided or mistaken alpha requires a certain strength all its own, one that is not generally fostered or recognized in our communities. A good beta must not be a yes-man or -woman to the resident alpha or Big Name Pagan. The SiC is in that rare position of being able to call out a community leader when they've violated the rules of the group. It can be with kindness and love, but it still must be done for the bonds of trust within the community to remain strong.

Sadly, these betas can get classified as suck-ups or toadies, or worse, suck-ups and toadies can be mistaken for SiC betas. The key here is that despite their focus on aiding the alpha, the second-in-command's ultimate loyalty is to the group. These betas will put the safety and well-being of the whole before their support of the alpha. Should an alpha turn bad, SiC betas will either be first in line to depose them and put a more worthy leader in their place, or lead as many people away from the toxic alpha as they can. One of the saddest things I've seen is a once-proud SiC come to terms with the fact that the alpha he supported was a narcissist. The charismatic alpha's grip on most of the group was too strong, but the SiC warned as many people as he could, and even became a founding member of an alternative group for those who wished to leave.

The Mediator/Paramedic: This is a place where beta leaders can really shine. Often, these betas are the folks that a group member or guest will feel most comfortable approaching if they have a problem. This is also the type of beta that can use the most support when they are first starting out, especially if they don't already have outside training in conflict mediation or what constitutes a reportable incident. Mediators need to learn how to receive accusations against other group members and not automatically dismiss them because of a power differential. With them rests the responsibility for ensuring that complaints are heard and survivors/victims are supported, especially if those complaints are against a community leader or BNP. Professional training in psychology or social services is a huge asset to Mediator betas.

Paramedic betas are most often found doing aftercare for particularly intense rituals. They help celebrants ground, center, and process their experience of the rite. They may also act as warders for a circle, keeping the participants physically and energetically safe. Again, training in this work from another beta is vital to the Paramedic's health and well-being. Burnout is probably highest here of any of the beta types.

The Stage Manager/House Manager: These betas most often show up in ritual situations. Just like a play, rituals have writers, actors, and (hopefully) directors. However, the positions equivalent to the stage manager and house manager are often neglected or even entirely absent. Betas inclined towards the Stage Manager role can make the difference between a smoothly-run ritual where participants are free to focus on the experience of the rite, and one where lack of preparation and Pagan Standard Time run rampant. Fire-keepers are probably the most visible and outgoing of the SM type (since celebrants setting themselves alight is usually discouraged), but many artisans can also fall into this category.

House Manager betas serve a similar function in that they tend to only be directly involved in rituals. These betas make sure everyone knows what time the ritual starts, that directions to the ritual site have been provided, and that folks are introduced to each other as they arrive. House managers may even lead an initial group meditation or team-building exercise to help establish common ground before entering ritual space. The hardest thing for these betas to do is to step up—often they want to help, but feel they are too junior in the group to make decisions.

The Editor/Project Manager: Here are the really, *really* behind-the-scenes betas. Generally they show up in larger, more established groups as administrative tasks become more and more necessary. These are the folks who run magazines, moderate the email lists, maintain the websites, and generally keep things running smoothly. They may make reservations and provide logistics for larger events. The Editor beta excels in herding cats and wrangling authors and artists towards the final goal of publication. Many of these betas come to the role naturally, being something of the "born organized" types. Delegation is an important part of their function, as well, and like the Second-in-Command, Project Managers in particular thrive on getting big jobs realized and completed.

So, what should the care and feeding of a beta look like? The first and most important thing is to realize that betas are emphatically not failed alphas. They have their own skill sets that need to be nurtured. The second thing to understand is that not all betas even want to be alphas. Sometimes a proto-alpha will take on beta-like roles as they train for a leadership position. However, it is important to remember that some betas are happy being just that: betas. Another problem is that many alpha leaders have trouble delegating. Betas, in general, are happy to take on a good portion of the workload, but they have to have permission to do so. This permission should not just come from the alpha in charge, but should be in accordance with established rules and norms of the group.

Lastly, if you are a beta, please realize that you are so important to the continued functioning of your group. You are the unsung heroes of our Groves, Covens, and Kindreds. Thank you for your service, and I hope you find the support and guidance that you need to continue doing what you do best.

Leaders Who Follow
Lisa Spiral Besnett

Apparently I'm a natural leader. At least that's what people tell me. Since I find myself often thrust into that role I've come to terms with it. Over the years I've found lots of ways to be a leader. I've had visionary ideas. I've been the one with the organizational skills. I've had the voice to carry the crowd. I've got the capacity to summarize and reframe a discussion so that it can move forward.

What I'm much more interested in is empowering others to be leaders. That's trickier. Giving up authority is not easy for anyone. It's even harder when people continue to look to you for cues, even when you've given someone else the title.

I have come to believe that the most important aspect of being in a leadership role is having the ability to follow. I have been the nominal leader in a group where a more charismatic person has actively undermined my authority. I have watched weaker leaders blossom when the more experienced leaders in the group turn their attention and trust as directed, and the rest of the group follows.

Especially in Pagan communities, leadership tends to be consensual, shared and in many ways "up for grabs." Of course there are traditions where rank and hierarchy prevail. There are places where holding eldership in the community carries the weight of authority. There are places where "known" or "Big Name" Pagans are always given authority over the local leaders. But even in these situations, leadership can shift when a strong personality steps up with an appealing vision.

Pagans tend to take our leaders in the moment, rather than in the long term. This is why it is essential for leaders as a group to support the nominal leadership. We can share that role if we are all working towards a common vision, long or short term. We will continue to build and collapse our communities if each time a new vision comes along leadership shifts and there is a power struggle for authority.

There are small ways to move a community in a direction that don't threaten existing leadership, but rather support it. There is leadership in being an advisor. There is leadership in reframing. There is leadership in being able to speak to leaders as a peer, human to human, rather than putting them on a soap box.

One of the easiest ways to be a leader who is also a good follower is to be willing to be first. This is different than needing to be first. We've all seen situations where leadership asked for volunteers or rituals where participants are invited to offer up. We recognize the "eager beavers" who need to be first, who need that spotlight. We've also seen the dead silence of reluctance to be first, and that's where leadership steps in. People who are leaders provide an example for the rest of the community, and give them permission.

I have been involved with the disability community for over 25 years. I have my own chronic issues. I have good days and bad days. One of the strongest leadership roles I have taken in my community is to sit down.

Disability awareness and need increase as the community ages. There are more and more participants who simply can't stand through an hour long ritual. There are more people who can't dance a spiral dance, especially if they are caught at the whip's end. But there is still a shame involved with needing support.

I find that if I sit down when I need to, it gives implicit permission for others to sit, or at least ask to be allowed to sit. I have attended circles where the leadership has made an effort to be conscientious. They offer a space for people to bring their chairs and sit. But the "context" of disability is not something that everyone who needs support responds to. Many people think "If I'm not in a wheelchair that doesn't mean me."

Even on good days I will sometimes take it upon myself to "be the first." I'll carry my chair to the assigned place and sit down. Most of the time, once I'm there, I will be joined by several others. They see someone who appears to be able bodied taking the space and that makes it more acceptable for them as well.

Doing this simple thing has made my local community both more aware and more responsive to the needs of less able bodied participants. Rituals tend to be planned with an eye to "take care of yourself" and "do what you can" rather than with an expectation of "everybody up." There is often a place established for participants who need to sit.

There is still work to be done. There is a difference between sitting out and participating while sitting that many people, especially those new to disability, don't seem to get. There are language issues around the word disability and around the shame. There are still community leaders who dismiss the need to accommodate.

Leadership isn't standing at the head of a parade, or at the head of a ritual, for an hour. It is a long term role with a long view and a sense of community need and willingness. It is a partnership role, both with other leaders and with the participants. It is stepping up with skills when they are needed as well as stepping back and being the example of a good follower.

Section 6
Building the Long Term Infrastructure of the Pagan Community

Age and Leadership
Annika Mongan

I have always wondered what it must have been like to be a part of the early Christian church, to meet the apostles, to see a little tribe of misfit disciples grow into a religion. I have often wished I could travel back in time, just to get a glimpse of the excitement, the challenges, and the rawness of a fledgling religion. I thought I would never know, but then I became a Witch.

It's not that I discovered a spell for time travel.

But in Paganism, I found a young religion with old roots in which many elders and founders of traditions are still alive. And we are also in a time in which our founders are aging and dying and a new generation is offering different interpretations and new ways of being Pagan. While we are culturally different, we have significant similarities with the early Christian church. Some of the letters that comprise the New Testament of the Bible were written at a time when early Christianity found itself at similar crossroads.

But we are a diverse and decentralized movement, and we have no scribes to document and critique our growth in texts that will become Holy Scriptures. We don't have (and we don't want) councils to define us. Our ideas and theologies are exchanged in the Pagan blogosphere and at festivals and conventions.

One of the best places to feel the pulse of our communities is PantheaCon, held in California every February. The programming often reflects hot topics in Paganism, and discussions take place that reverberate throughout the Pagan world for weeks and months after the convention.

Age was one of the themes that showed up strongly during the 2015 PantheaCon. Popular annual rituals were missing from the schedule because their leaders are now honored among our Mighty Dead. But there were also many new faces and a panel discussion, Turning the Wheel, which explored how to support young leaders. This is where my own struggle with age and leadership in the Pagan community began.

I came into Paganism in my early thirties after leaving behind a life as a Christian minister. Soon after finding my new path, I gravitated toward interfaith work. PantheaCon promised to be a great place for meeting other Pagans interested in interfaith work. At the Turning the Wheel panel I met student leaders in their twenties wanting to send a delegation to the Parliament of the World Religion's, a large international interfaith event. I left the panel discussion inspired and excited about networking with Pagans of all ages.

But then I went to the next event on my schedule.

I had found a listing in the PantheaCon program book labeled "Parliament for the World Religions" without any further description. I thought it would be an important networking opportunity, maybe a meet-up for potential Parliament attendees or a discussion group. I expected to meet and hopefully dialogue with Pagans from a variety of paths and a wide range in ages.

Instead, I was the youngest person in the room by a decade or two, and I could quickly see why. A presenter stood in the front of the room and narrated the history of the Parliament, leaving no room for discussion. Sometimes an audience member would interrupt the presenter with an anecdote from the 2009 Parliament or memories of the 1990s. I soon realized that almost everyone in the room had been to a previous Parliament and most of them knew each other. It felt alienating, as if I had just walked into a group of friends uninvited, so I spoke up and asked about ways to include young leaders, but I didn't feel heard.

After the event I blogged about my experience and my hopes for empowering young leaders, and I received many responses. Many young and middle-ages Pagans resonated with my reflection and shared similar experiences of their own.

But some older Pagans were quick to provide unsolicited and patronizing advice, often based on false assumptions, thus perpetuating the ageist culture I was critiquing in the first place.

Empowerment and Respect

When I wrote about making space for young leaders, it didn't occur to me that it could be interpreted as an attempt to push out older leaders. *The very idea of empowering youth was equated with disrespecting elders.* But empowerment and respect are neither mutually exclusive, nor are they scarce resources to be hoarded.

I once had the privilege of joining a magic class with students ranging in age from 23 to 87. It was incredible to work magic with those who were Pagans before I was born as well as those who were just starting out. There are challenges on both sides. Allowing the next generation to build on foundations that were carefully and lovingly laid can be a difficult rite of passage. For those just coming in, so full of energy and new ideas, it can be hard to listen and find a place in the turning of the wheel.

When I first came into the Pagan community I devoured books on Neo-Pagan history. To me it was like reading early church history and it blinded me to how young our religions still are. I was completely unprepared for *meeting* some of the "historical figures" I had read about. It was as if the apostles had stepped out of the pages of the Bible right into my hot tub to reminisce about the good old days.

I never thought I would come to know Pagan elders as teachers and some of them as friends. If I had been granted a one-stop time travel card, I would have redeemed it by going to see the beginnings of my religion, and here we are as Pagans *living* our early history.

Not many religions have the opportunity to deeply study their origins so soon after they were founded, and in some religious paths, learning about their origins is actively discouraged. We, on the other hand, have books and blogs written about our origins, archives of recordings and interviews with founders and elders, and those who still walk among us. It is true that focusing on the past and clinging to traditions can cause stagnation. But ignorance and disrespect are not the right antidotes.

While we take pride in our lack of scriptures and dogma, I hope we remain introspective about our history. Deepening our respect and gratitude for all that has gone into building this religion and community enables us to be innovative and build upon these foundations consciously. All of our new ideas are brought to life while standing on the shoulders of our ancestors.

So how *do* we empower young leaders while also respecting our elders?

The two are deeply interwoven. We respect our elders when we acknowledge their work, when we strive to understand their journey and listen to their wisdom. But we also honor them by allowing their work to continue, not as fossils to be admired, but as living and breathing traditions.

The next generation may not build upon their foundations the way older generations imagined, and allowing expectations to change can be painful. But there are times when the work of elders is best honored by making space for young leaders and the innovations they bring. A potential change in direction is scary and makes it hard to empower newcomers. But when we consider the alternative, the fossilization and atrophy of lovingly built foundations while young leaders scramble to erect new ones elsewhere, our communities are better off working through the difficulties together.

Different Kinds of Leadership

We don't have popes, deacons, pastors, vicars, or bishops. We have authors, bloggers, founders, priestesses and priests, but none have clearly defined positions of leadership. Those with published books, well-read blogs, and popular rituals—sometimes called "Big Name Pagans"—are assumed to be leaders, regardless of whether their skill with the pen or their energy in rituals translate to their ability or willingness to lead.

When we mention *leaders* in the Pagan community we picture teachers of particular traditions. But there are many different areas of leadership and not all involve teaching. When I first mentioned that I was stepping into leadership, I was told that I was rash and presumptuous, and far too inexperienced to be teaching in a Pagan tradition.

However, I never mentioned anything about teaching or asserting a position of spiritual leadership. Instead I was accepting the request to lead a particular group and to manage the logistics of the group's project. Even once I clarified that I had no intention of setting myself up as a spiritual expert, I continued to receive warnings from strangers that I was not fit to be a teacher.

Many of us come from religions in which we were taught to follow leaders who told us how to think and what to believe.

It is only natural that now we insist on being our own spiritual authority and are wary of the danger of self-proclaimed gurus. Unfortunately this has made us prone to tear down would-be leaders who are discouraged by the lack of support.

Other religions have leaders who are not providing spiritual guidance but serve by organizing events, managing the budget and books, and resolving conflict among members. Those responsibilities are often expected of our public figures, those who teach our traditions and lead our rituals, and many have burned out from the burden of being pushed into serving as administrators, event organizers, councilors, bookkeepers, and conflict managers.

Like myself, many emerging leaders, middle aged or younger, are looking to fill these roles. We are happy to leave the teaching of our traditions to our elders while being in charge of running an event or managing a group. Our styles of leadership may differ. While much of the wisdom and traditions passed down through elders is timeless, the way we implement them in our community, how we communicate and organize our groups, is changing rapidly. If we recognize the many different areas of leadership required to run a healthy community, we can avoid burnout of seasoned teachers while empowering new leaders to contribute their unique perspective and skills.

Age and Institutions

In my blog post about the PantheaCon presentation about the Parliament of the World's Religions, I mentioned my desire to see more young Pagans in interfaith work. In response I received comments attributing the absence of young Pagans to a lack of Pagan institutions that could provide financial support. Economic constraints and the need for better institutional support was also mentioned as a hindrance to young leaders at the panel discussion Turning the Wheel.

All of the comments came from an older generation of Pagans arguing the need for Pagan institutions for the *sake of the young*.

At the same time, elders lament the lack of institutions for themselves: communities to retire in, land to bury the dead. Elders longing for institutions for the aging as well as for the sake of the young. But what do young and middle-aged Pagans themselves want?

I know what we do not want. We do *not* want to see our Paganisms go the way of Christianity. We do *not* want paid clergy telling us what to believe. We do *not* want to sit in pews and listen to someone preach. But what about institutions that help us address issues of justice? Every year since I have attended PantheaCon the programming includes more offerings centered around issues of justice. In 2015 we had panels on racism, ageism, cultural appropriation, and capitalism.

As a young white person in a stable economic position with decent health and a very supportive community, I enjoy a high level of privilege. This means that I am not personally in need of Pagan institutions that offer scholarships, or that work for better accessibility at events, or that provide various forms of advocacy. Many Pagans younger than myself — or older, for that matter — are not so privileged. For instance, scholarships for young Pagans, which could enable some up-and-coming leaders to attend conventions and important events, are rare in our communities. At the same time, we have elders who served the Pagan community their whole lives but cannot afford to retire. Many rely on secular or Christian institutions as they age and will receive Christian funerals and burials.

Interestingly, the first institutions the early Christian church built were not churches. For more than three centuries, Christians met in homes, catacombs, or privately owned spaces. A few decades after Pentecost, i.e. the founding of the Christian church, institutions were built to benefit those in need, both Christian and otherwise. In the early days Christian institutions fed the hungry and clothed the poor — a community working together for justice, with no thought of domes or crystal cathedrals.

It is these kinds of institutions that I would like to see us build in our Pagan communities. Those who are well-off, able-bodied, and otherwise privileged may not need them, but we need them if we are to form communities that care for each other. I long to see Pagan eco-villages where our elders can retire and our young can grow up supported. I want to see us offer more scholarships for events and classes for those in need. I want to see us sponsor leadership training for new and young leaders. I want to see more places where we can bury our Beloved and Mighty Dead.

And yes, I want to see paid clergy, but not for imposing rituals on us, preaching or instilling doctrine. Leading ritual, preaching, and teaching are only aspects of what clergy practice in other religions. Clergy are also trained in leadership skills, mediation, and counseling. Those of us who can afford to do so pay for trained psychotherapists, so why not pay for spiritual counseling to support us (if we want it) *and others* in times of need? We may be able to find support from our friends or pay our therapist, but what about those in prison, in hospice, the homeless, traumatized, and poor?

Institutions are scary. The very word produces a knee-jerk reaction in many of us. We have seen them oppress, fossilize, and become irrelevant in other religions. It seems that we are even beginning to see the same within some of the few Pagan institutions we have. When organizations are preoccupied with reciting the achievements of their past, their descriptions read more like tombstones than invitations into living and thriving communities. But we have also seen new groups form, grow, and flourish, and then fall apart suddenly and painfully when their founders burn out or move on. Neither approach is sustainable.

If we are to build institutions that last, we need to learn from elders who have succeeded and failed and succeeded again. And we need to listen to younger generations, their needs, their ideas, their unique ways of expressing their Paganisms and support and empower them to step into leadership.

Building healthy institutions is shadow work. We have plenty of examples of oppressive and toxic institutions in our overculture. For us to succeed in re-envisioning and building healthy and sustainable communities of justice and empowerment, we will need all the collaboration we can get, of the old, the young, and of all of us in between.

No Free Lunch:
Building Community Has its Costs[25]
Rev. Dr. Karen Tate

Growing into being a Goddess Advocate I constantly heard about the need to build community, to have a temple, a physical space we could call our own. To some it could take the form of an outdoor space. Others wanted a brick and mortar building housing a school and healing center. And while some were against anything resembling organized religion, still others dreamed of buying an apartment complex or retreat center where the like-minded might live together and be mutually supported by community. Desire aside, with the exception of temples like the Goddess Temple of Orange County in southern California that runs 24/7 and a handful of others across the country and globe, our dreams rarely manifested. So if religious faith is often the foundation for building a community, let's examine if there are clues as to why it might be particularly hard for Pagans to move beyond small covens, circles, living rooms and the annual Pagan Pride event to build thriving communities. Let's start by first looking at a list of what I call the Big Picture Challenges we face.

So, if religious faith *is* the foundation for community, what happens when we don't have a universal liturgy, creation myth or a sacred text that unifies and provides cohesion for our beliefs? I've heard people leaving Goddess Spirituality or Neo-Paganism because they thought it lacked substance or they couldn't recognize its relevance in today's world. Rarely do we take our myths and use them to teach values for living. So finding Paganism lacking, they instead gravitated toward religions or spiritualities providing more organization, structure, meaning, and rules beyond following a Wheel of the Year or the Wiccan Rede. They often feel many of our groups do not teach much about what it means to be spiritual, or have healthy boundaries, or reflect upon if we're acting ethically. Believe what you will about the Emperor Theodosius I, but when he used

---

[25] Excerpted from Goddess Calling; Inspirational Messages and Meditations of Sacred Feminine Liberation Thealogy

Christianity as a glue to solidify the kingdom, (no, it wasn't Constantine as so many believe) he realized the importance of a common belief or thread to weave together disparate factions. And though most of us might hate religious dogma and value independent thinking, obviously it has its advantages over sectarian separatism.

Continuing along the lines of separatism, the mystery religion of Mithras, so popular in Imperial Rome, was quite the challenge to Christianity; however, one reason cited by some scholars for the religion not becoming more influential was women were excluded. When our goddess or Pagan groups are segregated by gender, do we not run the same risk? Women only groups take a particularly hard hit when you consider women still unfortunately make less money than men, therefore have less discretionary income, and it does cost money to build a viable community. So are women-only communities a recipe for failure when one also considers a woman cannot include her husband or male children in her spirituality, calling into question how deeply she can commit to the community, and does that not also hurt the community's long term sustainability? And some might question if it's ethical, spiritual, or wise to build a community based on what some see as sexist or discriminatory foundations.

I believe another major factor contributing to why we do not have larger communities is we do not use *fear to motivate*. No fire and brimstone and warnings of what might befall us if we are not baptized or accept a particular god as our savior. **So there's no penalty for not being Pagan.**

Next are our visibility issues. Where are the Pagan soup kitchens and missionaries visibly doing good works in the community to elevate Paganism and share the wisdom within? With the exception of a mere handful of leaders on the national and world stage, where are the pied pipers extolling the benefits of Paganism and advocating for Goddess ideals and values being the answer to many of humanities woes? Yes, we are at the Parliament of World Religions now, and we've recently won a spot at the table at the American Academy of World Religions, but why are there not more of us activated on the front lines fighting as Pagans for Gaia, religious tolerance, partnership, justice, peace, and human rights?

No doubt, it is because we have not yet won the battle of perceptions. Let us start by considering if our very labels need rehabilitation. The term Pagan is considered by many a term of derision used by Christians - a linguistic tool of persecution. A slanderous and a pejorative term for polytheists. Christian propaganda has similarly tainted the titles witch and priestess. And this insidious propaganda continues to exist. It is hard for some of us to come out of the broom closet and tout our beliefs without fear of some retribution because the very term Pagan has become so demonized or misunderstood in too many circles. Many of us do not or cannot use our own names publicly. We have to be careful not to have our photo taken at Pagan events and often with good cause. We all know that Christians have infiltrated all levels of government and public office. This often results in discrimination that sometimes makes getting 501c3 not-for-profit status, custody of children, housing, or even jobs more difficult if you are Pagan. When you consider these facts, no wonder we keep a low profile.

But being silent and not stepping up has its price too. It costs you in the allies you might never partner with and it costs you the understanding you might never *seed*. I don't think I'm the only one who watched the religious intolerance toward Muslims recently and did not think that backlash could so easily turn on us if some unbalanced Pagan did something stupid and it got national attention. We lack much-needed robust megaphones so we control our own messaging and not let other faiths dictate who we are to the rest of the world.

Another element, a double-edged sword if you will, both positive and a hindrance, is our belief we do not need any intermediary to access the Divine, hence, less need perhaps for an organized career clergy. That can result in no one stepping up long term, 24/7, professionally, taking on the mantle of spiritual leader or visionary to advance the community. There is also the perception among non-Pagans we have no clergy. How many have had difficulty ministering to the sick in hospitals or attracted curious looks when you've presided over handfastings, marriages or burials in public places?

Then there's money. My experience has been few Pagans seem to understand the importance of reciprocity or believe in tithing or donating toward the growth of a community or temple, while other faiths require congregants donate a portion of their income to their church. Period.

Which brings me back to our lack of physical brick and mortar temples, schools or healing centers. It's a Catch 22. If we are not visible in the community, if we do not appear to be in the legitimate business of religion with a center or place of worship on street corners, how can we expect to attract not just more congregants to carry out the work and pay the bills, but equally important, wealthy benefactors who might make healthy donations? If we are not perceived as credible and legitimate organizations, yes, even recognized by the government so that donors can receive tax deductions for their donations, then we also aren't eligible for all the help and tax benefits other religious groups enjoy. Just being associated with a recognized or traditional religious institution makes all the difference in so many practical ways, so we must realize the credibility bar for Pagans is so much higher to clear.

The City University of New York did a poll that showed when the many hybrids of goddess-oriented or earth-based spiritualities were grouped together, it was one of the fastest growing groups in the United States.* However, how many within these numbers actually take our faith seriously enough to make Goddess ideals, such as ecofeminism, equality, peace, nurturing, partnership, and fairness, to name just a mere few, integral to their everyday lives? And might there be some issues inherent to Pagan communities that never cause a problem in Christian churches, namely, the people curious about learning to manipulate energy and do magick. I hear complaints all the time that classes on sex magic, love spells, or prosperity rituals are guaranteed to fill while classes on service, ethics, politics and herstory are less likely to draw students. Another problem I doubt Christian communities face is that younger people don't join the neighborhood Church for shock value or to rebel against authority. I also suspect people come to Goddess church, or rituals, to be entertained, not do their spiritual work or learn a morality tale.

Taking this a step further, as Pagans, do we understand what it means to reconcile our spirituality with our politics and reflect those Goddess ideals in our choices, including in the voting booth? Do we believe it's important to have our values and beliefs recognized and our voices a part of a larger national dialog? Do many Pagans realize Goddess ideals offer a roadmap for a sustainable future? **We have a lot to do in the way of providing a baseline for education among Pagans everywhere.**

Now let's take a look at what questions we might ask before building a local community.

First, we will have to define what we mean by community. Who is in the community? How wide are we casting the net? Will we include all genders? Progressive Christians? Environmentalists? How will you recruit members? Will you actively seek out angels or benefactors? Will you buy or rent meeting space? Can you pay for all the peripheral costs involved?

How will your presumably legal religious business be structured? Hierarchy? Partnership? Council? Dictatorship of a charismatic leader? Rotation of leadership? Consensus or majority rule? Will you be a religious or educational entity?

What is the mission, ethics and vision of the community? Will you have a school and seminary? What will you teach beyond Wicca 101? Is it important to try to provide childcare and elder care? Do you have enough reliable and capable people to handle the teaching, administration, and spiritual guidance? Will these people receive a salary?

What is the responsibility of members? Will they be required to tithe? Teach? Volunteer? Attend classes on history, ethics, partnership and how to do their spiritual work? Will there be an ethical and fair way to work our grievances among members? Will your community try to be active in the greater community?

Will you have professional, career clergy? What will be their responsibility to the community and will they be monetarily compensated?

So there's a lot to think about. Some believe Pagan communities are in their infancy. There are not yet sufficient numbers of us to accomplish building such thriving and service-oriented communities. But we are making progress. We must remember Christians started long ago meeting in living rooms much like many of us do. They did not always wield the power and influence we see in their hands today. In fact, we might remind ourselves, there were no doubt times when they wondered if their fledgling faith might survive at all.

And our numbers are growing. The idea of the Sacred Feminine is becoming more mainstream everyday creating possibilities for many partnerships. Women's issues, very much a part of the politics of Goddess Spirituality, are on the radar screen of governments and organizations across the globe and have been cited as the moral imperative of our time. Progressive Christians are helping us fight the fight for a feminine face of god in liturgy and churches.

If we want to build a community that grows beyond our individual broom closets, covens, and annual Pagan Pride events, we must recognize there is a cost for this security and comfort. And Mother Nature, She provides the template, showing that ensuring a bountiful harvest to get us through both fat and lean times does not happen without work and a healthy respect and interdependence between human and Mother Earth. Nor does it happen without reciprocity. To grow a community, we must **plan** and **plant** and **tend** the **seeds** if we expect our garden to flourish. These seeds are our investments in the community and take the form of contributions by many in teaching, cooperation, thoughtfulness, tithing, energy and dedication. But first we must see if the land is fertile before we plant. We must ask, do we have the right ingredients in the necessary amounts and the knowledgeable farmers to cultivate our community? Are we willing to grow up, move beyond "Pagan time" and our infamous "herding cats" work ethic to move toward having a growing and sustainable community based on Goddess ideals?

These are just some of the considerations and questions we must ask ourselves and reflect on as we consider if the effort required will net a large enough return on our investment. One thing is for sure, there is no free lunch because building a community has its costs.

Only time will tell if we are going to grow into a movement that will help save the world and make our Mother proud. Only time will tell if we will be the instruments of her Sacred Roar.

End Note: The 2001 American Religious Identification Survey by the City University of New York

Section 7
Conflict Resolution and Dealing with Crisis in Groups

The Symptoms of
Second Degree Syndrome
Romany Rivers

Relationships between students and teachers are filled with peaks and valleys, plateaus, and tipping points. The journey is never smooth and unchanging; it is a cross country hike filled with challenge and beauty. The first year or so is always filled with great energy and enthusiasm, both student and teacher getting to know each other, exploring the path together, taking in the views and sharing the wonder of the world. There may be a few stumbles, a few occasions where students stray from the path prepared for them or when teachers stride ahead unaware of the student's difficulty navigating the terrain. Over time each challenge is met. Those who stumble are dusted off and helped to their feet; those who wander too far called back. As the journey unfolds, the path opens up to reveal all that we have already experienced and offer tantalising glimpses of future mysteries.

Then we reach our first peak, and our first major tipping point. The relationship changes. The teacher points the way down into the valley, deep into the darkness, and the student faces what lies before them. The teacher becomes the mentor, no longer paving the way but instead offering encouragement to the student as they pick their way carefully into the unknown. The student may stumble, slide, or fall and the mentor encourages them to get back up. The student may turn away from the difficult path and the mentor simply points the way back down. The student, once so comfortable on the path, may become fearful of the journey, tired of the journey or resentful of the difficulties. The mentor becomes the target of the student's frustration.

For those who follow the format of degree training, this tipping point most often occurs during the Second Degree, hence my fellow high priestess and I coined the phrase Second Degree Syndrome. The First Degree is the foundation of learning, most often the discovery of skills, techniques and traditions and the understanding of Divinity, of magic, of interconnectedness, of the Elements, of the power to create change.

The Second Degree is the point when that understanding moves from external knowledge to internal understanding. It is the time when we face the deepest parts of ourselves, when we uncover the truth of our actions and realise the reality that we create for ourselves. It is when the Divine becomes more real and manifest, far beyond hope, belief, and honor, and into a deep personal relationship.

It is most often when our lives get turned upside down and inside out that we shed our old skins and birth ourselves anew. The Second Degree is filled with challenge and change, and it is a very solitary journey even when learning within a group or coven.

The mentor steps back, no longer walking ahead and showing the way. The mentor may walk behind us or beside us, but it is up to each individual to find their own way into the deepest parts of themselves. This role change from teacher to mentor is necessary for the student to fully find their feet, but it can create a lot of tension and unpleasantness. When working one on one in an apprenticeship format, this tipping point may appear gradually and the relationship can keep its integrity through conscious awareness.

However, when working within a group, the tipping point can feel sudden and unpredictable. Several students can reach the same peak at the same time facing the same descent, and when one student moves over the tipping point they can grab all the others and take them with them. Instead of a gradual change in relationship with just one individual who can be given the time and energy to help them through the challenges, the mentor can now be faced with several students on an internal descent at the same time.

The personal issues and challenges raised during the Second Degree can be magnified as each student's issues collides with everyone else's issues, and like a snowball effect the more issues are raised, the faster the whole group descends, collecting more issues en route, moving faster and faster, out of control. This can lead to anger, hostility, resentment, in-fighting, lack of communication, challenges to authority or authenticity of the teachings, abuse of other students or the mentors, and unhealthy behaviour patterns that impact each individual's personal lives.

This is an unhealthy dynamic, and a hard one to bring back into balance. Having taught students one on one previously, we raised the topic of Second Degree Syndrome with our first large teaching circle. Even having discussed the potential problems, I was still overwhelmed at the incredible impact of many students going through the same experience at the same time. It was hard to spot the symptoms as they manifested because each student fed off of each other.

When I used a direct challenge to break up the behaviour of my first teaching circle and bring their focus back to their own personal journeys, I was surprised to find out that many of them did not even remember the discussions we'd had previously on the potential effects of Second Degree Syndrome. Interestingly, the few students that had avoided being dragged into the sliding group dynamics were the students who clearly remembered this discussion and had been consciously working to avoid being drawn into another's drama.

I was also surprised to find how much the hostility and aggression of the group impacted my own health and well-being. It raised deep seated issues for me that I had to face and deal with, whilst still attempting to mentor several people in challenging circumstances. Needless to say, this experience can be hard for both student and mentor, but as the group leader it is the mentor's role to encourage the relationship back into balance and work with all parties to resolve the conflict.

We cannot find a solution if we are not aware there is a problem. Therefore awareness of the symptoms of Second Degree Syndrome is important.

Cliques

We noticed that students would group together or pair off. Whilst this can be helpful in training, the same students constantly interacting with each other often resulted in issues being reflected back between them. One student, disgruntled with their journey, would seek affirmation and vindication through their clique, which in turn raised issues within those people or encouraged those people to fall into the same mindset regardless of where they were on their own journey.

Cliques also created tension with other students in the

wider group. Some students would feel isolated and pushed out of the community, some would fall into the 'us and them' mentality, and others would face playground politics as the popular and unpopular school kids' scenario was raised. Breaking up the cliques burst the bubble of security and affirmation that these students craved, exposed them to alternative situations and different mindsets, and slowed down the impact of students feeding off of each other's personal fears and issues.

Punctuality

Students experiencing Second Degree Syndrome would suddenly start arriving very early or very late to organised events and classes. Early attendees were unlikely to help out with the setup, would demand one on one attention prior to other students arriving, or would be verbally and energetically disruptive whilst mentors tried to organise and set up for the class. I personally found this very difficult as the time prior to the class or event was time I spent space clearing, creating an energetic environment to work within, centring and balancing myself, and creating a little 'down time' between my day to day life and my role as mentor. The presence of a student, especially one unwilling to participate in set up, created tension, a sensation of being rushed, and they generally invaded my personal space.

It also put other students on the back foot when they arrived, creating the feeling that they were either late and therefore flustering them, or making them feel as if they were not privy to something or being excluded from something important.

Students who arrived late would often disrupt the energy of a class already underway or would expect everyone else to await their arrival. Their presence would create delays in class content, would pull the whole group's attention towards them, and would feed their desire to be important within the group.

Starting early in the training process, be consistent and make sure that expectation of punctuality is reinforced. Lock the doors if necessary; prevent students from arriving early or late. Build a window of arrival time into class or events and give time for students to settle in, but beyond these fifteen minutes or so, make sure that students are turned away. We found that by instilling this expectation from the very beginning of the relationship, by the time that a student hit the Second Degree the idea of punctuality and the consequences of early or late attendance were fully integrated.

Of course, we still had the occasions where students arrived early or late due to life circumstances, but they usually called ahead to ask permission and we worked around that. Those who did not notify us were expected to wait outside or were turned away from class. We did lose a few students from this strict policy, but on the whole we found it created a better working environment for the rest of the group.

Interruptions and Challenges

Another common symptom is that of continual and increasingly aggressive challenges and confrontations within the group. We held an expectation that our students would challenge us as mentors and challenge the content of the classes in order to fully understand their own experiences, and healthy debate was always encouraged. However, we found that some students would become more aggressive in their challenges, talking over the mentor or other students, interrupting people as they discussed personal experiences, and raising topics outside of the current content in order to create conflict. Again, this form of behaviour constantly pulls the attention of all the other students back to one person, undermines the authority of those with experience, and challenges the authenticity of another's personal experience by demeaning the individual or criticising their spiritual understanding. This is potentially very damaging behaviour for other students, and this kind of hostility and aggression needs to be stopped as soon as it is seen.

It is advisable to create good ground rules for respecting those talking, teaching, listening, or raising questions from the very start of any group work. When personal experiences are discussed, a 'no interruption policy' should be put into place— using a talking stick if needed—to clearly define the roles and responsibilities of those talking and listening. (Mentors may have to learn the art of keeping those with a talking stick on track, curbing excessive talkers and making sure that everyone gets equal opportunity to speak.) Students who fail to adhere to the rules of respecting others must be spoken to privately and the expectation of their behaviour must be made clear.

It is not unusual for the most aggressive students to believe that by pulling them aside you, as the mentor, are targeting them, and this can be difficult terrain to navigate. Some students will believe that you target them because they challenge your authority or authenticity and this can feed into a delusion of importance — that they are right and you are wrong, that they have more experience and understanding than you, and that you fear them and their role within the group. Whilst some students with this mentality can be talked to and the conflict resolved, the most aggressive ones may have issues far beyond your role as a mentor and may require more specialised assistance. In this case, I would advise removing them from the group as the dynamic they create could be very harmful to others, and I recommend, where possible, additional support and services for them.

Withdrawal

In direct contrast to the overt signs of Second Degree Syndrome, another symptom is withdrawal. These students will withdraw into themselves, become uncommunicative, stop sharing their thoughts and feelings, and use their silence as a method of gaining personal attention. Body language can appear defensive, arms crossed across the chest, muscles tense, a lack of eye contact, and requests for participation met with shrugs or outright refusal. This is a difficult one to spot because it is not uncommon for someone to process deep spiritual or personal issues by withdrawing into themselves. Sometimes the only way that we can work through our experiences is by turning down the volume on the rest of the world and focusing on that quiet inner voice.

Students in this phase need attention and support so that they know they are not alone whilst they work out their issues. However, it can be easy to feed into the Second Degree Syndrome unintentionally. Students in personal process can be talked to and supported, but those with SDS feed on your energy and attention without making any effort to actually acknowledge or move through their issues. This detracts attention and energy from other students and can negatively impact the energy of the mentor.

The two undercurrents we discovered in withdrawn SDS students were resentment and externalisation of issues. These students have a tendency of blaming any personal issue or life challenge on external forces or other people (especially the mentor), and will not accept responsibility for their actions nor the consequences of their actions. Their resentment manifests in response to anyone appearing to be successful, happy or in control, or of anyone who is perceived of as getting more attention from the mentor or other students.

This form of SDS is usually only discovered once the mentor uses one on one techniques to uncover the reason for withdrawal. Private time away from the group can be a delicate balancing act between providing enough support to the student that they will work through their issues, and so much support that the student feeds off of the attention.

Firm boundaries for private sessions and one on one time must be established, and private time away from the group must be limited to avoid raising additional issues within the group or creating an expectation of the mentor to be 'on call' for certain students. Encourage withdrawn students to journal regularly, to get what is in their head out onto paper and to curb the potential build up of resentment. If the student shows a resentment of the mentor, consider reaching out to another leader or teacher to act as a mediator.

Power Plays

Power plays come in all forms, are very abusive, and can cause an otherwise healthy group to implode. We have witnessed students manipulating others, spreading gossip, creating their own 'secret' groups based on the teachings of our tradition, overtly challenging mentors, giving ultimatums to mentors and students, and generally trying to usurp positions of authority within the group.

I have one piece of advice for these kinds of SDS students — *cut them loose*.

We have tried to work with students displaying these

behaviours, knowing that they are revealing deep issues and often pulling shadow aspects to the surface. However, as a mentor or leader, we must consider the impact to the well-being of the entire group. The success rate of turning around an abusive member of the group is slim, and the energy it takes to do so means that the mentor has far less energy, time, and resources to support the growth and well-being of other students.

The risks of allowing someone who is obviously using power play techniques to continue and participate are too high. The damage that can be wrought from manipulating other students, who are often facing a challenging part of their own personal and spiritual journey, is too great. If you find yourself dealing with a student displaying this form of SDS, make the decision to stop the harm. By all means, pull the student to one side, highlight their behaviour and hope for change—give them a three strikes rule if that helps to define boundaries and expectations. However, don't shy away from making the tough call—if their behaviour does not change, remove them from the group.

Dealing with Second Degree Syndrome can also raise issues in the mentor or leader of the group. It takes a measure of awareness to observe your own personal responses to students with SDS, and to make sure that your responses are not enflaming the situation. Power plays, abusive behaviour and constant challenge and criticism can lead to emotional problems, feelings of doubt, inadequacy, insecurity, or increased defensiveness and anger.

Working with students in a one on one basis can give both student and mentor time to process any issues that arise, but the demands of working with a group can mean that there simply isn't enough time or energy to deal with every situation effectively. Learn to get support, seek counsel with other leaders and make sure that you, as a mentor, are getting enough time away from the situation for your own health and well-being.

Overcoming Second Degree Syndrome

The first step to overcoming SDS is to acknowledge that it is, to some degree, a natural part of the process of spiritual training.

There comes a point in a student's training when they must not only face their deepest issues, destructive behaviour patterns, and discordant energy, but also come to the understanding that their teachers, mentors, leaders and elders are in fact human with their own journeys, their own issues, and their own unique experiences and understanding. Realising that the people teaching you are also learning and are a work in progress just like you can be a shocking experience for some students, and can dramatically alter the student/mentor relationship.

An altered relationship, a change in behaviour, and some challenging experiences are to be expected as a part of the continual journey of self-awareness, spiritual understanding, and personal growth. Discussing the possibility of these experiences with students ahead of time allows for concerns and questions to be raised, and also helps to plant the seed of awareness within the students mind that will grow into understanding as and when the Second Degree Syndrome manifests.

Be aware of when changing behaviour and personal issues start to affect the group dynamics. Reach out to other teaching circles, covens, or groves for some external help and support in recognising the process of typically fleeting vs. potentially damaging SDS. We got excellent help and support from other groups who shared their own understanding of this challenging time in a student's development.

Regardless of how their training was structured, most other leaders and teachers immediately recognised the symptoms we were describing and shared their techniques for dealing with SDS in both individual and group context. Support from other groups outside of our own tradition also assisted us, as mentors, to step back from the issues and challenges, and to be conscious of not internalising the problems as they arose.

Guest Speakers

Bring in guest speakers and leaders of other traditions to provide different teaching styles, specialist content, and alternative perspectives for your students. A shake up in energy and removing focus from a sole mentor or teacher is a great way to break through the barriers of withdrawn or aggressive students whilst also providing potential resources for future growth. Having access to another leader can be invaluable in highlighting difficult group dynamics or behaviour patterns that the usual mentor may not have noticed, and it also provides support to the mentor or teacher by bringing in the benefit of external awareness. Having a support network of other experienced teachers and leaders can be beneficial for the mentor that needs to discuss issues personally, and can also provide good mediators for student/mentor private discussions.

Roles and Responsibilities

Give new roles and responsibilities to students. Many students experience SDS because of a need for control, often sparked by challenging life circumstances that make them feel as if they have no control. They become attention seeking and demanding, but this can actually be useful. Delegating set up, clean up, food preparation, or altar preparation duties to individual students can create a sense of control and responsibility, and foster a better understanding of the work 'behind the scenes'.

It can also give them the one on one attention they are seeking and provide space and time to discuss issues away from other students. Creating altars or being responsible for cleansing and preparing a group space offers the student the chance to connect with the Divine within, provides time to be calm and centred prior to class, and reduces the desire to manipulate the environment since it is an environment they helped to manifest.

Boundaries and Expectations

Develop boundaries and clear expectations from the beginning of your teacher/student relationship, and keep affirming and revisiting those boundaries throughout the relationship. Make clear and easy to follow rules about respecting other people's space, personal understanding, and contributions, as well as practical rules about punctuality, presentation and participation.

Some groups, especially in spiritual contexts, resist the idea of too many rules believing that they stifle the journey and personal experiences of the student; however in my experience rules are important. They create a foundation of understanding and discipline, and a framework that keeps everyone within the group safe from abuse. Abusive behaviour is never acceptable, and having clear rules about behaviour allows both student and mentor to know exactly what the consequences are for those who threaten the health and well-being of other individuals or the group as a whole.

Removing Members

Don't be afraid to make the tough decision to cut people loose. Recognise that not every student will continue their journey along the same path, and sometimes people must part ways. If a student starts displaying some of the symptoms of Second Degree Syndrome, consider providing one on one sessions to talk them through it and raise their awareness of their behaviour, or even call in another leader to act as mediator.

When you get to the point of witnessing a student that needs specialist support, therapy or counseling, make the effort to redirect them to appropriate support services and limit their access to the group teachings until they have a chance to work through their issues with a professional. If their behaviour threatens the safety of others, then remove them immediately. Do not be complicit in a culture of harm. Be strong enough to stand for a culture of integrity and honesty.

Self Reflection

Take a good, long look in the mirror and be very aware of your own behaviour. Lead by example and encourage the students to examine their own emotional responses to challenges and changing group dynamics. Seek additional support for your own health and well-being and remain conscious of the impact of giving too much time and energy without refilling your own well of wisdom.

Final Thoughts

Overall, the Second Degree Syndrome has a dramatic impact on group dynamics, but on a purely individual basis it can actually have some interesting benefits. When a student experiences SDS, they are bringing a huge amount of deeply buried issues to the surface at the same time which, although difficult to deal with, allows for a better understanding of oneself, of past patterns of behaviour and of repeated issues in personal, professional and spiritual relationships.

Like a violent storm, it is possible to get through SDS without any major damage and once the storm passes the air can feel much clearer. As with many situations in life, the trick is to be prepared. Prevention is better than a cure, so establish good boundaries early on and make sure everyone is aware of the potential impact from delving into the studies of the Second Degree. Be aware of the symptoms, start treatment early and get specialist or additional support if needed. Be prepared to cut out people who are causing harm to others, and act quickly and consciously to stop SDS spreading throughout a group.

Remember that you are not immune to the effects, and be aware of your own well-being. Above all else, use SDS to pass on an invaluable teaching to all your students: *Physician, heal thyself.*

Avoiding Demagoguery through Self-Differentiation: Avoiding Triangulation
Rev. David Oliver Kling

I don't believe I had ever heard the word "demagogue" before until someone called me one. After the confrontation in which I was called a demagogue, I had to go and look up the definition on Google and it came up with, "a political leader who seeks support by appealing to popular desires and prejudices rather than by using rational argument." To this day, I still struggle with what the implications of that accusation meant in the heart of the one who flung it at me.

Since that woeful day, I have felt it necessary to reflect upon my leadership style and work to develop my abilities as a leader in the hopes that I can avoid conflicts where epithets are issued indiscriminately. Throughout my varied experiences as a leader I have made mistakes, and it is through critical reflection of the self that we can learn how to develop into better leaders. The purpose of this essay is to provide the results of my reflections from my own leadership experience and offer these insights using Family Systems Theory as the reflection point in transitioning into good leadership practices.

Family Systems theory is a way of looking at behavior by focusing on the family "system" in which a person functions. Culbertson writes, "In systems thinking, a person is not a freestanding, constant entity but achieves her or his nature of the moment through interaction." Another way of looking at Family Systems theory is by looking at each "group" or "sub-group" in whom an individual belongs as an emotional system and the emotional state of each person within that system affecting the other people within that system. The anxieties of one individual within a system affect others within the system and systems tend to strive, knowingly or unknowingly, for homeostasis or harmony — often a dysfunctional harmony but harmony nonetheless. In this essay I will focus on the negative effect of triangulation and the benefit of self-differentiation.

Leadership Examples

The following four leadership examples reflect a time span of about sixteen years of leadership experience:

Example One (e.g.1)

At one point I was high priest of a closed Wiccan coven and Senior Druid of an ADF grove. I felt more invested in the grove because it was public and we served the community. I was getting burned out hosting coven "Wicca 101" every Friday night for several years and couldn't keep investing in both a coven and a grove. Doug and Susan, a couple and members of both the coven and the grove, approached me with concerns they had with Toby, my wife at the time. They both wanted to distance themselves from her and no longer wanted to remain in the coven but wanted to continue their involvement in the grove. Susan was the one who had the issue with Toby, and she had pulled Doug into the situation instead of talking directly to Toby. Likewise, Susan and Doug both approached me with their concern.

I knew that their leaving the coven would devastate Toby so instead of encouraging Susan to talk directly with her I came up with a "plan" to solve the problem and keep everyone friends. Since I had been focusing less and less on the coven I suggested to Toby that we disband the coven and focus on the grove. She was livid with the prospect of dissolving the coven and she eventually discovered the "plot" to dissolve the coven as a means of covering up the conflict that Susan had with her and I was eventually put into a position where I had to side with my wife. I lost two friends who had been important to me, and ultimately the marriage eventually failed.

Example Two (e.g.2)

This example occurred a few years after e.g.1. I was serving as Chief Druid of an AODA grove and it was right after our Yule ritual. We had just had a Sumble, a Norse ritual involving toasts and alcohol. After the Sumble I was talking with Robert, the grove treasurer. Robert was about twenty years older than I. He was someone whom I looked upon with deep respect as a fatherly figure in my life. During our discussion, he kept saying that we should require two signers for our checking account. Up to this point he and I were the only people who could withdraw money from the grove's checking and savings account but we could both sign individually. He wanted it changed to require both of our signatures.

I thought it was convenient having the treasurer write all of our checks himself and didn't want the added bureaucracy of requiring both of us to administer funds from the accounts. So I kept saying, "I trust you. One signer is enough." Robert had been drinking a lot that afternoon and I think I said, "I trust you" too many times. What transpired was a chaotic upheaval of emotion to which I thought for most of it that Robert was joking. When I realized he was serious I stood there dumbfounded, wondering about the definition of demagogue.

I left that grove event feeling very confused. Robert left the grove after that. He wrote me a cryptic apology in a letter but we never talked about that incident. We never talked again. His wife tried to remain a member of the grove but that only lasted about six months. Why did Robert want two signers on the account? What was his motivation for insisting on two signers for the account and why was he so passionate about insisting on this? To this day the reason remains a mystery.

Example Three (e.g.3)

This example occurred many years after e.g.2. I had finished college and was in graduate school (i.e., seminary). During graduate school I served a small Unitarian Universalist congregation as their consulting minister providing pastoral care to the congregation along with preaching and leading the Sunday service a couple of times a month along with representing the congregation within the local community. After a Sunday service I got an email from a member of the congregation who had been a very active member but had sporadic attendance since the birth of her second child. Her e-mail was very critical and complained that I had made too many changes to the regular style of their Sunday service. My contract indicated that I had complete autonomy in how I facilitated the

Sunday service. Likewise, she sent this e-mail not only to myself but also to all of the board members as well as long-standing and influential members of the congregation.

Overwhelmingly the board and influential congregation members sided with me and were upset with her sending this email. I followed the feelings behind everyone's actions. I ascertained that Kathy, who sent the email, had felt disconnected from the congregation that was important to her and she wanted to feel connected again and did not know how to fully reintegrate herself back into the congregation because of two small children taking up much of her time. The rest of the congregation was worried that I would take offence to her email and resign.

I thanked Kathy for her honesty and invited her to help me with some upcoming Sunday services. I started using hymns that were more familiar to the congregation as Kathy had suggested but continued some of my innovations that had been well received. In the end the conflict quickly dissipated and Kathy eventually became more involved with the congregation.

Example Four (e.g.4)

This last example occurred a couple of years after e.g.3. I had completed seminary and was about half way through a yearlong chaplain residency at a hospital in West Virginia. I was working day shift along with two staff chaplains. We all carried portable phones that worked throughout the hospital. I was up on the oncology floor visiting with patients and their families most of the day. A couple of hours before my shift was up I was sitting in the resident's office charting when I heard my name paged overhead by Greg, one of the staff chaplains.

I pulled out the portable phone I was carrying and the screen looked a little odd; the phones were a little old but functional. I turned it off and back on and then called Greg. He asked me where I was and I told him next door. I walked over to his office and Greg proceeded to interrogate me on where I had been and what I had been doing all day. His voice was elevated and accusatory. He asked if I had responded to a couple of calls that had come in and I advised him that I had not heard the overhead pages he mentioned nor had my phone rang all day.

He gave me a condescending look to which I finally sternly told him, "I may be a resident, but I am a professional. My phone must have been inoperable and I was unaware. This is a technical issue and not an issue of my competency as a chaplain."

Greg then proceeded to ask if me if I wanted to see a patient's family who was having a crisis and needed to talk with a chaplain. I told him I would go and then left to see the family member and listened to his problem and offered prayer and spiritual care. When I was finished I went back down to Greg and told him we still needed to resolve this issue. We were both a little calmer and we talked it through. He apologized for jumping to conclusions and I apologized for being defensive.

Triangulation, Anxiety, and Self-Differentiation

A succinct way of looking at triangulation is through the lens of your own life. Every person has been in a situation where someone has done something upsetting and in an effort to "feel better," and therefore alleviate anxiety, you run to a third party and start talking about the person who upset you. It doesn't fix the situation but makes you feel a little better. This is triangulation. It doesn't work in fixing the situation; it brings in another person into the problem making it more complex. Bohler writes, "Systems work best when people talk directly to one another... Triangles emerge when two people communicate to a third rather than each other." Emotional triangles perpetuate anxiety within a system and anxiety within a system is increased through emotional triangles.

Edwin Friedman defines differentiation with, "...the capacity to maintain a (relatively) nonanxious presence in the midst of anxious systems, to take maximum responsibility for one's own destiny and emotional being." A self-differentiated person will avoid emotional triangles and communicate directly with another. This involves being able to handle the often-uncomfortable feelings associated with direct conflict but which ultimately alleviates anxiety in the long term. The nonanxious, and therefore, self-differentiated leader isn't reactionary.

In an emotional system, whether that system be a biological family or a spiritual family like a coven or grove, the self-differentiated leader can effect change within the system by controlling his or her behavior and by controlling his or her own anxiety. People tend to be comforted by calm leaders, and anxious leaders tend to promote anxiety within organizations. The self-differentiated leader might cause some conflict in the short term but overall will promote a healthier organization.

Looking at the examples from my own leadership experience, we have examples of triangulation, heightened anxiety, and non-differentiation as well as self-differentiation.

In e.g.1 Susan's anxiety over her conflict with Toby was partially alleviated with her talking to Doug about her conflict. When this was not enough to alleviate her anxiety, it became necessary for her to triangulate me into her conflict. In turn I triangulated my anxious feelings of burn-out from trying to invest my time into two groups.

I should have been sharing my feelings with Toby over feeling burn-out instead of talking with Susan and Doug. When Susan and Doug approached me I should have advised them to talk directly to Toby in the hopes that they could work through their conflict; instead, bringing me into the conflict caused further anxiety and I wanted to fix the problem without involving Toby—effectively insulating her from their anxiety and my own.

This is a clear example of poor self-differentiation. I did not see myself as separate from the conflict and all I could see was "us," and I wanted to protect that "us." What resulted was Toby finding out about the conflict and the "conspiracy" to disband the coven, which she cherished deeply. Trust issues developed between Toby and I; likewise, the friendship she had with Susan and Doug came to an end.

In e.g.2 Robert undoubtedly confided in his wife over the real reason he wanted two signatures for the grove's accounts; however, he never confided in me as to the real reason. What resulted was my own unawareness of his feelings and him having my full confidence while he felt a conflict within himself. Was it shame that kept him from speaking candidly or was it fear of being judged? If Robert had talked to me about his true feelings then the conflict could have been alleviated and Robert and I could have maintained a friendship. Unfortunately, he was unable to overcome his anxiety and instead allowed his feelings to fester until they exploded.

Robert lacked the differentiation to speak openly about his feelings and preferred to leave the grove to keep his true feelings a mystery. I have tried reaching out to Robert over the years in an effort to mend this relationship but it has been futile and remains a mystery.

In e.g.3 we see an example of good self-differentiation. As the new minister of this congregation I did not have the years of investment that Kathy had with the other congregants. I chose not to react to her email in a way that incised conflict between her and I and the rest of the congregation, and I went directly to Kathy to discuss with her the nature of her email and to thank her for caring enough to send it. When congregation members became anxious, fearing I might resign, they triangulated their anxiety to me in the form of support.

While initially that support was flattering, it was fleeting because it was their anxiety and fear giving praise. By reaching out to Kathy I allowed her to remain connected to the congregation without feeling shame or regret for sharing her views. Kathy was unable to express her true feelings of feeling disconnected from the congregation so she triangulated her feelings in the form of her email to me, and I had to untangle those feelings and respond accordingly without creating further anxiety.

Likewise, in e.g.4 the conflict between Greg and I could have devolved into multiple emotional triangles with each of us going to a colleague to "vent" our frustrations about the other. Instead, I shared with Greg the feelings I had that had been building up for weeks over his condescension towards chaplain residents—a role he held a couple of years prior before he was hired full time as a staff chaplain. It took courage on my part to stand up to Greg and share with him what I was feeling and why I was feeling that way. I did so in a professional manner that respected his position as a staff chaplain but also honored my own position as a chaplain resident. By speaking directly with Greg we were able to come to place of mutual respect for one another which resulted in a friendship that remains today.

Conclusion

It has taken me several years to develop into the leader that I am today. I have done some things well, and very well; however, I have made mistakes. Some of my mistakes have been particularly painful and haunt me today. These mistakes have resulted in lost friendships and that is something I find tragic. Effective leadership is of the utmost importance for the Pagan community because people are the future of Paganism. How people interact and communicate with one another is critical in maintaining healthy and sustainable communities.

Being called a demagogue, "a political leader who seeks support by appealing to popular desires and prejudices rather than by using rational argument," is still troubling to me many years after being addressed in this manner.

I cannot go back in time and mend the events that spurned that verbal altercation but what I can do is continuously work on myself and maintain my own sense of self in a manner that promotes self-differentiation. It takes time and effort to develop into a good leader. The Pagan community needs good leaders and our future as a community depends on leaders being well grounded and capable who can reflect upon their mistakes and learn from them.

Works Cited:

Culbertson, Philip. *Care For God's People*. Minneapolis: Fortress Press, 2000.

Friedman, Edwin H. *A Failure of Nerve: Leadership in the Age of the Quick Fix*. New York: Seabury Books, 2007.

Friedman, Edwin H. *Generation to Generation: Family Process in Church and Synagogue*. New York: The Guilford Press, 1985.

Bohler, Carolyn J. "Essential Elements of Family Systems Approaches to Pastoral Counseling." *Clinical Handbook of Pastoral Counseling Volume 1*. Ed. Robert J. Wicks, Richard D. Parsons, and Donald Capps. New York: Paulist Press, 1993. 585-613.

Bleeding Heart Syndrome
Julia Maupin

One of the groups that I took over was already semi-established, and by that I mean it had lots of people but only a few active participants. The group needed a new surge of energy, with events and fun gatherings to participate in, and I was determined to offer it a chance for people who were forced into solitary existence to come out and meet others of like mind. I hoped to form a community amongst strangers; I had and still have the best intentions for this community.

Now, I'm very aware that I have what is commonly called 'bleeding heart syndrome,' which makes me want to take in every person that comes my way. I want to guide them and help them move on to the next portion of their lives. For some people it is fostering animals, but for me, I want to foster people. I want to give them hope and a sense of belonging, but I didn't realize just how potentially dangerous my 'syndrome' could be.

I had started a few social gatherings for people to sit around and explain their path, their beliefs and such. The group was becoming vibrant and fun; they wanted to come to learn things and share their knowledge. The group was starting to really shape up, but one person in particular called out to my bleeding heart.

He was thirty-something, working a simple job, and he was quiet and respectful. He contributed as needed and even donated a few items for another project I was working on for community education. He lived with his mother,(who I eventually met) who is a wonderful woman and as sweet as can be. We all had lunch together, laughing and chatting with one another. He was always there, always wanting to be an active member.

This relationship got to the point where I invited him and a few other members to a birthday party for my children. I was accepting him, in particular into my personal clan and circle of people. I felt that with just the right support system, he could really find his way.

Then one day, on an event he RSVP'd to, he ended up being a 'no-show', which was very rare for him. I called a co-organizer who lived near him to ask if she had seen or heard from him. I just felt like something was wrong. I logged into our website to see when he had logged in last, and it had been over a week, and the feeling fled deeper into the recesses of my stomach. The next day, after a few calls and emails, I had the co-organizer head to his work to check up on him. I care about my members; I'm going to do what is needed if I feel something is wrong. I was ready to jump in my car at a moment's notice if need be.

She eventually called me, but the news she gave me wasn't what I was expecting. That man, who had seemed so quiet and longed for community, who sat beside my children as they dove into their birthday cakes face first and gave a bag of gems and crystals to my son for his healing ritual after a long surgery — with intent and purpose to each stone — had been arrested by the state for two counts of Class X dissemination of child pornography.

This is punishable by an enhanced sentence of nine to thirty years, and I came to find out he was also a registered sex offender. I felt like this was my fault that I hadn't looked into his background; I just assumed it wouldn't be an issue. I just assumed the community I was trying so hard to foster, couldn't have someone like this in it.

The news shocked me to say the least, I couldn't believe someone like him could do something like *that*! What if he had gotten the urge to take it farther? What if, what if... the possibilities all started to run through my head. I started chastising myself for being a poor leader, for not looking out for the group and my family. For inviting someone with a history like this, that I didn't even bother to check because I was so consumed with my *need* to find and help people.

It's like an addiction — the bleeding heart needs to be fed and I didn't realize it until I choked on it. I had to take a step back to realize what I was doing and who I was really doing it for, and to find my boundaries. It rocked the community when I finally let them know; those closest to me felt just as I did, those on the outskirts of the group didn't say much, and others just didn't know how to respond.

My most active member, most dependable member, was a criminal, and of the worse kind in my mind. I processed the information and eventually I sent him an email knowing that he would not get it any time soon, but it felt better to write it. I let him know how much it hurt me, how much of my trust had been lost due to his actions and choices, and how things had changed.

I feel sorry for his mother. Part of me wonders if she knew, and then the bleeding heart tells me to reach out to her. To let her know that isn't her fault that her son made poor choices and has a problem that he is not ready to face. I haven't, but I feel I should.

In the end the group got quiet again, but that's okay. I've chosen to be more careful and that means having smaller group attendances and people I get to know better and about their past. This means I am truly putting safety first; I know I'll never cover every angle or possibility but I'm going to try.

Storms Aren't a Crisis, Just Weather
Lisa Mc Sherry

In classic sociology, small groups follow a consistent pattern of forming-storming-norming-performing and finally, adjourning[26] and most, if not all, magickal groups fall into this pattern as well. For the group leader, trying to navigate your group through the storms can feel like standing in the middle of a field in a lightning storm—shocking, dangerous, and traumatic. For a *new* group leader dealing with a storm can seem like the end of the world, with its unfamiliar tension and noise, discomfort and anxiety. Even seasoned leaders can be strongly rocked by a sudden storm The difference in how well everyone involved will come through it may depend on how well the leader can keep perspective: storms happen. They happen everywhere, all the time, and not only does almost everyone survive them, but they do a lot of ecosystems a world of good.

It has to happen eventually: Everyone stops being on the best behavior they brought to the newly-formed group, and suddenly conflict starts to arise. It's an organic part of realizing that members don't all share the same viewpoint, which was likely subsumed in the halcyon days of getting to know one another. Differences become more obvious and unsettling. Things you might wave away in a friendship or business acquaintance ('oh, that's just how she is') can seem more important than anything else in a magickal group, where 'love and trust' are vital components. Members may feel hurt or even betrayed when others seem to change into different people, not realizing that they are just getting to know them better—this is especially true in members who have self-esteem issues or difficult family lives. (Which seems to be just about everyone.)

It is no wonder that many new groups don't make it past the storming phase.

The real secret here is that a leader's task is to allow this stage to unfold, which may feel very difficult when it seems as if your authority is being challenged. This doesn't mean stepping

---

[26] "Developmental sequence in small groups." Tuckman, Bruce W. Psychological Bulletin, Vol. 63(6), Jun 1965, 384-399

back and not being present, far from it. Stormy weather in a magickal group requires leadership.

You may feel the need to create more and more rules in order to impose some kind of structure on something that is, essentially, uncontrollable. Resist this feeling. The path of wisdom allows for many viewpoints, and you want that diversity within your group. Instead, remind everyone of your ground rules for tolerance and respect, and maintain them. There is no reason a fiery dialogue can't also be civil, but it requires a basic sense of value for one another. This stage is also one in which it's good to remember that cultural and ethnic differences may interfere with understanding and make dialogues difficult. A good leader minimizes this, or at least sets a good example, by:

- Being aware of their own culture and doing the work to get rid of their inherent ethnocentrism (the tendency to judge all other groups according to your own group's standards, behaviors and customs).
- Recognizing differences as distinct without good/bad judgments attached.
- Showing respect for everyone.
- Being flexible and ready to adapt and adjust their behavior, without seeming insincere.
- Being tolerant by remembering that norms differ from one person to another.[27]

This is not a 'top-down' scenario, although members will take their cues from the leader. Members need to start working on their own processes of bending and molding their feelings, ideas, attitudes, and beliefs to suit the group's overall dynamic. They must move from a "testing and proving" mentality to one focused on problem solving and a general sense of 'working toward" a goal.

---

[27] Based on the list I developed for *Magickal Connections: Creating a Healthy & Lasting Spiritual Group*, New Page, 2007.

Members assist the process by:

- Being aware of their ethnic and cultural background and be willing to share its positive — and negative — aspects.
- Moving beyond good/bad judgments of other members.
- Showing respect for everyone.
- Being flexible and ready to adapt their behavior with honesty.
- Paying attention to their own biases and tolerant of others'.

Respect and civility is best modeled on an on-going basis, but you might consider doing a regular workshop or making it a part of your group intake process. Some 'rules' to follow might include:

- Do unto others as you would have done unto you.
- Do not let your silence condone disrespectful behavior.
- Accept that disagreement can exist without giving up your own convictions; what you may feel strongly others may disagree with just as strongly.
- Tone of voice matters; are you conveying what you want?
- Rely on facts, not assumptions.

One of the best collections of rules I've seen can be found at the University of Missouri's Show Me Respect website[28].

Group Activity: What is Respect?

Watch a half hour TV show or piece of a movie. Who was respectful/sexist/racist? Who wasn't? How do we know that (body language, interrupting, etc.)? Does respect mean different things to different people?

---

[28] Found at: http://civility.missouri.edu/civility-tips.php. Copyright © 2014. Curators of the University of Missouri. All rights reserved.

Group Activity: Where do I come from?

Have each member discuss at least five places they've lived and what they learned there. Have someone write down the commonalities and differences—are there more of one or the other?

Discuss ethnic or racial varieties within the group. Are there any? Are we making assumptions (for example, Juan has dark skin, are we assuming he is from Mexico or Central America?) How does age play a role in how we relate to one another?

These activities might be at periodic intervals (say, with the arrival of new members) or just when it seems it's been awhile since the last time. The important thing for leaders to remember is that to move out of the fire, members need to be able to listen to one another, without judgment and without interference.

Active Listening Isn't Just An Exercise

Active listening is a well-known technique, but often poorly understood and used in situations outside of the therapeutic one. It is also incredibly difficult to use when a magickal group is being shocked by conflict and high drama. Just imagine that Edgar called Iris an Earth Mother type in a fairly insulting tone and said he prefers the more ethereal Dana (100 lbs slimmer and 20 years younger) as a working partner. How is active listening going to make anyone feel better in this scenario? It's hard to be empathetic and objective when you are being talked about, and sharing on an intimate level—being able to be profoundly honest with one another—is absolutely necessary in a magickal group.[29]

But listening is important, because fundamentally we are building deep friendships. Knowing one another's hopes, dreams, quirks, likes, and dislikes are what will knit us all into a strongly connected group. Strong groups, the ones that transcend the inevitable fires of crisis and upheaval, have a strong sense of meaning: they support one another's spiritual

---

[29] I'll admit that in previous writings (specifically, *Magickal Connections*, 2007) I was a big proponent of active listening. The works of John Gottman have completely changed my mind.

aspirations.

In the above case there are things that can be learned on all sides: Edgar probably didn't mean to sound chauvinistic, but as a 45-yr-old single man brought up in England, he tends to 'glom on' to younger women as magickal partners. He had no idea that Dana only works with women because of a history of sexual and emotional violence with men in her life; this is her first time being in a magickal group with a man. Iris, with her 20+ years of magical practice, won't stand for being dismissed on the basis of her skills, but is so used to the body image that she accepts it — and his judgment — without question.

Lots for everyone to learn about one another, lots to heal all around. Some things won't completely heal, some will take years (if not decades), and some just a clarifying conversation. But until they are all listening to one another and not drawing unfounded conclusions, they will stay on the surface.

Here are some ways to improve listening skills:

1. Give the speaker your undivided attention. Look at them, make eye contact, and don't interrupt.
2. Make sure your body language is open and welcoming. Nod your head to show you understand what they are saying.
3. Once they finish speaking, wait a few seconds before saying anything. This gives you time to prepare your response and for them to feel like they were given space to say all they needed.
4. Do not plan out your response while they are talking. *This is the hardest habit to break, and the one that is the most distracting.* If you're planning a response, you're not listening. The observant speaker will be able to tell the difference in a listener who is tuned out and one who is focused on them. This is especially important when you're in the midst of a conflict and feeling a bit defensive.
5. Make sure you understood them by paraphrasing. I often will say, "what I hear you saying is . . .". Yes, it's obvious, it is also useful. At the same time, ask clarifying, open-ended questions.
6. Try to speak from your own place, and not for others. It's more useful to deal with the problem of how Janae always jumps in on the end of your sentences by telling her, "I really don't like how you do that," rather than starting out by accusing her of

disrespect. You might tell her it feels disrespectful as part of the discussion, but by keeping it to how you feel you can speak to what you know to be true.

Storms are Normal

As things heat up, group members are going to feel more comfortable voicing their opinion. They are developing a stronger Will, a key element in magickal workings–this should be a positive development! But to others, it can feel uncomfortable, as if there always needs to be a comfortable fit, making all other options "wrong".

As the leader your task is going to be to remember this: a storm passes. This is temporary, and not a crisis (at least, it doesn't have to be). Moreover, it will happen again and again. Magickal groups weather storms of varying degrees—if if only when they add new members—and you will all grow accustomed to the shifting energy, eventually.

It's even good for you.

A lack of healthy conflict is a strong indicator of a lack of trust between group members. Essentially, this stems from an unwillingness to be vulnerable and open with one another. Healthy conflict is the free and open exchange of ideas and perspectives. It leads to new learning, directions, and an overall stronger group commitment to whatever the spiritual goal is. Without that commitment, you end up with a lack of accountability and an inattention to results. It's like a chain with a link cracked or broken—the strength of the group deteriorates when healthy conflict is absent.

Just imagine this for your group:

1. You trust one another intimately.
2. You engage in unfiltered conflict around ideas and perspectives about how to accomplish tasks.
3. You commit to decisions and plans.
4. You hold one another accountable for delivering their part of those plans.
5. You focus on the achievement of those plans.

What a wonderful dynamic that is!

You may have noticed that I qualified conflict with the word "healthy", and this is a hard-won recognition that not all conflict is positive. In fact, sadly, there are some individuals who delight in creating conflict for the sake of chaos. We call them 'trolls' and there is a truly excellent website on how to spot them and deal with them[30].

Healthy conflict is rooted in respect. When I disagree with how to do our Lammas ritual I don't shut everyone down and say 'this is how we will do it, because I said so'--not unless I want to be laughed at. Instead I tell the group I'm not happy with how it's currently written, and can we talk about it? Sabbat rituals are formal in our group; they are very structured and have to work thematically within the overall solar year cycle we are working with. Changing one isn't simple, we might have to change several, and at the least we need to make sure our symbology is still accurate and telling the story we want. All of that needs to be discussed and we all need to be good with the results, even before we change a line of text.

Many of us come to magick with baggage—it's a process of transformation after all. A magickal group isn't a therapy group, but nonetheless a lot of spiritual and psychological growth tends to occur. Learning to deal with conflict in safe space that we created, with a family we chose, can be an immensely healing experience, not easy or calm in its evolution, but the end result is a healthier, happier human.

Working Magick

Working with many of the Fire God/desses can assist the group throughout this stage, especially when asking for wisdom to understand the deeper needs of the group. I like to work with Pele—She who dances the destructive lava up from the earth's core and in doing so creates new islands. You might want to do rituals with Her as a focus for a guided meditation—what what wisdom has She to offer? Or perhaps just work with her privately as the leader, using Her energy to augment your own as your group rebirths itself.

---

[30] Trollspotting, bichaunt.org/Trolls/index.html

If you work with Her, I offer this meditation:

(Use your preferred induction to enter a trance state.)

You find yourself walking along a shoreline, firm sand under your feet. To your right is a mass of vegetation, trees and tropical bushes. Begin to walk towards it. As you approach the vegetation, you see there is a path cleared that will lead you through this jungle. You walk, unhurried, taking note of the life teeming around you, the bright, tropical flowers, the hanging vines, the strong, healthy trees.

As you are walking, you get glimpses of a mountain through the trees. Your path opens before you, and you find yourself at the base of a large, dark gray mountain. It is smoking, and you think you can see a glowing light emanating from the top of it. It is a volcano. You know that although this volcano is active, it will not erupt while you are here; you are confident that you are in no danger.

You kneel at the volcano and feel at peace. You reach out your hand and feel it, taking note of its solidity, its texture, its temperature. You know that you will gain some great insight or knowledge at this volcano. As you wonder what that will be, you feel a presence behind you. You turn your head to look over your shoulder and you see the Goddess Pele standing behind you, watching you. Acknowledge her in your own words. She has something to tell you, if you will listen. Or perhaps, you have something to tell her, or to ask her. You can sense that she is willing to commune with you. You may do so.

When you are finished speaking with Pele, you say your goodbyes and, reaching out one last time to feel the steady warmth of the great volcano, you begin walking back through the path from which you came. With each step you feel yourself coming more and more to your own body, your own consciousness. Know that you will remember the message that you received from Pele today, whether it be in the form of words, images, or feelings.

Along with Fire deities, any Deity who deals with creating paths—Horus comes to mind—is also good to work with for guidance through this time. Again, you may wish to have the group work with Him directly, or just yourself.

If you work with Him, I offer this meditation:

(Use your preferred induction to enter a trance state.)
You find yourself walking on a deserted beach early in the morning of a summer day. The sand is hard beneath your feet, your footing firm, and the air is warm. The sky is crystal clear without a cloud in sight. The grains of sand beneath your feet shine from the sunlight and warm the soles of your feet. The sound of the waves beating against the shore echoes in the air.

You feel the warm, light breeze brush against your faces as you walk onward. Far off in the distance, you can hear the cries of sea gulls…You watch them glide through the sky, swoop down into the sea, and then fly off once again.

As you walk, the sun climbs into the sky, radiating warmth and comfort. Its light forms a bright path before you. As you walk forward you find yourself leaving the sand and ascending into the sky, rising up to meet the sun god, Horus.

Surrounded by warmth and filled with radiance, at His side you walk across the sky, traveling the path of the sun. As you travel, He may speak to you or you may ask a question. This is your time with Him.

You begin to realize that the light is growing cooler, dimmer, more blue in tone and texture. Your path begins to arch downward and, with grateful thanks for His wisdom, you once again find yourself walking along the beach. As you stare off into the distance, you see that the sun is beginning to sink into the horizon. The sky is turning brilliant colors of red…orange…yellow…while the sun sets, sinking down…down into the horizon. You feel very relaxed and soothed. You continue to watch the sun as it descends.

The beating of the waves, the smell and taste of the sea, the salt, the cries of the gulls, the warmth against your body – all of these sights, sounds, and smells leave you feeling very calm, refreshed, and relaxed.

Since much of the work being done in this cycle has to do with the will (and the Will), work with the solar plexus chakra can also be productive. This meditation has been useful for me in my work:

Breathe deeply and relax. Imagine an orange "energy ball" in front of your solar plexus. Make it the size of a basketball (or as large as you comfortable can while maintaining a strong, deep color all throughout). Breathe in through your nose and imagine the ball merging into your body and filling your body with orange light. You are glowing orange. As you are breathing in and out, know that you are filling your body with the empowering, shining light of self-esteem, willpower and courage with each breath. Do this for as long as you feel comfortable, and then imagine the orange light exhaling out of your body and merging with the light of everyday.

The first storm a leader encounters is frightening and upsetting; we rarely have the training needed to get through it unscathed. As terrible as it is, that storm was only the first of many we will encounter in our (hopefully) long time as leaders and in that time come to understand that they are, after all, just weather.

Bibliography

Curators of the University of Missouri. "20 Ways to Promote Civility and Respect." Web. 2 September 2014.

Mc Sherry, Lisa. *Magickal Connections: Creating a Healthy & Lasting Spiritual Group*, New Jersey: New Page, 2007. Print.

Petterson, David C. "Trollspotting." Web. 2 September 2014.

Tuckman, Bruce W. "Developmental sequence in small groups." Psychological Bulletin, Vol. 63(6), Jun 1965, 384-399. Print.

Circle Repair; Restorative Practices in Covens and Circles

Crystal Blanton

One of the most challenging elements to effective leadership can revolve around the demanding and frustrating task of dealing with conflict and supporting positive community dialogue. Navigating the dynamics of any group and mediating potential conflict could make the difference between a healthy community and one that is ripe for unhealthy engagement.

When thinking about the impact of these skills—or the absence of them—in our community, I began to think about the complexity of the community today.

As a social worker, I was trained in using a community model of restorative justice while working in the school system in Oakland, California. I had helped to support the use of restorative justice practices in urban environments before coming to the conclusion that this method of conflict mediation and community building could be useful in the Pagan community as well. What if we had a method to use that would help to maintain healthier relationships within our covens and groups? This was a question that I was asking myself as a social worker, and also as a part of the Pagan community.

Working towards sustaining healthy community means having the tools that are effective to use within those we lead and worship with.

Preventative work is important to the process of managing harmful dynamics, but prevention does not always stop potentially damaging situations from happening. Part of sustaining covens and groups is in our ability to repair what might be affected after a given situation and facilitating the building of community that is strong and viable.

Restorative Justice (RJ) is one of those systems of conflict mediation that has shown a lot of growth in popularity and implementation within justice systems, schools, and organizations. So then what is Restorative Justice and how can it support the Pagan community?

Crystal Blanton

Restorative Justice (RJ):

"The "magic" of restorative practices comes from a principled belief that when there is a breach in relationships, people can re-story their lives (often in gifted ways), given an active and supported responsibility to do so. It is clear from the research report, Restorative Justice: The Evidence, (Lawrence W. Sherman and Heather Strang, Smith Institute, 2007) that individuals can transcend large and small wrongs in a highly satisfactory way with improved long-term consequences when restorative practices are used. Our next question was: Could this opportunity be expanded from individuals to a wider sense of cultural harms?" – Christa Pierpont

"The philosophy of restorative justice is partially derived from the ways some indigenous cultures, such as the Maori, respond to conflict and harm. Rather than requiring retribution for wrongdoing, restorative justice seeks to encourage accountability, repair harm, and restore relationships. As a set of practices, it is best known for its use of a circle. The circle brings together the harmed, those who caused harm, and the community in which the harm occurred to respectfully share their perspectives, feelings, and concerns."- School-based restorative justice as an alternative to zero-tolerance policies: Lessons from West Oakland, Thelton E. Henderson Center for Social Justice

Restorative Justice is a system of conflict resolution that focuses on practices that work towards repairing the harm done in a community. Restorative Justice has a history of being used in the criminal justice system and has found its way into schools, the workplace, and even some religious organizations. Modern Restorative Justice practices are usually traced back to the mid 1970's as a part of victim/offender programming that became widely utilized in correctional facilities. The primary purpose of this type of program in the prisons was to support the repairing of harm that happened after a crime disrupted the relationships within a community or society. The focus, being more about the repairing of harm, is not about the right or wrong of the situation and more about how supported dialog can help in the goal of community and societal reparation in a way that the criminal justice system alone cannot.

Although these types of systems started to gather steam and recognition in the 70's, there is a long history of these types of practices and many people disagree on the origins of restorative justice as a whole. Many of the elements of Restorative Justice circles come from different native and indigenous cultures that many are familiar with. Actually sitting in a circle and the use of a talking piece are from practices much older than the 1970's.

As this system has transformed to fit other communities, we see that the uniqueness in this conflict model is that it encourages mutual understanding and individual accountability to forge the potential for some level of repair.

The benefits of using restorative practices are maximized by the facilitation of open and honest dialog around conflict and interpersonal relationships. The opportunity for understanding, empathy, and the restoration of harmed relationships offer another layer of insight on the many ways conflict can affect interpersonal relationships and community relationships in intended and often unintended ways. We do not exist in isolation, and restorative justice practices help to highlight just that.

Restorative justice gives an opportunity to create safe space, aiding to a foundation that promotes healing and open communication. The opportunity to explore problems and concerns, hopes and goals together can be something so engaging and hopeful when communities need it the most.

All parties have to be willing to engage in the process and work towards resolution and understanding. This is not a system that can be enacted by force, it requires an amount of willingness that must enter into the circle with each person. The process can be lengthy but powerful in dissolving conflicts in any community, including the Pagan community. Well-done RJ practices not only help to restore community after a conflict but can help to create community as well.

There are several different types of RJ activities and programs but the "circle", or peacekeeping circle, is one of the most widely utilized.

The Three Pillars of Restorative Justice:

Harms and Needs: RJ focused more on the harm that is done to a person or community versus the action itself. While laws focus on the crime, RJ focuses on the harm done to others and what is now needed as a result. In covens and groups it would focus less on the actions of the coven members and more on how said actions impact or harm the community of the coven.

Obligations: This point reinforces that thought that each person has an obligation and responsibility to his or her community. With this obligation comes the responsibility of understanding the harm that is created in a community, how actions affect others, and being accountable to try and correct some of the wrongs that have been created as a result.

Engagement: This point in the pillar refers to the participation of all the "stakeholders", or affected people, in the decisions that will lead to the outcome, and what is required to restore balance to the community.

Methodology

A restorative circle has several elements to it that help to support the flow of energy towards healing and restoration. Setting the tone starts prior to the process of the circle but has very important implications on the way that the participants engage. Identifying a calm and safe place to do the RJ circle, creating a supportive atmosphere, and creating the center of the circle are very important elements. The center of the circle always reminds me of an altar and has some of the same significance as an altar does within many Pagan practices. It is a focal point for the ceremony, it is a means to outline the type of energy that will be expended and it sets a tone to the desired outcome.

Often times there will be a cloth laid out, some flowers, pictures, objects, or other decorations in the center of the circle to support the flow of the energy. I found that this worked very well when doing restorative justice with other Pagans, and the correlations with Pagan circles supported people in respecting the space.

Another aspect of the circle that is very important includes the use of the talking piece. In Peacemaking Circles; From Crime to Community, Pranis, Stewart and Wedge state, "The talking piece generates and then sustains an inclusive dialogue. To those who are quiet, shy, or struggling to find their voice in a group space, the talking piece offers an opportunity to share what's on their mine and hearts. Conversely, to those accustomed to asserting their views, the talking piece offers an opportunity to listen and ponder. The talking piece opens doors of communication not only outwardly among those in the Circle but also inwardly for each participant by lending a focus for inner reflection".

The use of the talking piece in circles becomes one of the more valued tools of the facilitator. Using it as a means of respecting the voice of the speaker, and allowing space for all to be heard, helps to regulate and minimize talking over one another and escalating conversations.

The Circle Keeper is the facilitator of the process, and unlike other systems of community building or conflict resolution, the Circle Keeper is not above the participants in the circle. The Circle Keeper is considered a part of the community and working *with* the community to lead them through the process.

The Restorative Justice format that I use has several components in it; the opening, agreements, questions/activities, appreciations, and closing. Each part of the circle is just as important as the next, and all parts add to a collective outcome that is created in the process.

The opening can be a variety of things that include a poem, song, passage from a book, prayer or something that helps to open the circle to the theme of the engagement. After opening the circle, it is often customary to welcome everyone to the circle, talk about the purpose of having the circle, and discuss the use of a talking piece in the process.

This then is a segue to a discussion about circle norms (rules) for the circle.

I usually come prepared with several norms (rules) that I feel are important to incorporate into the circle to keep the space safe and open for healthy connections. Some of the ones that are commonly used include one person speaking at a time (one mic), assume positive intent, speak from the heart (honesty), no put-downs, and remaining open to new information. Often times the circle keeper will pass around the talking stick to get input from those participating in the circle and potentially add some norms or values to the list.

The next step in the process includes what I call the

"meat" of the circle. This is where the questions and activities are introduced. I was trained to consider this as a slow unfolding process, slowly going down the rabbit hole to the core of the topic being explored. It is important to choose questions that are clear and precise, and give a container for responses to be able to flow in the circle. Some examples include questions that draw out ideas and discussion, yet are structured.

- One statement or phrase to describe how you feel about (insert topic)
- Two to three sentences about how the situation made you feel
- One word, one statement or one phrase to describe what you want to see from (insert topic).

Questions should flow energetically and for that reason it is good to have them pre-written out. Just like in any energetic process, you are asking questions or supporting exercises that lead to the peak, and then unwind the energy back out from the center again to close; imagine a labyrinth.

Depending on the people in the circle, and the reason for doing the circle, the Circle Keeper may decide to loosen up on the structure of the questions and allow communication to flow. This level of openness requires clear circle norms and a facilitator that is willing to hold the boundaries of the norms as the communication continues in the circle.

After winding back to the surface, an activity or exercise to push towards conclusion and closing are important. Agreements are the next part of the process, supporting the community in making shared agreements that they can individually and collectively keep. This is an opportunity for the community to hold themselves, and one another lovingly accountable for the next steps together.

Agreements should be tangible and supportive to the outcome of healing and community. Choosing agreements like "thinking about things" are not good ones because they are not easily measured or easy to hold one another accountable for. I often support agreements that are actionable and observable. Agreements like checking in at the beginning of every meeting regarding plans, emailing once, montly discussions, or exploring a book together to address a specific relationship curve; these are all more actionable agreements that can be measured and work towards a outcome of restoration.

Then the process leads to acknowledgements, where members of the circle acknowledge one another for what they have brought to the process. It is highly encouraged that everyone participates in this portion, even if things have not reached a conclusion. Restorative practices are an exercise in creating or restoring relationships, and so often times the *process is the outcome*, meaning that this is not about traditional conflict resolution. When doing a community-building circle or a harm circle, understanding that RJ practices are meant to support long-term solutions is important; it is not a quick fix.

After acknowledgements, a closing poem, phrase, mantra, or exercise is utilized to close up the circle and give a definite ending to the process for that moment. It is often suggested that follow up circles are done to continue to process and support healthy relationships.

This is a very quick and simplified outline of what community restorative justice or restorative practices look like. This is not meant to be an in-depth training on leading circles or to make you an expert. This serves as a snapshot of how restorative justice circles are ran, and can be used easily in Pagan communities to support healthy and sustainable relationships. In-depth RJ training requires several days of training and a lot of practice, but the more we are introduced to the process, the easier we can create common language and practice these skills.

Important Tips and Reminders about an RJ/Peacekeeping circle:

- Circle Keepers are the facilitators of the circle that support the process.
- Setting the atmosphere for cooperation and healing can be essential to outcome.
- Using a talking piece helps the circle to focus on one person at a time so that everyone is heard.
- Collaborating as a group on what values will be upheld is important in facilitating towards respect and common understanding.

- Circle Keepers should have a list of questions that are to be used in the circle to assess and facilitate the discussion around the harm done.
- Having a prepared inclusion activity or question can be good practice.
- All circles should end with some agreements that the community agrees on and helps in restoring the effected relationships. These agreements can include follow up actions to be taken or even tangible ways of moving forward in the relationships.
- Closing of the circle is done with appreciations of those who have participated; participants can choose someone in the group or the group as a whole.
- Depending on the number of participants, an RJ circle could take up to two hours. It is not a process we necessarily want to rush because the key is that everyone is heard. It is also important to note that a circle keeper will have the responsibility of keeping the circle moving when a person gets stuck on a point or people start to interrupt the speaker.

Restorative Circle Activity:

Here is a workable scenario to show how the "meat" of the RJ circle can be creative and productive. Below are the activities and questions that I have used in several circles, and in workshops illustrating restorative practices.

   Scenario: Everyone has been in the same working group for a while. A member has left the group and the emotions have created confusion and divided everyone in the coven.

- Participants will have access to plates and markers. Everyone will write on his or her plate the value that is important to bring into this circle. All plates will be placed in the middle of the circle with the altar after each participant states why they chose that particular one.
- Each person will have a piece of yarn. Go around the circle and each person will tell something that is important about relationships that their ancestors taught them or stood for. After sharing, that person will tie one end of the yarn to the

person next to them. Once around the circle, the circle of yarn will be placed on the ground around the plates to support containing that energy in the circle with the values that are important to everyone.

This portion can be done after the circle norms are done and as a transition into the questions and "meat" of the circle.

Questions for circle:

1. Choose one emotion or feeling to describe how you feel about the current situation in the group.
2. How are you affected by the loss of our coven mate?
3. How has this situation harmed the circle?
4. What would help to restore the balance of the group? (circle keeper take notes)
5. What is one thing you would send with the departing coven member to take on her journey to ensure success on her path?

- Agreements (take from question of what would restore group)
- Acknowledgments
- Closing

Resources:

Zehr, H. (2002). The Little Book of Restorative Justice (The Little Books of Justice & Peacebuilding). Good Books.

Pranis, K., Stuart, B. & Wedge, M. (2011). Peacemaking Circles: From Crime to Community. Living Justice Press.

Boyes-Watson, C. (2008). Peacemaking Cricles & Urban Youth; Bringing Justice Home. Living Justice Press.

http://www.tolerance.org/blog/talking-circles-restorative-justice-and-beyond

http://www.circle-space.org/2010/06/24/the-restorative-justice-talking-piece-tangible-and-physical-abstract-and-soulful/

http://www.restorativejustice.org/

Section 8:
Recognizing and Dealing with Burnout

When Leaders Need to Step Back From Community
Margo Wolfe

Several years ago, I decided to step back from a group I was leading. I cited several reasons for my departure, including an underlying conflict that was brewing that I felt was not worth a fight, but mostly it was due to fatigue and a feeling of stagnation. The work that I was preparing was not performed adequately and I felt I was spinning my wheels. I needed to leave. I sat down with my group and explained calmly that I needed to step back and that I had full confidence in their work and their ability to transition to a group without me.

The story is different for each person, yet the feelings are strangely similar. I say person instead of leader, because many senior personnel in the Pagan community don't even realize they are leaders until someone says that word to them. They will often shake their head, look at the ground, and softly say, "No, I'm not a leader. I just do what I need to do for my community, my group." Leaders lead for a reason. That reason could be their extensive knowledge, profound experience, winning personality, bursting creativity, but if anything it is their energy that others see as enriching and captivating. But they are people, spiritual people first, who shoulder responsibilities far beyond what others imagine.

Unlike other denominations of spiritual practice, Pagans often have to chart their own path of education and leadership. It is only recently that we've begun to see more readily available forms of learning that are filled with leadership trainings. I'm certainly not saying they didn't exist; they most definitely did, but practices were often localized to a specific group or tradition. Leaders are created, sometimes by recreating the wheel each time a new person gingerly steps forward.

It is when times become difficult that I turn to the practices and advice of other religious communities that offer assistance in leadership training. Because of their vast experience, these denominations recognize that leaders and those who serve can lose the joy of serving when the process becomes merely a task that needs to be performed. I find some comfort that we, at least in this way, are seeking the same guidance.

It is more often these types of leaders, the ones who dedicate so much time to their work and not enough time to their own well-being, that need to step away from community for a period of time or even forever. This comes in many forms, but how each form is addressed is instrumental in how each community reacts to this change and how that group can continue once those leaders remove themselves, gently, from the fray.

Knowing When to Leave

Determining the real or even hidden reasons why this break is necessary will help to determine what type of break a leader needs. In "Why youth pastors leave around the 2-3 year mark", blogger Jody Livingston states that there are several reasons why burn-out exists, especially in ministerial roles. He states that not building sustainable relationships can make the work more difficult because there is little room for growth or even commitment[31]. I hear tales of disconnect between leaders and their groups because a distance has been created for some reason. Rooting out these types of causes will help to soothe any alienation once the split between leader and group is established.

Burn-out is nothing to be ashamed of, and as Pagan leaders we need to dialogue more about this in order to come to terms with our own perceptions of ourselves as leaders, especially as volunteer leaders. In *Reboot your life*, the authors discuss the concept that we are living as "a nation on the verge of burnout." Allen, et al. cite a 2009 Gallup poll that states that Americans are working more hours than they did 20 years ago and that does not include any work outside of a day job[32]. Granted, many Pagan leaders view their work as a "labor of love" and that is certainly the case for myself, but it still is a labor that cuts into any time for rejuvenation and creative growth. We need a break.

---

[31] Livingston, Jody, "Why Youth Pastors Leave Around the 2-3 Year Mark." *www.thelongerhaul.com.*
[32] Allen, Catherine, et al. *Reboot your Life* (New York: Beaufort, 2011), 12.

Disillusionment is another reason why leaders step aside. Leaders may feel that the work they are doing is not enough or that group members don't appreciate the work, respond in a way in which the leader sees demonstrates their love for their workings, or maybe the response overall hasn't been as prolific as intended. Some leaders lament that they feel the work is not enough, so they try to cram in even more, trying to please the people they serve. It becomes a never-ending loop of fatigue.

Whatever situation leads to this feeling of hopelessness and withdrawal is common and perhaps taking a step back is a good way for a leader to regroup and decide on a future course. Planning ahead can be difficult when a group is just trying to keep up with the next event, the next ritual, or the next class. Taking a step back, where breathing become one of the main goals, helps to put so much in perspective that a vision can take shape.

Sabbatical for Self

When I took my break, stepping back from the work and the rituals, I slept. I caught up on my rest, read a few books, and then wondered what I was supposed to do next. My entire existence was wrapped up in my leadership roles and I didn't plan on not knowing what to do with all the available time. I found I was wandering around, physically and metaphorically, unsure of my direction or actions. I made no advanced plans, no understanding, just sitting on the sofa channel-surfing thinking that I was actually resting. I wasn't. I was lost.

There are many books on taking a sabbatical, but the most influential one for me is *Walden*. Thoreau examines rest, reflection, simplification, and so many other introspective aspects that fit so well with our Pagan philosophies. He states "I went to the woods because I wished to live deliberately, to front only the essential facts of life, and see if I could not learn what it had to teach, and not, when I came to die, discover that I had not lived. I did not wish to live what was not life, living is so dear; nor did I wish to practice resignation, unless it was quite necessary. I wanted to live deep and suck out all the marrow of life, to live so sturdily and Spartan-like as to put to rout all that was not life, to cut a broad swath and shave close, to drive life into a corner, and reduce it to its lowest terms."[33]

Thoreau didn't escape the whirlwind of the world and just sit in the woods enjoying nature. However wonderful that sounds, his experiment yielded a great deal of reflection and a host of ideas that, to this day, help people to cope with their hectic lives.

All aspects of leadership can pervade day-to-day life and even impede personal spiritual practice. When you decide to step back, you want to consider what you will do with that time so that it reflects a positive transition of growth and renewal. Make a plan before you leave, knowing that the journey might ebb and flow. Without a direction, though, the time will not be as restful as you might think. Days can blend together and a person with too much free time will feel they should return to their post, even when they haven't had ample time to rest. There are several ways you can plan without overwhelming yourself even more, while finding your breath.

Meditation is often the first thing to go when leaders feel overwhelmed with organizational and logistical concerns of their leadership practices. Re-establishing a daily and focused meditative practice is one way to reconnect to your spiritual practice and discovering a new path or reflecting on the past work.

Intensive journaling: reflective writing has always been a part of the group work I have done. After workings or rituals, each group member spends time journaling their experiences and then shares with the group what they found significant. As the leader, I would scribble something down then set to work, refilling tea cups quietly and holding the space for them so that they are not disturbed. Once they are done, I would guide the discussion, and only minimally focus on my own reflections. When on sabbatical, you have the opportunity to do intensive journaling, setting aside time to just sit, reflect, write down your thoughts, doodle, stand up and walk around the room, write some more. Whatever process happens without worrying about what else needs to be done. I often couple my intensive journaling sessions with talking aloud to myself while I work

---

[33] Krutch, Joseph W. ed. *Walden and Other Writings by Henry David Thoreau*. 3rd ed. (New York: Bantam, 1982), 168.

through some thoughts. When a thought gets stuck, I will get up and perform some physical task like weeding a flowerbed or cleaning a room. They helps me to process as well. Keep in mind that self-examination is good, but too much self-examination also holds us hostage. Like the legend of Sankofa, the bird who examines his tail feathers before flying forward, we look to the past to help with the future. Reflect and move on.

Personal and spontaneous ritual: My personal practice suffers when I take on too many leadership roles. I know so many others who also let their practice fall by the wayside in favor of giving more time to their community. A spiritual sabbatical is that time to resume those practices and feed yourself through reflective and spontaneous ritual.

I have a friend who had to remove himself from a leadership role because he was just burned out. Drama erupted in the community and, while he expertly handled the situation, it left him drained of all connection to deity. He removed himself quietly and completely, and planted himself in the middle of nature. He took weekly, sometimes daily hikes into state parks, local and regional trails, and hide-a-way locations, documenting all of the glory and beauty of Gaia in his photography. It was a marvel to watch this spontaneity of growth and communion happen for him. His travels and hiking continue, but now he feels ready to once again take up the reins and organize work for his community.

Enjoying the leadership of others: While working to mentor and teach others, developing and running rituals, and generally planning events, leaders can forget that they can learn a lot from the work of comparative authors and presenters. While many people want to completely distance themselves from their work during sabbatical, it can be refreshing, after you've caught your breath, to read the works of other leaders. I recommend you be as diverse as possible, picking up volumes in subjects from other religious persuasions. Gaining a bit of perspective will often give you insights into your own work.

Daily Breaks

Maybe you don't need to completely step away. Maybe you just need to turn off. Pagan leaders are on-call just like pastors of other faiths, tending to the emotional needs of their web and feeding their work. To find balance, you need to something that feeds you in another way and pulls a curtain around the chatter of email and texts. Establish yourself as a person first and a Pagan leader second. Don't give away your cell number to everyone. Have a separate email account that you check only once a day or even every other day. Step away from Facebook, especially if it tends to stir more conversations. While all these bits of technology are so useful in networking, marketing, and planning they are also part of the work. Don't let them become part of your play, too.

When Taking a Break Becomes a Battle

One of the problems associated with taking a break is that there is the perception that our Pagan community is fragmented, especially now that our elders and founders are crossing over the veil. At one particular conference, a presenter called for more Gen-Xers to do more: write and publish more, organize more, take their place in the circle where others have retired. As a Gen-Xer myself, I have heard this call a thousand times throughout my life. Gen-Xers are told they are lazy and want everyone else to do everything for them. Now is not the time to take a break, they scream; now is the time for action. We respond in full force, continuing to do more and attempt to live up to the great leaders who plowed this path for us. But the focus of work is shifting, and the old ways of organizing, event planning, and even writing are changing, so our message is clouded over and our efforts hindered.

Strong leaders, good leaders, do step back when necessary. They do take time for themselves and care for their well-being. This sometimes means a lengthy sabbatical in order to hover over the circle and gain a new perspective. Starhawk writes in *The Empowerment Manual*, that "Elders get to be elders by exhibiting good judgment, being able to put the good of the group before their own personal benefit or profit, being able to look ahead, anticipate problems and deflect disasters."[34] For

---

[34] Starhawk. The Empowerment Manual: A Guide for Collaborative Groups (Gabriola Island, BC: New Society, 2011), 60.

some leaders, this may mean to step away and let others tend to the community, to allow a shift in the power, and give others room to find their voices.

When you are spinning your wheels, maybe this is the time to stop...and breathe...and find a new perspective that could open the way for fresh energy and creativity into your leadership. Maybe it doesn't have to be forever. Taking a break is just another way of providing continuing leadership to those who wish to follow and build alongside you.

I know that stepping back can be a herculean task for some leaders because of the interdependent web we build. I found that to be problematic myself when I decided to step away from a group. It became a mess. They refused to let me leave and even tried bargaining with me to stay. The entire group fell apart and I feel, to this day, the guilt of allowing that happen. In the end, though, I think it was a learning process for me. As a leader I can only be completely responsible for my own spiritual growth. I can continue to be a mentor and educator, guiding people toward their goals, but in the end the path they choose it up to them. I cannot make them drink the water.

My experiences are mixed and are not meant to discourage anyone from stepping back when they need to breathe, but to help any guilt dissipate if that action causes drama to brew. The best any leader can do is make a plan, not rush into any action, and help the group transition. A sudden departure frightens people and emotions overrun the process.

Finally, maybe a paradigm shift needs to happen. In the end we need to take care of not only ourselves, but one another. We need to tend to each other on a regular basis, so that the lengthy sabbatical or even the complete step-away is not always necessary. Stawhawk writes that when leaders take on heavy responsibilities, others can be assigned to take care of that leader, making sure they have food, drink, a hand to hold in trying times, and a ride to perform difficult tasks. She acknowledges that people might not like the concept of personal care, but when leaders take on difficult responsibilities, either in ritual or in mundane work, then their care becomes part of our service. When we tend to our leaders, then they can continue to tend the spiritual needs of the community[35].

Finding Your Peace

Whatever the reason, whatever is needed, our Pagan leaders must take the time necessary to refresh, regroup, or re-envision their role. Working and resting with intention are what can make our work meaningful and invigorating. When our leaders need to step back, our community needs to honor that need.

---

[35] Ibid. 62.

Take a Break or Burn Out
Philip Kessler

Sometimes you have to take a break or you burn out.

No one really likes to admit it when they have overdone it; especially people who are looked up to as authority figures or leaders. That simple little word "no" is one of the hardest things to say, and it seems to get harder and harder to say the closer you are to burnout. Take it from me, I've been there.

Not too many years ago I found myself at the point of burnout. I had been working 40+ hours a week, running a weekly Pagan discussion group, leading a coven, publishing a monthly newsletter, and trying to have a social life. Unfortunately, the social life is what came in last on that list. Not only did I have a distinctive lack of social life, my romantic life had spiraled into oblivion — a hot and fast relationship fizzled out mere months after starting.

One evening, while the members of the discussion group were assembling in the living room, I was hiding in my bedroom in total darkness and crying my eyes out. My ex was in the room with me, trying to encourage me to come out and lead the discussion. I knew I should have been in the living room ready to get things underway. I knew that people were depending on me to lead them in meditation and an educational discussion. My heart wasn't in it, or I should say my heart wouldn't let me do what my mind knew I should be doing. (One of the group members made matters worse by making a big stink about my needing a mental health break. Needless to say, she wasn't often at future gatherings.)

After that I took a break. I'd had an emotional break down and knew that I needed time to recover. People still depended on me to be a spiritual leader for them, to advise them in many different parts of their lives. As a discussion group facilitator and a newsletter publisher, I had to step back. If I couldn't be there for myself, I knew I couldn't be there for anyone else.

I know. How could I be a leader or advisor to someone when I was taking such a break? I had to drop one or two things from my routine in order to have some time for myself. One of the group's long term members stepped up to the plate and began hosting the weekly meditation and discussion group at her home, relieving me of that obligation while I tended to my own personal well-being.

Five years before that evening I had taken a five year hiatus from being a leader in my community. My life had spiraled out of control. The reason was not because I was doing too much, but because I wasn't doing enough.

And the Pendulum Swings Awry

I had been in a four year relationship. During those four years all I did on a spiritual level was lead a weekly discussion group. I was allowing my partner to control everything else I was doing. I was the main breadwinner in the house; I was working nearly around the clock as a manager at a convenience store, and I was focusing most of my free energy on my partner. Four years of turning my life over to someone else was probably the biggest mistake I have made yet.

After I came out of this five year hiatus, I dove right in and tried to do more than I probably should have, and that's what led to my breakdown several years later.

The Pendulum Swings Back

Now, most would say that I am doing too much again. I work 40+ hours a week as a store manager, I do three radio shows every Sunday, blog on a semi-regular basis, I write for various publications on a regular basis and I own an online business. What I am not currently doing is trying to lead a discussion or meditation group, and my coven has gone inactive. I still provide spiritual advice and leadership to those who depend on me, but I do not go out of my way to do those things right now.

I take a regimen of vitamin and mineral supplements and herbal treatments for stress, anxiety, and depression. I was recently diagnosed with high blood pressure (big surprise) and am on medication to control that. I pay more attention to what I take into my body, and I focus on my spiritual well-being more than I have in the past.

Sometimes as leaders we forget to take care of ourselves. Tending to our coven, grove, or circle is very important. Each member has unique spiritual and emotional needs. People demand our attention; they want us to help make them feel good. We spend a lot of time tending to those needs and forget about our own. It is somewhat like a medical doctor or a psychologist. Like a doctor, we are often our own worst patients/congregants.

Spending time taking care of ourselves seems selfish to some. Especially when what we are doing for ourselves seems to have nothing to do with spiritual well-being. Sitting in front of the TV vegging out with a glass of wine or a bottle of beer apparently has nothing to do with spirituality. Curling up with a collection of short stories or even a paranormal romance doesn't appear to have anything to do with taking care of our emotional well-being, however, taking time for ourselves, tending to our own spiritual and emotional needs, is taking time for ourselves. Regardless of what "meaningless" and "mindless" entertainment we do.

Relaxation, self-care, meditation, healthy diet, exercise, and plenty of sleep are all great ways to tend to your own needs. No matter who you are. As a leader, as someone that people look to for guidance and instruction, remembering to focus on you is important.

I don't mean to sound as if I am saying that you should be selfish and ignore the needs of your students, coven members, and congregants. Far from it, but you do need to take your own needs, emotional and spiritual, into account when you are tending to the needs of others. Sometimes you just have to say no to people - even those who depend on you the most.

What is a Break?

Saying no is not a bad thing. That is something that I have spent a long time learning to understand. In the past I said yes to just about everyone who came to me with a problem, a spiritual issue or an emotional need. I thought that if I said no I was failing my students or my congregants. Even when I was doing intuitive readings on a professional level I was hesitant to say no when someone needed more than a basic reading. It was even harder to say no when they needed much more work than I could provide in one or even five sessions.

I recently had a conversation with my tradition's founding High Priestess about this very topic. "A break!?" she asked. "What's a break? My home town was destroyed, I didn't get a break. My High Priest died, I didn't get a break." For over twenty years she has been leading a ragtag group of people through the ins and outs of our various flavors of Paganism. In those two plus decades she's not really been able to take a vacation from being a leader. Even in the hardest of situations, she's been on call 24/7/365.

That said, I do see her doing self care. She might not get a several hours-long or even days-long break from being a leader, but she does get to relax sometimes. She goes fishing, either alone, with a student, or her partner. She dives into a book or series of books and devours them. She'll veg in front of the TV and watch Supernatural. She'll hang out at the covenstead and drink with the other coveners.

I've spoken with leaders of covens, groves, circles, even tradition heads, about what it is like being a leader. They all agree that there never seems to be enough time to do everything that needs to be done to support their group. They do their best. Often times they wind up neglecting their own self-care.

One leader I have become friends with, after years of not Seeing eye to eye on a lot of things, was forced to take an extended hiatus. She worked in the IT department of the local university and lost her balance. She instinctively reached out to keep herself from falling and completed the circuit between two mainframe stacks, short circuiting her brain. She had to relearn how to do everything - talk, walk, and feed herself. She now has a "pacemaker for the brain" to keep her brain functioning at near-normal capacity. During her medically necessary hiatus she had handed many of her responsibilities to other priestesses within the Church. Now that she is back to near-normal capacity she has reclaimed many of her duties, but has learned that her students and priests/esses can handle much of the work load when necessary.

Keys to Avoiding Burnout:

There are many things that we can do to avoid burnout. Perhaps the most important thing is to understand what the word "no" means. It doesn't mean that you don't care. It doesn't mean that you don't want to help the person. It does mean that you need to take time for yourself. It does mean that caring for you is just as important as caring for them. As my HPS likes to say, "What part of 'no' don't you understand? Is it that big open space in the 'o'?"

Meditation and exercise are keys to not only keeping your mind and body healthy, but to avoiding burnout. Meditation sessions can mean specific music, guided visualization, and all the other stuff you might use with a group, and it can also mean just taking a few minutes a day, or more often, to sit quietly and clear the mind. Taking the time to acknowledge what is around you and in you, what you need to address for the day and what you can put aside for another time.

Sample Meditation

Find a quiet place to sit and relax. If you choose to meditate at the beginning of the day, you can do so while still in bed. If you prefer to meditate at the end of the day before going to sleep, you can lay down in your bed. If you like to use music for meditation, please do. Make a selection of music or ambient sound that works for you.

Close your eyes and take three slow, deep breaths. In through nose, out through your mouth (or the other way around if it makes sense to you). As you breathe in, see in your mind's eye a pure healing light entering your body and as you exhale, see the murky and dark energy of the stressors of your day leaving. After you have done this simple breathing exercise, take a few moments (or minutes) to acknowledge your body. Feel and see the various parts of your body that might be hurting, focus some of that healing energy on to those parts and relax them as much as you can. After you have gone from head to toe (or toe to head) you can take some time, however much you want or need, to sift through your thoughts and clear out those things you don't need or that are dragging you down. Focus some of that healing energy from earlier on to those things that are negative connections in your life, this will help cut those connections. Focus some of your time and energy on boosting your strengths and desires.

After a time, when you feel it is right or needed, you can return to the present, to the here and now. Repeat the breathing exercise from the beginning as you bring yourself out of your trance or meditative state. You can now go about your day or curl up with a good book and go back to bed.

Note: this simple meditation can be done at any time of day or night. All you need is a few minutes of quiet time.

Physical Exercise and Meditation

As to exercise… We all hear about the benefits of exercise. From our doctors, from physical therapists, from friends, from complete strangers. Even on social media and the news. There is no denying that some form of regular exercise is a good thing for your body and your mind and spirit. If you are a person who has a relatively sedentary lifestyle - sitting behind a desk all day or driving a school bus - then exercise is even more important. Walking or jogging are two easy forms of exercise. A walk around the block, or down to the end of the road to get the mail, are pretty easy to do. They are low impact and get the blood pumping. Exercise that raises your heart rate, even if only a little, is extremely beneficial.

Yoga and other forms of meditational exercise are great. You don't have to join a gym or lift weights to exercise. If you are like me and work on your feet all day long, exercise is still important. Experts tell us that exercise is above and beyond your daily routine at work. If you put in several miles a day on your feet, sling cases of water or bags of ice, you are not exercising. You are working. I like to take a walk as often as I can. Get out and enjoy the air (on nice days) and get my heart rate up. I've got joint and back issues, so I don't do running or even jogging, but I do get out and move around.

You can combine the ideas of meditation and exercise into one. Yoga and martial arts often combine meditation with the physical acts involved in those routines. Beyond martial arts and yoga, there are other means of combining exercise and meditation; long walks, using exercise equipment. Often when I go out for a walk I do so in a slight trance state, low level meditation. I am mindful of my surroundings, but take advantage of the physical activity to also clear my mind. Many of the relaxation techniques that I use to better control my blood pressure or low level trance work and mindful meditation. Jon Kabat Zinn is my go-to author and lecturer for mindful meditation.

Entertainment

Entertaining yourself, taking a break from reality is another good way to take care of you. Most reading this are Pagans of some flavor or another. As Pagans we often read, and read, and read. Much of what we read is how-to and reference materials. Taking a little time out of your day or week to spend with your nose buried in a book (fiction or nonfiction) is a great way to relax and get away from it all. Whatever you enjoy reading is good. Be it fantasy, science fiction, historical fiction, or even smut.

Along with reading, watching TV or a movie can be a good break. As I mentioned earlier, my HPS likes to sit down and watch Supernatural for a break from everything. Entertainment is important. We may think that spending every waking minute on the Coven or discussion group, or whatever service we provide to our community, is the most important thing in our lives. It isn't always.

Family, Friends, and Relationships

With all of the time we spend with our Coven mates or congregants, we sometimes neglect spending time with our family and friends. I've found myself so out of the loop with what is going on in my family or friends' lives that I have missed weddings, birthdays, and special parties. I've even lost time with my mother when she has been visiting because I had overbooked myself. We just might have to schedule time with our families to get into the habit of spending time with them again. I'll give you an example of what I mean here: I work a minimum of 48 hours a week. That comes out to one full day off and a very short day in the middle of the week. With everything else that I do, I have little time for being social with family, let alone with my friends. I have to schedule it. Sounds bad, doesn't it?

For leaders in our community that have spouses and children, not spending time with them can be very detrimental to the family dynamic. When I was a kid we made it a point to have at least one meal a day together as a family. Usually that was supper. We'd all sit around the table and be together. It's worth making the effort to have time together without any electronic devices. However, sometimes family time involves sitting in the same room and not talking. Sitting around the living room playing games or updating our statuses might not seem like quality time, but at least you are together.

As humans we are generally social animals. There are some that are just as happy to go weeks or months without seeing another living person, but even the most introverted person needs social interaction from time to time. And I am not talking online social networks. Going out for coffee or dinner with friends is a great means of taking time for yourself - taking a break from the must-do's of being a leader in the Pagan community.

Vacations and Attending Events

I've had the opportunity to go to Pagan festivals and other events over the years. Most of the time I take those opportunities as vacation time, even though I do take advantage of being around so many Pagans and like-minded individuals to learn, to share, and to discover new things, and I'm still doing a lot of networking. I hike the grounds, spend time with friends, and explore other worlds of Paganism. Most of the time I go with friends and we have a great time. We camp out, eat home cooked meals around the fire, and share stories, songs, and laughter.

I also vend at Pagan events with a friend, and this is not a vacation. But we do take advantage of not being in our usual surroundings and let ourselves relax whenever we can. We stay in a hotel, go out to eat, share a bottle of wine or mead, and have a good time in the evening. Other than setting up, running the booth, and tearing it down, we have plenty of opportunity to go around and meet new people and reunite with old friends.

Self-Care and Benefiting Community

I'd like to ask you, the reader, to take a moment here and think. Does any of this sound selfish? Does it sound like you are ignoring your responsibilities? Or does it sound like you are doing things to better yourself and be able to better give of yourself to your community?

Whatever you might do to take time for yourself, as long as it is healthy it is good. Take a soaking bubble bath, relax to some good music, read a book. You may be amazed at how much better you feel. With the understanding of self-care for yourself you can now go and share some of those ideas and techniques with your students, with your community. You can show that taking care of yourself not only benefits you but your community.

The Day Guacamole Saved My Priestesshood

Courtney Weber

If you dropped into our apartment one sunny, Saturday morning this past spring, you might have thought our cat died. It was perfect "park-weather," as we say in NYC, and my partner and our cats were in perfect health. Yet, I was weeping uncontrollably into my partner's arms. I had a Coven meeting that afternoon and obviously, I did not want to go.

"I'm going to quit," I sobbed into my partner's shirt. "I can't be responsible for guacamole anymore."

I was burned out.

Burn-out: the state of being over-tired and unable to rejuvenate the required enthusiasm or energy for your work. It's the point beyond being tired for too long. A worn-out person asks for help when something seems like too much. A burned-out person is too worn out to even ask. Fatigue can be cured with some rest, time away, or redistributing duties. But burn-out lingers long after a restful break is concluded. If being tired is seeing the vital light in someone's drive go dim, burn-out is that light being extinguished completely.

It is serious, and it is a serious huge threat to Pagan communities. Larger religions have infrastructure, staff, and resources to support their leaders to help avoid the burn-out that can decimate their communities. But if you're reading this, you probably don't need me to explain that the majority of Pagan leaders do their work voluntarily, on top of a regular job and family duties, keeping plates stacked very high with work that means a great deal to them, but takes a great deal from them. Pagan communities are familiar with leaders throwing up their hands and walking away after a small infraction in their community. Some become physically ill. Others, depressed. Great leaders leave their people and it's often said to be a product of ego, life, or "basic instability" within Pagan culture. Maybe it's true, but it's quite possibly the dreaded demon Burn Out.

My burn-out happened in the way Hemingway described

the journey to bankruptcy: gradually and then suddenly. I didn't mean to lead a community. I became a Priestess because I loved the work of the Gods and underwent initiation in order to know more. Receiving the crown set a light on my head somewhere in the Universe. People came to find me and sought to learn from me all that I sought to learn from the world. I was in love with my life and my role. I couldn't believe that the inclusive, powerful, magnanimous community I found myself in existed, let along that I was at the helm of it.

I wanted a perfect Magickal experience for all who came through my door. I coordinated every detail of ritual, from the invite to the execution, and prepared food for every guest— amenable to all food intolerances and preferences. As we formed into a formal group, I checked in with members throughout the week to make sure they were happy and well. If I didn't have an answer to a member's Magickal question, I researched and found the answer for that person, myself. I baked birthday cakes and sent out weekly emails listing all event dates and details as well as personal announcements and who needed energy blasts that week. I attended workshops and festivals with the sole purpose of finding tools to make the group, which had become a full-fledged Coven, even stronger. I proofread job-hunting Coveners' resumes. I helped people find roommates or apartments. I hid in my workplace bathroom to take calls from Coveners having horrid days. I counseled during lunch hours. I organized retreat weekends. I organized fundraisers to bring over guest speakers, who I then housed and set-up speaking engagements for them to make some money.

Our Coven blossomed and eventually grew a solid "outer-court" of people who wanted ritual and fellowship, but not the formality of a Coven. As we attracted more people, we needed bigger spaces for our Sabbats, which required room rentals and promotion. My own Magickal development got a cameo once in awhile, of course.

Despite the crazy levels of responsibility, I was in heaven. I didn't feel the need to have the Magickal experiences my Coveners and guests received. The gift for me was in the giving. I put all of my time and attention outside of my day job into building my community. I nestled roots into New York City. Rents were definitely cheaper in other places and life qualities much higher, but I found a home in the madly crowded place, among those worshipping life beneath the concrete and the Gods within the infrastructure. The whole Pagan community was alive in NYC—I had a hand in making it shine. We supported each others' work and in time, had an unofficial "Council of Elders" going on, a friendship between leaders all devoted to supporting Pagan life.

This meant I really couldn't go to any ritual or gathering in the city without some semblance of responsibility handed to me, but that again was a joy and a privilege. I was doing something truly important with my life.

Naturally, it wasn't always a gleeful Spiral Dance. Homophobia and poverty directly threatened many persons within our community. Occupy Wall Street lifted the rock on some of the ugly truths plaguing our city and world—the now archetypal 1% was ruining things and the rest of us may have had numbers, but few answers. Hurricane Sandy hit and while it was a glorious showing of solidarity in which we pitched in to help our city, it also brought out Shadow, pain, and strife between individuals. Tempers were short, feelings were hurt, the shape of groups changed. A valued leader died suddenly one autumn day, and I looked at the grieving faces of our Pagan urban population—we'd been through so much and I had no answers as to why the Gods had seemed to so carelessly abandon us. I relished support from my fellow leaders, but we were all equally tired and drained. The only natural thing to do was to plan the next ritual, organize the next Sabbat, keep on with The Keeping On.

As I write this, I see now a reflection of a whole community that shared the fatigue with myself and the other leaders. Its manifestation, however, came in the form of complaints and tirades.

In the early days, I received long emails from people, expressing their joy in having found our community, but those gave way to quibbles on social media about ritual locations being "too far away" or the timing being "too early" or "too late." Within my own Coven, I heard less about personal epiphanies and more about disappointments over not getting a birthday cake when I hadn't had time to bake or money to buy one. I stopped planning the annual retreat when I felt I was spending more time talking Coveners through who would be sleeping where and who would be on dinner/clean-up duty than I was creating opportunity for communing with the land. But then I started receiving more complaints about the retreats' absence than I'd ever received feedback about it being a positive experience. Coveners stopped coming to me for help interpreting dreams or concocting spells, and more to share their disappointment that other Coveners had not come to their parties or called them when they felt like talking to someone.

I did my best to help people work out their differences with compassion and understanding, trying to see it as a "Spiritual Task in Working Together." Once, while suffering a migraine, I spent a whole evening performing a healing ritual for a Covener whose feelings were hurt in a misunderstanding with other Coveners. The Covener loved the ritual, but the misunderstanding was never resolved and gave way to more, the Covener finally leaving in anger.

I began to resent my responsibilities.

Outside of my Coven, regular Sabbat attendees became more demanding. One young man, furious that I'd not noticed his week-long absence from Facebook, said that I was much more "CEO of a corporation" than a Priestess. Another wrote me a series of angry emails for not using my email lists to advertise his classes or attend them, myself: "Priestesses should show more support of their communities." One young woman stopped coming to our events because a regular attendee said something that hurt her feelings at a party I hadn't even been invited to, and when I didn't address it, felt "unsupported." Nearly every week included a conversation with someone bothered by someone or something in the community. I was nervous and anxious before public rituals, often losing patience with my ritual team and laying sleepless after the rituals wondering what I could have done to make more people happy.

I no longer felt like a spiritual leader. I felt like a Pagan Customer Service hotline.

I needed a plan and suggested to my Coven and our community that complaints only be brought to me if they were accompanied by a suggested solution. Most agreed it was a good plan. My Coven was very willing to help. Several then suggested that I work on delegating a few more of my responsibilities. I recognized that my own ego was at work against met: Trying to be the best via doing it all wasn't really making me a good leader, only a busy—and cranky—one.

"You just need to delegate more!" is something most leaders have surely heard but I would imagine it's a solution more commonly offered by those who haven't had to delegate and don't know how much work delegation creates!

Delegation did help shoulder the work-load and certainly minimized complaints. Someone who has felt the pinch and pull of organizing a public Sabbat is less likely to complain about the presence (or lack of) bacon among the potluck dishes in the Fellowship portion at a different function. However, I stayed busy and tired. I was often asked to "look over" plans for the things I'd delegated, or give up a few hours in the evening for a call or coffee date as someone wanted to "run a few questions" by me. Some were reasonable, such as help in securing a park permit. But some involved talking someone through nerves about leading a ritual, or finding someone else to fulfill the duties when someone was suddenly unable to do something (and then comforting the person who had to drop their leadership role if they felt guilty about it). It didn't change my role in the broader community as a "Go-To" person. Even if I were attending a ritual as a guest, I spent incredible amounts of time responding to texts and emails with some version of "I'm not leading this one. You'll need to talk to the person in charge, *and that person is not me.*"

Delegating created more work. It was easier to simply do the task myself.

Delegating also did not stop complaints from filtering to me. Although we had our new rule of, "Bring your solutions with your complaints," many were often masked as, "This isn't a complaint, I'm just sharing my thoughts…" It was a fine line for me in being a compassionate, listening ear, and once again being the sink basin into which all troubles flowed. Magick and the Spirit world had become something I gave barely a nod to. There was too much work to be done in the Coven and community to develop my Magickal skills or any sort of educational framework. I was too busy doing the work of a Magickal community to do the Work which brought the community together in the first place. I saw it as merely the reality of supporting a large community. I could provide the basin in which Magick could grow, but individuals would need to find Magick on their own. There was no longer any room on my plate to help connect people with Spirit. But people seemed dissatisfied and the more complaints I received, the more resentful I became.

This past year, things became quite intense in my personal world. My first book was accepted for publication while I was working full time and taking nearly nightly Tarot clients. My partner had just graduated school and was looking for work, but I was still the bread-winner, keeping our lives going while scrambling to finish a manuscript. Once the manuscript was complete, I was laid-off from my fulltime job. I funneled all of my energies into finding Tarot clients and teaching Witchcraft classes, somehow managing to keep my end of the bills up, when there wasn't a fulltime job to be had between the two of us. I tried to keep my Coven and our public work thriving. I asked for help when I needed it, but was running out of the energy to even ask.

Also at this time, I was starting to do more work in the Pagan activism sense. The battle over hydraulic fracturing ("fracking") in New York State was coming to a head and many Pagan leaders in the community wanted our collective groups to respond. The work re-inspired me. Without the fulltime job, I had more time to devote to this cause than many others and found myself as the primary organizer. I did not mind as my soul was ringing again for the first time in a very long time. Combining ritual with activism and fellowship parties in support of eco-justice initiatives was deeply fulfilling. Many of my Coveners joined me in the cause, finding it equally inspiring.

I was glad to see this develop, but I found even more new problems. The rituals and events were not officially Coven-sanctioned but separated, and I did not use our normal collective decision-making process. I simply did what I wanted. Participating Coveners were upset that their ideas weren't included or that a non-Covener was given a role they typically embodied. Other Coveners were angry over the presence of cameras and press, as our normal functions were strictly camera-free. I had become High Priestess wherever I went with my Coven and community, including our social outings.

The moment guacamole saved my Priestesshood—by almost destroying it

I went to a party with several of my Coveners, hosted by a Covener who made a batch of delicious guacamole, which vanished within minutes. One Covener did not get any guacamole and was mad. They made a passing, but deliberate, complaint about the lack of guacamole—directly to me.

I froze in my steps and shook with anger. It wasn't my house. It wasn't my party. It wasn't a Coven function. *And I wasn't the one who ate the last of it, either.* Why was that complaint coming to me????

It was such a small thing, but I still needed to spend several minutes breathing deeply (and chugging a beer) until I could speak without screaming. I tucked it away, as it was a party after all! I did not bring it up to the Covener as it seemed too silly to spend the time discussing. Life is short…it seemed better to let it go, but it didn't stay gone for long.

A few months later, I attended a faith-leaders' summit. We sat in small groups, sharing our leadership challenges. One woman, rejected by her Christian family for being a lesbian but still became a Christian minister, spoke of counseling rape victims from Uganda. Another leader, younger than myself, talked about finding Spirit in scrubbing the floors of a homeless shelter. The third person spoke of her mission work in Central America and witnessing first-hand the effect of the drug trafficking world on children. These three kept strong, dry eyes through their stories, but I cried—partly for the content of their experiences, but mostly for the shallowness of mine:

"It's a challenge for me as a leader when people complain about guacamole."

Now, let's go back to me crying over needing to go to a Coven meeting. I was reeling from the extraordinary conference and had opened my computer to a long email from a disgruntled Covener complaining about the choice of meeting locations. After reading it, then came the tears and the raging threats to quit.

Other ministers fed the hungry and fought the system, but what was I doing? Was I spending my life catering to the entitled? Was I enabling the spoiled? What was I doing with my life? I put ten years into one of the most expensive cities in the world. I had no savings. I lived thousands of miles from my family. I had no garden to grow my vegetables and heard the wheezes of buses and growls of motorcycles far more than songs of birds—but I'd done it all to build a community that I once loved but in that moment, fully despised. My partner had given up a life in a beautiful place to come to me in NYC so I could continue my Priestess work, and there we were—both barely making ends meet and for what? To make sure there was always enough fucking guacamole wherever I went?

I was done.

Quitting and moving 3,000 miles away was desperately appealing, but it would have been a move in weakness (as well as cost a ton of money we didn't have). I couldn't quit until I tried, one more time, to fix the situation. That afternoon, I shared my concerns that our Coven was no longer a place of Magick and that expectations needed to change. They listened, compassionately, but when I cited the guacamole incident as an example of an overarching problem, the party's hostess sighed and said, "I should have bought more avocados."

But more avocadoes wasn't the answer. Increased production does not slow expectation. If anything, it leads to expecting even *more* and even greater disappointment when desires are not met. I realized I needed to dig deeper.

I meditated on my Priestesshood as though it were a tree. I saw the "Entitlement" "Expectations" and "Whining" as rotten fruit, existing because a deep need was not being fed. I saw the trunk of my Priestesshood as sick and tired, the roots twined and twisted, all drawing from a tiny pool of water deep beneath the soil—and it was absolutely dry. The pool was me—my finite resources of being a single person and being able to supply all of the nourishment for the giant tree that was both my Coven and community. It was impossible. Yet I understood that early in my Priestesshood, I set myself up as the answer to every need when I was not. If I, and my community, were going to continue to thrive, a recalibration was necessary.

I started by writing an email to my Coven, defining my role similar to a job description:

As your HPS, I am responsible for:

- Cultivating safe, sane, and responsible space for private, Magickal, personal and Spiritual growth within the Coven.
- Organizing, leading, or delegating leadership of six public Sabbats for our community, supporting two private Sabbats for the Coven.
- Keeping two relatively even-keeled public social media pages: one private Coven page and one public community page.
- Being available to each of you for Magickal, Spiritual, or Personal Support as needed.

I also stressed that I was *not* responsible for social functions, or necessarily being the lead organizer for Pagan functions outside of our Coven (meaning: Find your own ride to the festival). I explained the importance of my doing things separately from our Coven, and Coveners were entitled to the same influence or privacy of our Coven functions simply because I was in charge. Outside of the Coven, I also wrote several blog posts about what my specific responsibilities were as a public Priestess—and what they were not—to the broader community.

I received apologies, praise, and words of thanks. They were kind and certainly appreciated, but unnecessary. The spiraling pipeline to my burnout was my responsibility. Maybe in the early days, I felt like I owed myself to the world. Maybe it was a leftover martyrdom complex of my Christian upbringing, but whatever the case, I had built myself into the role of "Do All" and therefore, that was what my Coven and community expected of me. In the interest of helping, I grabbed the reins of individuals' accountability, and in the process, I robbed them of their own development.

Basically, I failed my Coven and community.

The failure was not in that I hadn't addressed every need they had, but in that I presented that it was possible for me to do so. I had promised wings and wheels when I only had two feet and one heart, and then became angry at people who expected me to fly.

In Witchcraft, we recognize balance and limits. We do not advocate boundless sacrifice as other religions might. Again, Burnout is a real, serious threat to Paganism. Unfortunately, when leaders burn out, the finger is often pointed at the community. In truth, all too often communities are treated like shops and leaders like cashiers: "Give me what I want, how I want it, simply because I want it." It reinforces the same consumer mentality that is devouring our planetary habitat. But leaders not only allow this dynamic, we often create it. We are not The Goddess. We may be *of* the Goddess, but we as individuals are not the Divine source from where all things come. We are fleeting, mortal beings with finite resources, just as the living earth.

It is up to us to set the precedent that our communities are living entities that need nurture, pruning, space to grow, but also knows when to cocoon and regenerate. It is our responsibility to set boundaries and it is the community's responsibility to respect them. We cannot ask our communities to respect our boundaries if they are not set, first.

But in order to do this, each leader must be truly aware of what our specific roles are first—and what they are not. By being the All-Purpose, we perpetuate the "add-to-cart" philosophy that all things asked for are provided for those who ask, which essentially distracts from true blessing when it is bestowed and leaves the soul starving, focusing more on what it did not receive.

Some resources are renewable, but all are finite without knowing the boundaries. Nothing is boundless except the Divine. All things of this world, in the physical and mortal exist with finite limitations. By treating ourselves as finite resources, we reinforce the idea of boundaries, of living with respect for resource and understanding of limits. Limits may not be "nice," but they are kind and they are true. By drawing the lines early, your groups may be smaller, but your participants fuller.

I still have a long way to go. Large ships don't make rapid u-turns, large groups don't change old habits overnight. I started with myself—making my sole job in my Coven and community to create Magickal space for the participants. I suggest prosperity and home spells, but don't help find roommates or job postings. I share information about others' events, but I don't answer emails or texts with questions about events that aren't mine. I am firm and adamant when someone complains about something unrelated to the specific Coven task at hand: "Not my problem, my love!" or gently remind people that nothing gets addressed without suggested solutions.

There's also a sense in which a functioning Coven is one who forgives. We as leaders are going to make mistakes, but we must own them and not be afraid to recalibrate when necessary. We must leave space to reroute our roots to keep our fruits healthy.

Guacamole drew attention to the source of my spiritual starvation and in it, ultimately saved it. Now, my biggest concern over guacamole is making sure *I* get some of my own, but leave enough left behind so that others can feed themselves, which is each our own true responsibility to one another.

Conclusion
Taylor Ellwood

Two years ago (at the time of publication) I sat down for lunch with Shauna and as we talked I realized I'd found the co-editor I needed for this anthology. I wanted to put together an anthology on Pagan leadership, but I didn't have the connections I knew would be helpful in getting such an anthology published. I had literally met Shauna the week before at Pantheacon 2013, and we'd promised that we'd get together for a meal at Convocation 2013. As I got to know Shauna it became very clear to me that she had the connections, but more importantly the passion for leadership that is essential for putting a project like this together. As a result I pitched the anthology to her and explained why I felt it was needed. She agreed with me and consequently two years later, this anthology was published. My thanks goes to Shauna for helping to pull this anthology together and reach out to the various people she knew to help turn it into a reality.

We aren't the only ones who feel passionate about leadership, as is evidenced by the essays you've finished reading. Each of the contributors shared their hard earned experience and wisdom so that you as a reader can learn from both their triumphs and mistakes on your own leadership journey. My hope is that you've taken your time to read each article and digest what you've learned.

The real challenge of leadership is found in experience, and so while these articles can be a guide, ultimately you have to just go out there and be a leader and make your own mistakes, as well have your own triumphs. The privilege of leadership is that gives you a chance to make an impression on your community and help the members in it. The responsibility of leadership is recognizing that what you do has an effect on the people you are leading and you have to take responsibility for those effects, good or bad and then learn from those experiences.

May you take from this anthology what you need in order to become a better leader. The leadership journey, like many other journeys, never really stops. There isn't a point where you just arrive and that's it for the journey. This book provides some guidance on your journey and hopefully inspires you to continue onward.

Taylor Ellwood
November 2015
Portland Oregon

Bios

Sable Aradia (Diane Morrison) has been a traditional witch most of her life, and she is also a licensed Wiccan minister and a Third Degree initiated Wiccan priestess in the Star Sapphire tradition. She is the author of "The Witch's Eight Paths of Power: A Complete Course in Magick and Witchcraft" (Red Wheel/Weiser, 2014) and a blogger at PaganSquare, the Patheos Pagan channel, and Gods & Radicals. To make ends meet she reads Tarot, teaches workshops, makes music, writes speculative fiction, maintains an Etsy shop and works part time at a bookstore. She lives in Vernon, BC, Canada with her two partners and her fur babies. http://www.sablearadia.com

H. Byron Ballard is a West North Carolina native, teacher and writer. She has served as a featured speaker and teacher at Sacred Space Conference, Pagan Unity Festival, Pagan Spirit Gathering, Southeast Wise Women's Herbal Conference, Glastonbury Goddess Conference and other gatherings. Her essays feature in several anthologies, she blogs and writes a regular column for Witches and Pagans Magazine. Her book "Staubs and Ditchwater" debuted in 2012 and the companion volume "Asfidity and Mad-Stones" was published in Oct. 2015. Byron is currently at work on "Earth Works: Eight Ceremonies for a Changing Planet". Contact her: info@myvillagewitch.com

Lisa Spiral Besnett writes and speaks about spirituality and spiritual practices. She's been an active presence in the Twin Cities Pagan Community (Paganistan) for over 30 years. She has lead public rituals, taught, mentored, and served on a number of Pagan organization's boards of directors. Lisa Spiral has presented workshops and been a featured guest at festivals and national conferences. Her two books: Manifest Divinity and When Gods Come Knocking: An Exploration of Mysticism from a Deity Based Perspective are available through Immanion Press. Her weekly blog posts can be found at lisaspiral.wordpress.com.

Crystal Blanton is a social worker, activist, writer, priestess, mother and wife from the Bay Area. Blanton is a board member for the Solar Cross Temple and the 2015 Keeper of the Light for the Pagan Alliance. She is the author of several published books and the editor of several anthologies discussing topics of diversity within the Pagan community. She writes for the Wild Hunt, Sage Woman, and the Daughters of Eve blog. She is also the founder of the 30 Day Real Black History Challenge and website, promoting understanding and reflections of the experiences of Black people throughout history. Blanton is passionate about the integration of community, spirituality and healing from our ancestral past, and is an advocate for true diversity and multiculturalism within the Pagan community. She continues to work in her local community, and within the Pagan community, by facilitating and participating in discussions on topics of social justice, diversity, leadership, harnessing cultural magic and the use of restorative justice practices to empower the community voice.

Rev. Catharine Clarenbach: From the time she—age 5—tried to explain the nature of God to her best friend, Catharine Clarenbach has been a spiritual and religious seeker. Catharine has led groups in Earth Religious and Roman Catholic communities for over 30 years. She was ordained a Unitarian Universalist minister in April 2015 and has also been blessed by shared spiritual life in Quaker, Reform Jewish, and African Diaspora communities. Catharine's ministry through her site, The Way of the River (www.thewayoftheriver.com), brings together a regular blog and newsletter with spiritual direction and classes on discernment, spiritual practice, and meditation. She is also a regular blogger on Patheos' blog, Nature's Path, where she writes about religious expressions through a UU-Pagan lens.

Kenn Day is a professional post-tribal shaman, working and living in Cincinnati, Ohio with his beloved wife and daughter. He has been a familiar face at midwestern neo-pagan events since the mid 80's, offering workshops and rituals. He is the author of two books on post-tribal shamanism: Dance of Stones: A Shamanic Road Trip and Post-Tribal Shamanism: A New Look at the Old Ways, both from Moon Books. Kenn also offers a series of workshops in which he passes on the shamanic teachings he has received and is founder of Sheya, an initiatory Mystery tradition.

Rev. Bill Duvendack is a lifetime student of the western mysteries, an internationally known astrologer, author, presenter, and psychic. He is ordained through Circle of Light Independent Spiritualist Church and is currently president.

He's president of the Astrological Association of St Louis, a member of NCGR, BOTA, and the Fellowship of Isis. He writes monthly and daily horoscopes, teaches classes on astrology and occultism, meets clients, and divines using astro-dice and tarot at various locations. He has presented in venues including libraries, colleges, high schools, the Pagan Picnic, Pagan Pride, Pantheacon, Babalon Rising, The Aquarian Organization of Astrologers, The International Left Hand Path Conference, and Oak Spirit Sanctuary. He has made many appearances on television, radio, newspapers, podcasts and has been interviewed by the NY Times and RTE 1. Essays have appeared in many publications, and magical writings have been translated into 6 languages. For more information, please consult: www.418ascendant.com.

Taylor Ellwood is the Managing non-fiction editor for Immanion Press as well as the author of Pop Culture Magic 2.0, Manifesting Wealth as many other books. He resides in Portland, Oregon with his wife, 2 kids, and 6 cats, where he also runs the magical experiments community. For more information about him, visit www.magicalexperiments.com

The Rev. Melissa Hill is a priestess in the Ár nDraíocht Féin Druidic tradition. She is dedicated to building sustainable, local, pagan communities that heal the soul of the land and the people who live upon it. She is a founding member of Cedarsong Grove, ADF and an active participant in a number of local and national pagan organizations. As a writer, farmer, artist, and ritual leader she hopes to create a better way to live and love. As a spirit-worker she works with both spirits and people to find balance and to help them come in to right relationship with each other. Learn more about her vision at dandelionladyseeds.blogspot.com.

Melanie Howard is the co-author of Psychic Tarot with Nancy Antenucci, co-founder of the former Blessings and Breathing Center in Hastings, Minnesota, and an avid Tarot reader and creator of unique spreads. She is also the author of several children's books. Melanie currently resides in Burnsville, Minnesota, with a Lhasa pug named Joe-Joe. Please visit Melanie's Tarot blog at http://way-ward-tarot.blogspot.com/ for more information about Melanie, and also access to more contract documents for spiritual gatherings and groups.

KaliSara has been a Pagan for 20 years, heading several circles and spiritual discussion groups during that time. She co-hosts Pagan-Musings Podcast and Pagan Weekly News with her long-time friend, RevKess. KaliSara has authored books, essays and blogs in between chasing her husband, Stormcrow, two kids, Thing 1 and Thing 2, and a cat.

Philipp Kessler, aka RevKess, is a podcaster, radio personality, and blogger. He podcasts through Pagan-Musings Podcast Channel on BTR, co-hosts Murphy's Magic Mess on KZUM-Lincoln (NE), and blogs for Pagan Activist, DiversiTree, and his own review site revkessreviews.wordpress.com. He is a founding member of the Pagan Alliance Nework (paganalliancenetwork.spruz.com) and a long standing elder in the Covenant of Kernunnos Tradition. RevKess can be heard on a variety programming through PMPChannel.com and can be found on Facebook, Twitter, and Google+.

David Oliver Kling is a graduate of Wright State University holding a B.A. degree in Religious Studies and a B.A. degree in Philosophy. He has a Master of Divinity from Methodist Theological School in Ohio with a specialization in Black Church and African Diaspora Studies. While in college he worked as Director of Religious Education at the Unitarian Universalist Fellowship of Yellow Springs and while in seminary he served the Delaware Unitarian Universalist Fellowship as consulting minister. He is currently working as a hospice chaplain in Northeast Ohio, as well as the Chair of the Ministry, Advocacy, and Leadership Department at Cherry Hill Seminary. Additionally, he is ordained and endorsed for specialized ministry by Sacred Well Congregation. His religious background includes Christianity, Wicca, Druidry, Gnosticism, and Roman Paganism. His academic interests include Black Church studies, comparative theology, pastoral care and practical theology.

Shauna Aura Knight is an artist, author, ritualist, presenter, and spiritual seeker, Shauna travels nationally offering intensive education in the transformative arts of ritual, community leadership, and personal growth. Her work is inspired by the mythic stories of heroes, swords, magic, and the shadows we each face. She is the author of The Leader Within, Ritual Facilitation, and Dreamwork for the Initiate's Path, and her work is included regularly in CIRCLE Magazine and numerous Pagan anthologies. She's also the author of urban fantasy and paranormal romance novels, and her mythic artwork and designs are used for magazine covers, book covers, and illustrations, as well as decorating many walls, shrines, and other spaces. Shauna is passionate about creating rituals, experiences, spaces, stories, and artwork to awaken mythic imagination. http://www.shaunaauraknight.com

Christine Hoff Kraemer received a PhD in Religious and Theological Studies from Boston University. She is an instructor in theology at Cherry Hill Seminary, a practitioner of religious witchcraft, and author of Seeking the Mystery: *An Introduction to Pagan Theologies* (2012) and *Eros and Touch from a Pagan Perspective: Divided for Love's Sake* (2014). She blogs for the Patheos.com Pagan channel at Dowsing for Divinity (formerly Sermons from the Mound, www.patheos.com/blogs/sermonsfromthemound).

Rev. Judith Laxer is a modern-day mystic who believes that humor, beauty and the wonders of nature make life worth living. The founding Priestess of Gaia's Temple, an inclusive, Earth-based Ministry, Judith also enjoys a successful private practice as a psychic, spiritual counselor, hypnotherapist, shamanic practitioner and teacher of women's mysteries. A keynote speaker and author of Along the Wheel of Time: Sacred Stories for Nature Lovers [Booktrope Publishing], Judith has presented classes and workshops on the re-emergence of the

Divine Feminine since 1993 at conferences nationally. She dedicates her work to restoring the balance between feminine and masculine energy in our culture.www.judithlaxer.com, www.gaiastemple.org

Phoenix LeFae is equal parts blue eyed wanderer and passionate devotee of the Goddess. She is a restless seeker of knowledge, always yearning to learn more, dig deeper, and dive into the wild. Phoenix suffers from the whims of her Divine muse, and in that suffering experiences joy that manifests in writing, ritual, teaching, and song. Initiate of the Reclaiming Tradition of Witchcraft, Phoenix has had the pleasure of teaching and leading ritual globally. Her heart, mind, and soul are dedicated to helping others find their spiritual path and return to a place of wholeness. Ultimately, beyond titles, traditions, or trainings, Phoenix is a simple spiritual seeker looking for the Power of the Goddess in all things. Find her at www.phoenixlefae.com or at her shop www.milk-and-honey.com

Julia Maupin is an aspiring humanitarian, philomath and occultist. She works as a Spiritual Advisor for Finding Jewels and has done so professionally since 2010. Her current focus is on sustainable community and co-living applications for families and friends. She founded Strawberry Moon Coven, an eclectic Wiccan circle with focus on family, and volunteers for various groups both online and in person. She writes for a small smattering of semi-annual newsletters which range in topic from psychedelic societies to community outreach and small scale farming. She is currently working on the formation of a co-living community and resides in Waterloo, IL along with her husband, three children and a revolving door of house guests and friends. You can find her on Facebook, Twitter and Google+

Catriona McDonald is an Ovate Grade member of the Order of Bards, Ovates & Druids, and a proud denizen of the Assabet River bioregion of central Massachusetts. She regularly facilitates rituals for the Mystic River Grove, has presented workshops at the OBOD East Coast Gathering, and has been published in a number of devotional anthologies. Further Druidic ramblings can be found on her blog, The Druid's Well, at http://thedruidswell.com.

Lisa McSherry is a priestess and author living in the Pacific Northwest with her husband and furchildren. She is the author of two books, The Virtual Pagan (2002) and Magickal Connections: Creating a Lasting & Healthy Spiritual Group (New Page, 2007) and has contributed to several more. The leader of JaguarMoon Coven (www.jaguarmoon.org), she is also the editor for Facing North (www.facingnorth.net) a site for reviews of interest to the Pagan/new age/ alternative spirituality community.

Annika Mongan is born and raised an evangelical Christian in Germany, Annika Mongan joined the Jesus Freak movement as a teenager and became a passionate evangelist and worship leader. After attending Bible College in the U.S., she was ordained by a Southern Baptist church and sent out to convert Pagans. On the road Annika was confronted with religious diversity, from the Amish casting demons out of school busses to Roman Catholic priests breaking into government buildings. Her disillusionment with fundamentalism eventually led her to Witchcraft and she moved to California where she founded an intentional Pagan community. When she is not networking, doing interfaith work, or volunteering for too many events, Annika spends her time studying what causes religious transitions and writing about her experience.
Blogs: http://www.patheos.com/blogs/bornagainwitch/ http://witchesandpagans.com/pagan-culture-blogs/cross-and-pentacle.html

Manny Tejeda-Moreno is a professor and social scientist. His doctorate is in business with a specialty in leadership, organizational behavior, statistics and measurement. His scholarship has been focused in research methods, leadership and diversity. He also has a masters degree in psychotherapy and works on issues in support of LGBTQ youth. Manny was born in Cuba and raised in the American South. Manny has been in the Pagan community for almost four decades. He is a witch and was raised as a child of Oyá. He is a monthly columnist for The Wild Hunt: A Modern Pagan Perspective. He enjoys spending time in the deep wild and is encouraged by the Balance within the natural world enjoys storms and the night. He is a beekeeper, orchid-grower and builder of bat houses. Manny is married and splits his free time between the Florida Swamps and the Atlantic Ocean.

Syren Nagakyrie is a Polytheistic Goddess-centered Witch and Priestess, a feminist, herbalist, writer, and radical bridger of worlds. She is the founder of the Shekhinah Mountainwater Memorial Fund, a co-founder of Mother Grove Goddess Temple, and serves on the board of Gods&Radicals. She works professionally in non-profits and social justice and is available for consultations. Syren blogs in several places on the web and can be reached at siren.nagakyrie@gmail.com. Currently Syren is content in the PNW; as her heart sings for the sea and her body yearns for the mountains, her spirit is that of the Wandering Hermit.

Mya Om is a Witch, Author, Attorney and recent transplant to the Windy City. Mya has spent her life seeking, learning and teaching magickal arts. You can find Mya online https://www.mrleeauthor.com

Diana Rajchel has acted as a volunteer organizer for Twin Cities Pagan Pride and now runs Bay Bridge Pagan Society in San Francisco, CA. She is the author of three books, including Divorcing a Real Witch. She identifies as more "priestess" than "Wiccan." Find out more at http://blog.dianarajchel.com.

Selina Rifkin, L.M.T., M.S. is a writer on holistic health, permaculture, and Paganism. She is a licensed massage therapist and author of The Referral Guide for Complementary Care, a book that describes twenty-five different healing modalities. In 2006, she completed a Masters program in nutrition with a focus on traditional foods and the work of Weston A. Price. Currently, Selina is the Executive Assistant to the Director of Cherry Hill Seminary, the first Pagan seminary to offer Master's degrees. She has been Pagan since her teens. She blogs at PaganSquare.com at Cauldron to Kitchen (http://witchesandpagans.com/pagan-culture-blogs/selina-rifkin.html).

Jade River is the Co-founder of the Re-formed Congregation of The Goddess--International; the first legally incorporated tax-exempt religion serving the women's spiritual community. She is the creator of the Women's Thealogical Institute the first organization to nationally offer in-depth training for women seeking training in Goddess religion and for some ordination as Priestesses. She is the author of several books including: Tying The Knot: A Gender-Neutral Guide to Handfastings or Weddings for Pagans and Goddess Worshippers, To Know: A Guide to Women's Magic and Spirituality, and a number of other publications dealing with the Goddess and women's spirituality. Website: http://www.rcgi.org Email: rcgiorg@yahoo.com

Romany Rivers is a British born Witch, Artist and Reiki Master residing in Canada. Author of Poison Pen Letters to Myself and The Woven Word: A Book of Invocations and Inspirations, Romany is also an avid contributor to blogs, magazines, community books and anthologies including Witchcraft Today 60 Years On and Naming the Goddess.

Raine Shakti is a writer, spiritual artist, and a Doctorate of Divinity candidate at Ocean Seminary College. She works professionally in the communications and training field and her best professional experiences are when she is able to empower people. She has spent the last four years reclaiming her life and her inner warrior. Part of this journey was becoming an ordained priestess with the Fellowship of Isis. Her Matron deities are Nephthys who has helped her become a true virgin woman, the Morrigan who has taught her what it means to be sovereign, and Yemaya who has taught her the strength in having a loving heart. To read more about Raine visit her site at http://www.boudicarising.com.

Sophia Kelly Shultz was born and raised in suburban Philadelphia, artist and writer Sophia Kelly Shultz is best known in pagan circles for her gods-inspired art such as "Hollie's Green Man," and for her publication "The Stone Circle Oracle: Transformation Through Meditation" (Schiffer Publishing, 2013). Sophia has been associated with Four Quarters Interfaith

Sanctuary for ten years, and has served on its Board of Directors for the past five years. She is also active in event planning, and has been made Vendor Coordinator. She, her husband, two dogs, and a very smart, very bad cat live in an old house packed with books and rocks occupying a steep Pennsylvania hillside. Both her costumes and needlework are award-winning.

Her artwork can be viewed at http://badgersoph.deviantart.com On Facebook, look under Sophia Kelly Shultz or Stone Circle Oracle. She can also be contacted by email: sophianan@aol.com. More information on Four Quarters can be found at: www.4qf.org.

Karen Tate: As an independent scholar, speaker, radio show host, published author, sacred tour leader and social justice activist, Karen's work for three decades has been inspired by her interests and passion for travel, comparative religions, ancient cultures, women's herstory and the resurging interest in the rise of the Feminine Consciousness. Her work combines feminism, spirituality and uplifting women, all of which are highlighted in her projects.

Her first book, Sacred Places of Goddess: 108 Destinations has garnered prestigious endorsements, while her second book, Walking An Ancient Path: Rebirthing Goddess on Planet Earth, was a finalist in the National Best Books of 2008 Awards. Her newest book, Goddess Calling: Inspirational Messages and Meditations of Sacred Feminine Liberation Thealogy, has received rave reviews from her mentors and peers. Her fourth book, the anthology, Voices of the Sacred Feminine: Conversations to ReShape Our World, includes the wisdom of noted visionaries and scholars who she has interviewed on her radio show of the same name.

Karen has been named one of the Top 13 Most Influential Women in Goddess Spirituality and a Wisdom Keeper of the Divine Feminine Movement. Tate's work has been highlighted in the Los Angeles Times, Seattle Times and other major newspapers. She is interviewed regularly by the media and has hosted her own internet radio show for the last nine years, Voices of the Sacred Feminine Radio, considered a treasure trove of insight and wisdom for our time. Her work has segued into writing, producing and consulting on projects which bring the ideals and awareness of the Sacred Feminine into the mainstream world through television and film. She can be seen in the new documentary, Femme: Women Healing the World, produced by Wonderland Entertainment and actress, Sharon Stone and Dr. Tate has been chosen as a presenter at the upcoming Council for the Parliament of World Religions. Website: www.karentate.com

Jhenah Telyndru is the founder and Morgen of the Sisterhood of Avalon (www.sisterhoodofavalon.org), and Academic Dean of the Avalonian Thealogical Seminary. She is the author of "Avalon Within: A Sacred Journey of Myth, Mystery, and Inner Wisdom", "The Avalonian Oracle: Spiritual Wisdom from the Holy Isle", "Journeys to Avalon: Immrama to the Holy Isle" CD of guided meditations, and the creator of a unique embodiment meditation system found on the "Trancing the Inner Landscape: Avalonian Landscape Postures" DVD. She presents workshops across North America and facilitates journeys to sacred sites in the British Isles with Mythic Seeker Spiritual Pilgrimages. Jhenah holds a master's degree in Celtic Studies from the University of Wales, Trinity St. David. She welcomes your contact through her website (www.ynysafallon.com).

Peggy Thompson graduated with a degree in Anthropology and Criminology in 2008. While attending college, she was one of the founding members of Cleveland State Pagans where she worked to increase the visibility of Pagans on campus and to dispel myths. Peggy has coordinated many different public events. She has also been invited to teach at conferences to share her knowledge of Paganism and Organizational strategies. This year she was invited back to Cleveland State to speak to a class on Paganism. Currently, Peggy is the High Priestess of her own small group in Lakewood OH. She also sits on the boards of Rising Sun Outreach Ministry, and the Open Hearth Foundation. Through these organizations she works to encourage other leaders and strengthen Pagan Communities. She can be reached at peg.e.thompson@gmail.com or via her Facebook page under peg.e.thompson.

Samuel Wagar is a 3rd Degree Wiccan HP (1985), community activist, founder of Pagans for Peace (1982-2002), of a national Wiccan Church (1991 - Congregationalist Witchcraft Association of Canada, which now has three provincial daughter churches) and CWABC (2004), of Gathering for Life on Earth festival (1993-present), author of four books, MA in Canadian History (SFU 2006) now Doctor of Ministry student, chaplain at University of Alberta, former election candidate (NDP 1994, Green Party 1996). 58 year old cis-gendered divorced heterosexual man from a working-class/lumpen rural background, raised by a single mother, the oldest child of six, born in Canada into a Protestant Anglican family, a gifted child grown up, moderately blessed by Attention Deficit Disorder, an introvert masquerading as an extrovert. His ethnic background is English, German, and Mohawk. samwagar@shaw.ca www.cwaalberta.com.

Courtney Weber is a Priestess, writer, Tarot advisor, activist and practicing Witch in New York City. She is the High Priestess of the NYC Chapter of Novices of the Old Ways--a progressive Witchcraft community. She is the author of Brigid: History, Mystery, and Magick of the Celtic Goddess and Tarot for One: How to Read Your Own Tarot, both through Weiser Books. She blogs at www.thecocowitch.com and on Witchesandpagans.com ("Behind the Broom: What the Books Don't Tell You"). She is the designer and producer of Tarot of the Boroughs, a photographic Tarot deck set in New York City. She lives in Manhattan with her husband and cats. @thecocowitch

Margo Wolfe is a writer and educator who leads various groups in Northwest PA and New York. Currently, most of her work is with teens and young adults. Her writings and reflections can be found at walkingwithteens.com and torstone.org.

Get More at Immanion Press

Visit us online to browse our books, sign-up for our e-newsletter and find out about upcoming events for our authors, as well as interviews with them. Visit us at http://www.immanion-press.com and visit our publicity blog at: http://ipmbblog.wordpress.com/

Get Social with Immanion Press

Find us on Facebook at:
http://www.facebook.com/immanionpress

Follow us on Twitter at
http://www.twitter.com/immanionpress

Find us on Google Plus at
https://plus.google.com/u/0/b/104674738262224210355/

CPSIA information can be obtained
at www.ICGtesting.com
Printed in the USA
FSOW01n0904230116
15965FS